Frommer's®

W9-BYI-637

P O R T A B L E

New York City

2009

by Brian Silverman

Here's what critics say about Frommer's:

"Amazingly easy to use. Very portable, very complete."

—*Booklist*

"Detailed, accurate, and easy-to-read information for all price ranges."

—*Glamour Magazine*

WILEY

Wiley Publishing, Inc.

Published by:

WILEY PUBLISHING, INC.

111 River St.
Hoboken, NJ 07030-5774

ISBN 978-0-470-28968-6

Editor: Kathleen Warnock
Production Editor: Jana M. Stefanciosa
Cartographer: Andrew Murphy
Photo Editor: Richard Fox
Production by Wiley Indianapolis Composition Services

Front Cover Photo: Statue of Atlas in Rockefeller Center

For information on our other products and services or to obtain technical
support, please contact our Customer Care Department within the U.S. at
800/762-2974, outside the U.S. at 317/572-3993 or fax 317/572-4002.

Wiley also publishes its books in a variety of electronic formats. Some content that appears in print may not be available in electronic formats.

Manufactured in the United States of America

5 4 3 2 1

Contents

List of Maps

ACKNOWLEDGMENTS

My editor, Kathleen Warnock, with her guidance and support, helps make working on this book a pleasure rather than a chore and for that I am very thankful. I'd also like to thank Gail Eisenberg for her tireless fact checking of this very fact-filled book.

ABOUT THE AUTHOR

Brian Silverman is a freelance writer whose work has been published in *Saveur, The New Yorker, Caribbean Travel & Life, Islands,* and *Four Seasons.* Among the many topics he writes about are food, travel, sports, and music. He is the author of numerous books including *Going, Going, Gone: The History, Lore, and Mystique of the Home Run,* and the *Twentieth Century Treasury of Sports.* For Frommer's, he has written Complete, Portable, and Budget guides to New York City, as well as *New York City For Dummies.* He lives in Manhattan with his wife and children.

AN INVITATION TO THE READER

In researching this book, we discovered many wonderful places—hotels, restaurants, shops, and more. We're sure you'll find others. Please tell us about them, so we can share the information with your fellow travelers in upcoming editions. If you were disappointed with a recommendation, we'd love to know that, too. Please write to:

Frommer's Portable New York City 2009
Wiley Publishing, Inc. • 111 River St. • Hoboken, NJ 07030-5774

AN ADDITIONAL NOTE

FROMMER'S STAR RATINGS, ICONS & ABBREVIATIONS

Every hotel, restaurant, and attraction listing in this guide has been ranked for quality, value, service, amenities, and special features using a **star-rating system.** In country, state, and regional guides, we also rate towns and regions to help you narrow down your choices and budget your time accordingly. Hotels and restaurants are rated on a scale of zero (recommended) to three stars (exceptional). Attractions, shopping, nightlife, towns, and regions are rated according to the following scale: zero stars (recommended), one star (highly recommended), two stars (very highly recommended), and three stars (must-see).

In addition to the star-rating system, we also use **seven feature icons** that point you to the great deals, in-the-know advice, and unique experiences that separate travelers from tourists. Throughout the book, look for:

Finds	Special finds—those places only insiders know about
Fun Fact	Fun facts—details that make travelers more informed and their trips more fun
Kids	Best bets for kids and advice for the whole family
Moments	Special moments—those experiences that memories are made of
Overrated	Places or experiences not worth your time or money
Tips	Insider tips—great ways to save time and money
Value	Great values—where to get the best deals

The following **abbreviations** are used for credit cards:

AE	American Express	DISC	Discover	V	Visa
DC	Diners Club	MC	MasterCard		

FROMMERS.COM

Now that you have this guidebook to help you plan a great trip, visit our website at **www.frommers.com** for additional travel information on more than 4,000 destinations. We update features regularly to give you instant access to the most current trip-planning information available. At Frommers.com, you'll find scoops on the best airfares, lodging rates, and car rental bargains. You can even book your travel online through our reliable travel booking partners. Other popular features include:

- Online updates of our most popular guidebooks
- Vacation sweepstakes and contest giveaways
- Newsletters highlighting the hottest travel trends
- Podcasts, interactive maps, and up-to-the-minute events listings
- Opinionated blog entries by Arthur Frommer himself
- Online travel message boards with featured travel discussions

Planning Your Trip to New York City

In the pages that follow, you'll find everything you need to know to handle the practical details of planning your trip in advance: airlines and area airports, a calendar of events, resources for those of you with special needs, and much more.

1 Visitor Information

Before you leave home, your best information source (besides this book, of course) is **NYC & Company,** at 810 Seventh Ave., New York, NY 10019. You can call © **800/NYC-VISIT** to request the *Official NYC Guide* detailing hotels, restaurants, theaters, attractions, events, and more. The guide is free and will arrive in 7 to 10 days. (*Note:* I've received complaints that they sometimes take longer.)

You can find a wealth of free information their website, **www. nycvisit.com**. To speak with a live travel counselor, call © **212/484-1222,** weekdays from 8:30am to 6pm EST, weekends from 8:30am to 5pm EST.

You will need a decent map of the city, and also a transit map, which you can get at the **Times Square Visitors Center,** 1560 Broadway, between 46th and 47th streets; © **212/869-1890;** (www.timessquare nyc.org) or at most larger subway stations. Look inside the back cover of this book for a map of most of the Manhattan subway lines.

FOR U.K. VISITORS   The **NYCVB Visitor Information Center** is at 36 Southwark Bridge Rd., London, SE1 9EU (© **020/7202-6367**). You can order the Official NYC Visitor Kit by sending an A5-size self-addressed envelope and 72p postage to the above address. For New York–bound travelers in London, the center also offers free one-on-one travel-planning assistance.

2 When to Go

Summer or winter, rain or shine, there's always great stuff going on in New York City, so there's no real "best" time to go.

Culture hounds might come in fall, winter, and early spring, when the theater and performing-arts seasons reach their heights. During summer, many cultural institutions, especially Lincoln Center, offer free, alfresco entertainment. Those who want to see the biggest Broadway hits usually have the best luck getting tickets in the slower months of January and February.

Gourmands might find it easiest to land the best tables during July and August, when New Yorkers escape the city on weekends. If you prefer to walk every city block to take in the sights, spring and fall usually offer the mildest and most pleasant weather.

New York is a nonstop holiday party from early December through the start of the New Year. However, keep in mind that hotel prices go sky high during the winter holidays, and the crowds are almost intolerable. If you'd rather have more of the city to yourself—better chances at restaurant reservations and shows, easier access to museums and other attractions—choose another time of year to visit.

Bargain hunters might want to visit in winter, between the first of the year and early April. Sure, you might have to bear some cold weather, but that's when hotels are suffering from the post-holiday blues, and rooms often go for a relative song—a song in this case meaning a room with a private bathroom for as little as $150. AAA cardholders can even do better in many cases (generally a 5%–10% savings if the hotel offers a AAA discount). However, be aware that the occasional convention or event, such as February's annual Fashion Week, can sometimes throw a wrench in your winter savings plans. Spring and fall are traditionally the busiest and most expensive seasons after holiday time. Don't expect hotels to be handing you deals, but you still might be able to negotiate a decent rate.

The city is drawing more families, and they usually visit in the summer. Still, the prospect of heat and humidity keeps some away, making July and the first half of August a significantly cheaper time to visit than later in the year; good hotel deals are often available.

At Christmas, expect to pay top dollar for everything. The first 2 weeks of December—the shopping weeks—are the worst when it comes to scoring an affordable hotel room; shoppers from around the world converge on the town to catch the holiday spirit and spend, spend, spend. But Thanksgiving can be a great time to come: Business travelers have gone home for the holiday, and the holiday shoppers haven't arrived. It's a little-known secret that most hotels away from the Thanksgiving Day Parade route have empty rooms, and are usually willing to make deals to fill them.

If you want to know how to pack just before you go, check the Weather Channel's online 10-day forecast at **www.weather.com**; I like to balance it against CNN's online 5-day forecast at **www.cnn.com/weather**. You can also get the local weather by calling ℂ **212/976-1212.**

New York's Average Temperature & Rainfall

	Jan	Feb	Mar	Apr	May	June	July	Aug	Sept	Oct	Nov	Dec
Daily Temp. (°F)	38	40	48	61	71	80	85	84	77	67	54	42
Daily Temp. (°C)	3	4	9	16	22	27	29	29	25	19	12	6
Days of Precipitation	11	10	11	11	11	10	11	10	8	8	9	10

NEW YORK CITY CALENDAR OF EVENTS

The following information is always subject to change. Confirm before you make plans around a specific event. Call the venue or the NYCVB at ℂ 212/484-1222, go to www.nycvisit.com, or buy a copy of **Time Out New York** for the latest details.

For a huge list of events beyond those listed here, check http://events.frommers.com, where you'll find a searchable, up-to-the-minute roster of what's happening in cities all over the world.

January

Restaurant Week. Twice a year some of the best restaurants in town offer three-course prix-fixe meals at *almost* affordable prices. At lunch, the deal is $24.07 (as in 24/7), while dinner is $35. Some restaurants in 2008 included standouts such as Aquavit, Fiamma, and Union Square Café. Call ℂ **212/484-1222** for info, or visit **www.nycvisit.com**. Late January.

February

Chinese New Year. Every year, Chinatown rings in its own New Year (based on a lunar calendar) with 2 weeks of celebrations, including parades with dragon and lion dancers, plus vivid costumes. The parade winds throughout Chinatown along Mott, Canal, and Bayard streets, and along East Broadway. Call the **NYCVB hot line** at ℂ **212/484-1222** or the **Asian American Business Development Center** at ℂ **212/966-0100.** Chinese New Year falls on January 26 in 2009, and it's the Year of the Ox.

March

St. Patrick's Day Parade. More than 150,000 marchers join in the world's largest civilian parade, as Fifth Avenue, from 44th to 86th streets, rings with the sounds of bands and bagpipes. The parade usually starts at 11am, but go early if you want a good spot. Call ℂ **212/484-1222.** March 17.

Easter Parade. Once upon a time, New York's gentry came out to show off their tasteful but discreet toppers. Today, if you were planning to slip on a tasteful little number—say something delicately woven in straw with a simple flower—you will *not* be the grandest lady in this springtime hike along Fifth Avenue, from 48th to 57th streets. It's more about flamboyant exhibitionism, with hats and costumes that get more outrageous every year, and anybody can join in for free. It generally runs Easter Sunday from about 10am to 3 or 4pm. Call ✆ **212/484-1222.** April 12, 2009.

April

New York International Auto Show. Here's the irony: You don't need a car in New York, yet this is the largest car show in the U.S. Held at the Javits Center, many concept cars that will never roll off the assembly line but are fun to dream about are on display. Call ✆ **800/282-3336** or visit **www.autoshowny.com** or **www.javitscenter.com**. Call for dates.

TriBeCa Film Festival. Conceived in 2002 by the unofficial mayor of TriBeCa, Robert De Niro, the festival has grown in popularity and esteem every year. In 2008, the 12-day festival featured over 250 films and included such events as a Family Festival Street Fair, music performances and art exhibitions, and outdoor "drive-in" films. Call ✆ **212/941-2400** or visit **www.tribecafilmfestival.org**. Last week in April/early May.

May

Fleet Week. About 10,000 Navy and Coast Guard personnel are "at liberty" in New York for the annual Fleet Week. You can watch the ships as they dock at the piers on the west side of Manhattan, tour them with on-duty personnel, and watch some dramatic exhibitions by the U.S. Marines. Even if you don't take in any of the events, you'll know it's Fleet Week because those 10,000 sailors invade Midtown in their white uniforms. It's wonderful— just like *On the Town* come to life. Call ✆ **212/245-0072,** or visit **www.fleetweek.navy.mil** (your best source for a full list of events) or **www.intrepidmuseum.org**. Late May.

June

Parades, parades, parades. During the summer there is a parade for almost every holiday, nationality or ethnicity. June is the month for (among others) the sometimes raucous but very colorful **Puerto Rican Day Parade** and the **Lesbian and Gay Pride Week and March,** where Fifth Avenue goes wild as the LGBT community celebrates with bands, marching groups, floats, and plenty of panache. The parade starts on upper Fifth Avenue around 52nd Street and continues into the Village, where a waterfront dance party with fireworks cap the day. Call (C) 212/807-7433 or check **www.hopinc.org**. Mid- to late June.

Shakespeare in the Park. The Delacorte Theater in **Central Park** is the setting for first-rate free performances under the stars—including at least one Shakespeare play each season—most often with stars on the stage. For details, see "Park It! Shakespeare, Music & Other Free Fun," in chapter 5. Call (C) **212/539-8500,** or visit **www.publictheater.org**. June through August.

July

Independence Day Harbor Festival and 4th of July Fireworks Spectacular. Start the day amid the crowds at the Great July 4th Festival in lower Manhattan, then catch Macy's fireworks extravaganza over the East River (the best vantage point is from FDR Drive, which closes to traffic). Call (C) **212/484-1222** or Macy's Visitor Center at 212/494-3827. July 4.

Lincoln Center Festival 2009. This festival celebrates the best of the performing arts from all over—theater, ballet, contemporary dance, opera, even puppet and media-based art. Recent editions have featured performances by Ornette Coleman, the Royal Opera, and the New York Philharmonic. Schedules are available in mid-March, and tickets go on sale in May or early June. Call (C) **212/546-2656,** or visit **www.lincolncenter.org**. Throughout July.

August

Lincoln Center Out of Doors. This series of free music and dance performances is held outdoors on the plazas of **Lincoln Center.** Call (C) **212/875-5766** or 212/546-2656, or visit **www.lincolncenter.org** for the schedule (usually available in mid-July). Throughout August.

Harlem Week. The world's largest black and Hispanic cultural festival spans almost the entire month, to include the Black Film Festival, the Harlem Jazz and Music Festival, and the Taste of Harlem Food Festival. Call (C) **212/484-1222.** Through August.

U.S. Open Tennis Championships. The final Grand Slam event of the tennis season is held at the Arthur Ashe Stadium at the USTA National Tennis Center at **Flushing Meadows Park** in Queens. Tickets go on sale in May or early June. The event sells out immediately because many tickets are held by corporate sponsors who hand them out to customers. You can buy scalped tickets outside the complex (an illegal practice, of course). The last few matches are the most expensive, but you'll see more tennis early on, when your ticket allows you to wander the outside courts. Call ℂ **866/OPEN-TIX** (it's always busy) or 718/760-6200 well in advance; visit **www.usopen.org** or **www.usta.com** for information. Two weeks around Labor Day.

September

West Indian–American Day Parade. This annual Brooklyn event is New York's largest and best street celebration. Come for the costumes, pulsating rhythms (soca, calypso, reggae), folklore, food (jerk chicken, oxtail soup, Caribbean soul food), and two million hip-shaking revelers. The route can change from year to year, but it usually runs along Eastern Parkway from Utica Avenue to Grand Army Plaza (at the gateway to Prospect Park). Call ℂ **718/467-1797,** or visit **www.wiadca.org**. Labor Day.

October

Big Apple Circus. New York City's homegrown, performing-arts circus is a favorite with children and anyone who's young at heart. Big Apple is committed to maintaining the classical circus tradition with sensitivity, and only features animals that have a traditional working relationship with humans. A tent is pitched in **Damrosch Park** at **Lincoln Center.** Call ℂ **800/922-3772,** or visit **www.bigapplecircus.org**. Late October through January.

Greenwich Village Halloween Parade. This is Halloween at its most outrageous. Drag queens and other flamboyant types parade through the Village in creative costumes. The route has changed over the years, but recently it has started after sunset at Spring Street and marched up Sixth Avenue to 23rd Street or Union Square. Call the *Village Voice* Parade hot line at ℂ **212/475-3333,** ext. 14044, visit **www.halloween-nyc.com**, or check the papers for the exact route so you can watch—or participate—if you have the threads and the imagination. October 31.

November

New York City Marathon. Some 30,000 runners from around the world participate in the largest U.S. marathon, and more than a million fans cheer them on as they follow a route that touches all five New York boroughs and finishes at Central Park. Call ℂ **212/423-2249** or 212/860-4455, or visit **www.nyrr.org**, for info and applications. First Sunday in November. November 2, 2008.

Radio City Music Hall Christmas Spectacular. A rather gaudy extravaganza, but lots of fun, this event stars the Radio City Rockettes and a cast that includes live animals (just try to picture the camels sauntering into the Sixth Ave. entrance!). For information, call ℂ **212/307-1000,** or visit **www.radiocity.com**; you can also buy tickets at the box office or via Ticketmaster's **Radio City Hot Line** (✆ **212/307-1000**), or visit **www.ticketmaster.com**. November through early January.

Macy's Thanksgiving Day Parade. The procession from Central Park West and 77th Street and down Broadway to Herald Square at 34th Street continues to be a national tradition. Huge hot-air balloons in the forms of Rocky and Bullwinkle, Snoopy, the Pink Panther, Bart Simpson, and other cartoon favorites are the best part. The night before, you can usually see the big blow-up on Central Park West at 79th Street; call in advance to see if it will be open to the public. Call ✆ **212/484-1222** or Macy's Visitor Center at 212/494-2922. November 27, 2008.

Lighting of the Rockefeller Center Christmas Tree. The annual lighting ceremony is accompanied by ice skaters, singing, entertainment, and a *huge* crowd. The tree stays lit 24/7 until after the New Year. Call ✆ **212/332-6868,** or visit **www.rockefellercenter.com**. Late November or early December.

December

Holiday Trimmings. Stroll down Fifth Avenue and you'll see a 27-foot sparkling snowflake floating over the intersection outside **Tiffany's,** the **Cartier** building beribboned with red bows, wreaths warming the necks of the **New York Public Library**'s lions, and fanciful figurines in the windows of **Saks Fifth Avenue** and **Lord & Taylor.** Madison Avenue between 55th and 60th streets is also a good bet; **Sony Plaza** usually displays something fabulous, as does **Barney's New York.** Throughout December.

Christmas Traditions. In addition to the **Radio City Music Hall Christmas Spectacular** and the New York City Ballet's staging of *The Nutcracker,* traditional holiday events include *A Christmas Carol* at **The Theater at Madison Square Garden** (✆ **212/465-6741** or www.thegarden.com; for tickets, ✆ **212/307-7171** or www.ticketmaster.com). At **Avery Fisher Hall** is the National Chorale's singalong performances of Handel's *Messiah* (✆ **212/875-5030;** www.lincolncenter.org) a week before Christmas. Don't worry if the only words you know are "Alleluia, Alleluia!"— you'll get a lyrics sheet. Throughout December.

Lighting of the Hanukkah Menorah. The world's largest menorah (32 ft. high) is at Manhattan's **Grand Army Plaza,** Fifth Avenue and 59th Street. Hanukkah celebrations begin at sunset, with the lighting of the giant electric candles. December 21, 2008.

New Year's Eve. The biggest party of all is in **Times Square,** where raucous revelers count down the year's final seconds until the ball drops at midnight at 1 Times Sq. This one, in the cold surrounded by thousands of drunks, is a masochist's delight. Call ℂ **212/768-1560** or 212/484-1222, or visit **www.timessquare nyc.org**. December 31.

3 Tips for Travelers with Special Needs

FOR FAMILIES

Good bets for the most timely information include the "Weekend" section of Friday's *New York Times,* which has a section dedicated to the week's best kid-friendly activities; the weekly *New York* magazine, which has a full calendar of children's events in its listings section; and *Time Out New York,* which also has a great weekly kids section with a bit of an alternative bent. The *Big Apple Parents' Paper* is usually available, for free, at children's stores and other locations in Manhattan; you can also find good information from the folks behind the paper at **www.parentsknow.com**.

The first place to look for **babysitting** is in your hotel (better yet, ask about babysitting when you reserve). Many hotels have babysitting services or will provide you with lists of reliable sitters. If this doesn't pan out, call the **Baby Sitters' Guild** (ℂ **212/682-0227;** www.babysittersguild.com). The sitters are licensed, insured, and bonded, and can even take your child on outings.

TRAVELERS WITH DISABILITIES

New York is more accessible to travelers with disabilities than ever before. The city's bus system is wheelchair friendly, and most of the major attractions are easily accessible. Even so, **always call first** to be sure that the places you want to go to are fully accessible.

Most hotels are ADA-compliant, with suitable rooms for wheelchair-bound travelers as well as those with other disabilities. But before you book, **ask lots of questions based on your needs.**

Hospital Audiences, Inc. (ℂ 212/575-7676; www.hospital audiences.org) arranges attendance and provides details about accessibility at cultural institutions as well as cultural events adapted for people with disabilities. Services include "Describe!," which allows visually impaired theatergoers to enjoy theater events; and the invaluable **HAI Hot Line** (ℂ 212/575-7676), which offers accessibility information for hotels, restaurants, attractions, cultural venues, and much more. This nonprofit organization also publishes *Access for All,* a guidebook on accessibility, available free-of-charge on the website **www.hospitalaudiences.org**.

Another terrific source for travelers with disabilities who are coming to New York City is **Big Apple Greeter** (𝕮 212/669-8159; www. bigapplegreeter.org). All of its employees are well versed in accessibility issues. They can provide a resource list of city agencies that serve those with disabilities, and they sometimes have discounts available to theater and music performances. Big Apple Greeter even offers one-to-one tours that pair volunteers with visitors with disabilities; they can even introduce you to the public transportation system if you like. Reserve at least 1 week ahead.

FOR SENIOR TRAVELERS

New York subway and bus fares are half-price ($1) for people 65 and older. Many museums and sights (and some theaters and performance halls) offer discounted admittance and tickets to seniors, so don't be shy about asking. Always bring an ID card.

Many hotels offer senior discounts; **Choice Hotels** (which include Comfort Inns, some of my favorite affordable Midtown hotels), for example, gives 30% off their published rates to anyone over 50, if you book your room through their nationwide toll-free reservations number (not directly with the hotels or through a travel agent). For a list of Choice Hotels, visit **www.hotelchoice.com**.

Many reliable agencies and organizations target the 50-plus market. **Elderhostel** (𝕮 800/454-5768; www.elderhostel.org) arranges worldwide study programs (including some in New York City) for those ages 55 and over.

FOR GAY & LESBIAN TRAVELERS

Gay and lesbian culture is as much a part of New York's identity as yellow cabs, high-rises, and Broadway theater. Indeed, in a city with one of the world's largest, loudest, and most powerful GLBT populations, homosexuality is squarely in the mainstream.

The **Lesbian, Gay, Bisexual & Transgender Community Center,** known as "The Center," is at 208 W. 13th St., between Seventh and Eighth avenues (𝕮 212/620-7310; www.gaycenter.org). The center is the meeting place for more than 400 LGBT organizations. The online calendar lists hundreds of happenings—lectures, dances, concerts, readings, films—or call for the latest. Their site offers links to gay-friendly hotels and guesthouses in and around New York, plus tons of other information; the staff is friendly and helpful in person or over the phone.

Other good sources for lesbian and gay events are the two free weekly newspapers, *Gay City News* (www.gaycitynews.com) and the

New York Blade (www.nyblade.com), and the free magazines *HX* (www.hx.com), *Next* (www.nextmagazine.com), and *GONYC* (www.gomag.com), which is lesbian-oriented. You'll also find lots of information on their websites.

The International Gay and Lesbian Travel Association (IGLTA; ℭ 800/448-8550 or 954/776-2626; www.iglta.org) is the trade association for the GLBT travel industry, and offers an online directory of gay- and lesbian-friendly businesses and tour operators.

Gay.com Travel (www.gay.com/travel) provides current information about gay-owned, -oriented, and -friendly lodging, dining, sightseeing, nightlife, and shopping in every important destination worldwide. British travelers should click on the "Travel" link at **www.uk.gay.com** for advice and gay-friendly trip ideas.

4 Playing It Safe

Sure, there's crime in New York City, but millions of people spend their lives here without being robbed or assaulted. In fact, New York is safer than any other big American city and is listed by the FBI as somewhere around 150th in the nation for total crimes. While that's encouraging for all of us, it's still important to take precautions.

Men should carry their wallets in their front pockets and women should keep hold of their purse straps. Cross camera and purse straps over one shoulder, across your front, and under the other arm. Never hang a purse on the back of a chair or on a hook in a bathroom stall; keep it in your lap or between your feet, with one foot through a strap and up against the purse itself. Avoid carrying large amounts of cash. You might carry your money in several pockets so that if one is picked, you won't be without cash. Skip the flashy jewelry and keep valuables out of sight when you're on the street.

Panhandlers are seldom dangerous and can be ignored. If a stranger walks up to you on the street with a sob story ("I live in the suburbs and was just attacked and don't have the money to get home" or whatever), it's likely a scam. Be wary of an individual who "accidentally" falls in front of you or causes some other commotion, because he or she may be working with someone else who will take your wallet when you try to help. And remember: You *will* lose if you place a bet on a sidewalk game of chance.

SUBWAY SAFETY TIPS In general, the subways are safe, especially in Manhattan. There are panhandlers and questionable characters like anywhere else in the city, but subway crime has gone down to 1960s levels. Still, stay alert and trust your instincts. Always keep a hand on your personal belongings.

When using the subway, **don't wait for trains near the edge of the platform** or on extreme ends of a station. During non–rush hours, wait for the train in view of the token-booth clerk or under the yellow DURING OFF HOURS TRAINS STOP HERE signs, and ride in the operator's or conductor's car (usually in the center of the train). Choose crowded cars over empty ones—there's safety in numbers.

Avoid subways late at night, and splurge on a cab or take the bus after about 10 or 11pm.

5 For International Travelers

VISAS

The U.S. Department of State has a **Visa Waiver Program (VWP)** allowing citizens of the following countries to enter the United States without a visa for stays of up to 90 days: Andorra, Australia, Austria, Belgium, Brunei, Denmark, Finland, France, Germany, Iceland, Ireland, Italy, Japan, Liechtenstein, Luxembourg, Monaco, the Netherlands, New Zealand, Norway, Portugal, San Marino, Singapore, Slovenia, Spain, Sweden, Switzerland, and the United Kingdom. (*Note:* This list was accurate at press time; for the most up-to-date list of countries, consult **www.travel.state.gov/visa**.) Canadian citizens may enter the United States without visas; they will need to show passports (if traveling by air) and proof of residence, however. *Note:* Any passport issued on or after October 26, 2006, by a VWP country must be an **e-Passport** for VWP travelers to be eligible to enter the U.S. without a visa. Citizens of these nations also need to present a round-trip air or cruise ticket upon arrival. E-Passports contain computer chips capable of storing biometric information, such as the required digital photograph of the holder. (You can identify an e-Passport by the symbol on the bottom center cover of your passport.) If your passport doesn't have this feature, you can still travel without a visa if it is a valid passport issued before October 26, 2005, and includes a machine-readable zone, or between October 26, 2005, and October 25, 2006, and includes a digital photograph. For more information, go to **www.travel.state.gov/visa**.

Citizens of all other countries must have (1) a valid passport that expires at least 6 months later than the scheduled end of their visit to the U.S., and (2) a tourist visa, which may be obtained without charge from any U.S. consulate.

As of January 2004, many international visitors traveling on visas to the United States will be photographed and fingerprinted on arrival at Customs in airports and on cruise ships in a program created by the Department of Homeland Security called **US-VISIT.** Exempt from the extra scrutiny are visitors entering by land or those that don't require a visa for short-term visits. For more information, go to the Homeland Security website at **www.dhs.gov/dhspublic**.

MEDICAL REQUIREMENTS

Unless you're arriving from an area known to be suffering from an epidemic (particularly cholera or yellow fever), inoculations or vaccinations are not required for entry into the United States.

CUSTOMS
WHAT YOU CAN BRING INTO THE U.S.

Every visitor older than 21 years of age may bring in, free of duty, the following: (1) 1 liter of wine or hard liquor; (2) 200 cigarettes, 100 cigars (but not from Cuba), or 3 pounds of smoking tobacco; and (3) $100 worth of gifts. These exemptions are offered to travelers who spend at least 72 hours in the United States and who have not claimed them within the preceding 6 months. It is forbidden to bring into the country almost any meat products (including canned, fresh, and dried meat products such as bouillon, soup mixes, and such). Generally, condiments, including vinegars, oils, and spices, coffee, tea, and some cheeses and baked goods are permitted. Avoid rice products, as rice can often harbor insects. Bringing fruits and vegetables is not advised, though not prohibited. Customs will allow produce depending on where you got it and where you're going after you arrive in the U.S. Foreign tourists may carry in or out up to $10,000 in U.S. or foreign currency with no formalities; larger sums must be declared to U.S. Customs on entering or leaving, which includes filing form CM 4790. For details consult your nearest U.S. embassy or consulate, or **U.S. Customs** (www.customs.ustreas.gov).

WHAT YOU CAN TAKE HOME FROM THE U.S.

Canadian Citizens: For a summary of Canadian rules, get the booklet *I Declare*, from the Canada Border Services Agency (© **800/461-9999** in Canada, or 204/983-3500; www.cbsa-asfc.gc.ca).

U.K. Citizens: For information, contact **HM Customs & Excise** at © **0845/010-9000** (from outside the U.K., 020/8929-0152), or consult their website at **www.hmce.gov.uk**.

Australian Citizens: A helpful brochure, available from Australian consulates or Customs offices, is *Know Before You Go*. For more information, call the **Australian Customs Service** at ℂ **1300/ 363-263,** or log on to **www.customs.gov.au**.

6 Money

You never have to carry too much cash in New York, and while the city's pretty safe, it's best not to overstuff your wallet (although always make sure you have at least $20 for a taxi on hand).

In most Manhattan neighborhoods, you can find a bank with **ATMs** (automated teller machines) every couple of blocks. Even in neighborhoods that aren't well served by banks, most delis and bodegas have ATMs (which usually tack on a service charge in addition to any fees your own bank charges).

ATMs

The easiest and best way to get cash away from home is from an ATM. The **Cirrus** (ℂ **800/424-7787;** www.mastercard.com) and **PLUS** (ℂ **800/843-7587;** www.visa.com) networks span the country. Look at the back of your bank card to see which network you're on, then call or check online for ATM locations. Be sure you know your personal identification number (PIN) and daily withdrawal limit. *Note:* Remember that many banks impose a fee every time you use a card at another bank's ATM. In addition, the bank from which you withdraw cash may charge its own fee. To compare banks' ATM fees within the U.S., use **www.bankrate.com**. For international withdrawal fees, ask your bank.

CREDIT CARDS & DEBIT CARDS

Credit cards are the most widely used form of payment in the United States: **Visa** (Barclaycard in Britain), **MasterCard** (Eurocard in Europe, Access in Britain, Chargex in Canada), **American Express, Diners Club,** and **Discover.** They also provide a convenient record of all your expenses, and they generally offer relatively good exchange rates. You can withdraw cash advances from your credit cards at banks or ATMs, provided you know your PIN.

Visitors from outside the U.S. should inquire whether their bank assesses a 1% to 3% fee on charges incurred abroad.

It's highly recommended that you travel with at least one major credit card. You must have one to rent a car, and hotels and airlines usually require a credit card imprint as a deposit against expenses.

ATM cards with major credit-card backing, known as **"debit cards,"** are now a commonly acceptable form of payment in most stores and restaurants. Some stores enable you to receive "cash back" on your debit card purchases, allowing you to get extra cash when you make a purchase. The same is true at most U.S. Post Offices.

TRAVELER'S CHECKS

Traveler's checks are widely accepted in the U.S., but international visitors should make sure that they're denominated in U.S. dollars; foreign-currency checks are often difficult to exchange.

You can buy traveler's checks at most banks. Most are offered in denominations of $20, $50, $100, $500, and sometimes $1,000. Generally, you'll pay a service charge ranging from 1% to 4%.

The most popular traveler's checks are offered by **American Express** (© 800/807-6233; © 800/221-7282 for card holders—this number accepts collect calls, offers service in several foreign languages, and exempts Amex gold and platinum cardholders from the 1% fee.); **Visa** (© 800/732-1322)—AAA members can obtain Visa checks for a $9.95 fee (for checks up to $1,500) at most AAA offices or by calling © 866/339-3378; and **MasterCard** (© 800/223-9920). If you choose to carry traveler's checks, keep a record of their serial numbers separate from your checks. If they are lost or stolen, you'll get a refund faster if you know the numbers.

7 Getting There

BY PLANE

Three major airports serve New York City: **John F. Kennedy International Airport** (© 718/244-4444) in Queens, about 15 miles (1 hr. driving time) from midtown Manhattan; **LaGuardia Airport** (© 718/533-3400), also in Queens, about 8 miles (30 min.) from Midtown; and **Newark International Airport** (© 973/961-6000) in nearby New Jersey, about 16 miles (45 min.) from Midtown. Information about all three is available online at **www.panynj.gov**; click on the "All Airports" tab.

Even though LaGuardia is the closest airport to Manhattan, it has a bad reputation for delays and terminal chaos, in ticket-desk lines and baggage claim. You may want to use JFK or Newark instead.

Almost every major domestic carrier serves at least one of the New York–area airports; most serve two or all three. Among them **American** (© 800/433-7300; www.aa.com), **Continental** (© 800/525-3273; www.continental.com), **Delta** (© 800/221-1212; www.delta.com), **Northwest** (© 800/225-2525; www.nwa.com), **US Airways** (© 800/428-4322; www.usairways.com), and **United** (© 800/864-8331; www.united.com).

In recent years, there has been rapid growth in the number of start-up, no-frills airlines serving New York (and 2008 brought the demise of some of them, so check and see whether the following are still flying when you are planning your trip). You might check out Atlanta-based **AirTran** (𝒞 800/AIRTRAN); Denver-based **Frontier** (𝒞 800/432-1359; www.flyfrontier.com), Milwaukee- and Omaha-based **Midwest Airlines** (𝒞 800/452-2022; www.midwestairlines. com), or Detroit-based **Spirit Airlines** (𝒞 800/772-7117; www. spiritair.com). The JFK-based cheap-chic airline **JetBlue** ✦ (𝒞 800/ JETBLUE; www.jetblue.com) has taken New York by storm with its low fares and classy service. The nation's leading discount airline, **Southwest** (𝒞 800/435-9792; www.iflyswa.com), flies into MacArthur (Islip) Airport on Long Island, 50 miles east of Manhattan.

TRANSPORTATION TO AND FROM THE NEW YORK AREA AIRPORTS

For transportation information for all three airports (JFK, LaGuardia, and Newark), call **Air-Ride** (𝒞 **800/247-7433**), which offers 24-hour recorded details on bus and shuttle companies and car services registered with the New York and New Jersey Port Authority. Similar information is available at **www.panynj.gov/airports**; click on the airport at which you'll be arriving.

The Port Authority runs Ground Transportation Information counters on the baggage-claim level at each airport where you can get information and book transport. Most transportation companies have courtesy phones near the baggage-claim.

Generally, travel time between the airports and Midtown by taxi or car is 45 to 60 minutes for JFK, 20 to 35 minutes for LaGuardia, and 35 to 50 minutes for Newark. Always allow extra time, especially during rush hour, holiday travel times, and if you're taking a bus.

TAXIS   Despite significant rate hikes the past few years, taxis are still a quick and convenient way to travel to and from the airports. They're available at designated taxi stands outside the terminals, with uniformed dispatchers on hand during peak hours at JFK and LaGuardia, around the clock at Newark. Follow the GROUND TRANS-PORTATION or TAXI signs. There may be a long line, but it generally moves pretty quickly. Fares, whether fixed or metered, do not include bridge and tunnel tolls ($4–$6) or a tip for the cabbie (15%–20% is customary). They do include all passengers in the cab and luggage—never pay more than the metered or flat rate, except

AirTrains: Newark & JFK—
The Very Good & the Pretty Good

First the very good: A few years ago, a rail link revolution-
ized the process of connecting by public transportation to
Newark-Liberty International Airport: **AirTrain Newark**,
which now connects Newark-Liberty with Manhattan via a
speedy monorail/rail link.

Even though you have to make a connection, the system
is fast, pleasant, affordable, and easy to use. Each arrivals
terminal at Newark Airport has a station for the AirTrain, so
follow the signs once you collect your bags. All AirTrains
head to **Newark International Airport Station**, where you
transfer to a **NJ Transit** train. NJ Transit will deliver you to
New York Penn Station in Midtown.

The trip from my apartment on Manhattan's Upper West
Side to the Newark Alitalia terminal, for example, was under
a half-hour and cost me less than $14 ($11.55 for the AirTrain
link via Penn Station plus $2 for the subway to get to Penn
Station). That's a savings of at least $35, compared to what it
would have been if I took a cab, not to mention the time I
saved. NJ Transit trains run two to three times an hour during peak travel times (once an hour during early and late
hours), and depart from their own lobby/waiting area in
Penn Station; you can check the schedules on monitors
before you leave the airport terminal, and again at the train
station. NJ Transit tickets can be purchased from vending
machines at both the air terminal and the train station (no
ticket is required to board the AirTrain). The one-way fare is
$11.25 (children 4 and under ride free). On your return trip
to the airport, the AirTrain is far more predictable, time-wise,
than subjecting yourself to the whims of traffic.

Note that travelers heading to points beyond the city can
also pick up Amtrak and other NJ Transit trains at Newark
International Airport Station to their final destinations.

for tolls and a tip (8pm–6am a $1 surcharge also applies on New
York yellow cabs). Taxis have a limit of four passengers, so if there are
more in your group, you'll have to take more than one cab.

- **From JFK:** A flat rate of $45 to Manhattan (plus tolls and tip)
  is charged. The meter will not be turned on and the surcharge

Now the not-so-very good: A few bumpy years after opening in 2003, after years of anticipation and $1.9 billion, AirTrain JFK is beginning to operate more efficiently. Though you can't beat the price—only $7 if you take a subway to the AirTrain, $12 if you take the Long Island Rail Road—you won't save much on time getting to the airport. From midtown Manhattan, the ride can take anywhere from 40 minutes to 90 minutes, depending on your connections. Only a few subway lines connect with the AirTrain: the A, E, J, and Z; the E, J, Z to Jamaica Station and the Sutphin Blvd.–Archer Ave. Station; and the A to Howard Beach/JFK Airport Station. The MTA is contemplating adding connections to the AirTrain in lower Manhattan sometime in the next decade, though there's not much they can do now to speed up the trip.

A word of warning for both AirTrains: If you have mobility issues, mountains of luggage, or small children, skip the AirTrain. You'll find it easier to rely on a taxi, car service, or shuttle that can offer you door-to-door transfers.

For more information on AirTrain Newark, call ℂ **888/ EWR-INFO,** or visit **www.airtrainnewark.com**. For connection details, click on the links on the website, or contact **NJ Transit** (ℂ **800/626-RIDE;** www.njtransit.com) or **Amtrak** (ℂ **800/USA-RAIL;** www.amtrak.com).

For more information on AirTrain JFK, go online to **www. airtrainjfk.com**. For connection details, click on the links on the AirTrain website or the MTA site, **www.mta.nyc.ny.us/ mta/airtrain.htm**.

will not be added. The flat rate does not apply on trips from Manhattan to the airport.
- **From LaGuardia:** $24 to $28, metered, plus tolls and tip.
- **From Newark Liberty:** The dispatcher gives you a slip of paper with a flat rate ranging from $30 to $38 (toll and tip extra),

depending on where you're going. New York yellow cabs aren't permitted to pick up passengers at Newark. The yellow cab fare from Manhattan to Newark is the meter amount plus $15 and tolls (about $69–$75, a few dollars more with tip). New Jersey taxis can't take passengers from Manhattan to Newark.

PRIVATE CAR & LIMOUSINE SERVICES   Private car and limousine companies provide 24-hour door-to-door airport transfers for roughly the same cost of a taxi. The advantage they offer is that you can arrange your pickup in advance and avoid the hassles of the taxi line. Call at least 24 hours in advance (earlier on holidays), and a driver will meet you near baggage claim (or at your hotel for a return trip). You'll probably be asked to leave a credit card number to guarantee your ride. You'll likely be offered the choice of indoor or curbside pickup; indoor pickup is more expensive but makes it easier to hook up with your driver (who usually waits in baggage claim bearing a sign with your name on it). You can save a few dollars if you arrange for an outside pickup; call the dispatcher as soon as you clear baggage claim and then take your luggage to the designated waiting area, where you'll wait for the driver to come around, which can take anywhere from 10 minutes to a half-hour. Note that curbside traffic can be chaotic during prime deplaning hours.

Vehicles range from sedans to vans to limousines and tend to be relatively clean and comfortable. Prices vary slightly by company and the size of car reserved, but expect a rate roughly equivalent to taxi fare if you request a basic sedan and have only one stop; toll and tip policies are the same. (*Note:* Car services are not subject to the flat-rate rule that taxis have for rides to and from JFK.) Ask when booking what the fare will be and if you can use your credit card to pay for the ride so there are no surprises at drop-off time. There may be waiting charges added if the driver has to wait for you due to flight delays when picking you up, but the car companies usually check on your flight to get an accurate landing time.

I've had the best luck with **Carmel** (© **800/922-7635** or 212/666-6666) and **Legends** (© **888/LEGENDS** or 212/888-8884; www.legendslimousine.com); **Allstate** (© **800/453-4099** or 212/333-3333) and **Tel-Aviv** (© **800/222-9888** or 212/777-7777) also have reasonable reputations. (Keep in mind, though, that these services are only as good as the individual drivers—and sometimes there's a lemon in the bunch. If you have a problem, report it immediately to the main office.)

For a bit more luxury and service, the best option I've found is **Luxor Limo** (© **866/990-4111;** www.luxorlimo.com), where the cars are spacious and the drivers as reliable as you will find, and with rates not much higher than the above companies.

These car services are good for rush hour (no ticking meters), but if you're arriving at a quieter time of day, taxis work fine.

PRIVATE BUSES & SHUTTLES   Buses and shuttle services provide a comfortable and less expensive (but usually more time-consuming) option for airport transfers than do taxis and car services.

Super Shuttle serves all three airports; **New York Airport Service** serves JFK and LaGuardia; **Olympia Trails and Express Shuttle USA** serves Newark. These services are my favorite option for getting to and from Newark during peak travel times because the drivers usually take lesser-known streets that make the ride much quicker than if you go with a taxi or car.

The blue vans of **Super Shuttle** (© **800/258-3826;** www.super shuttle.com) serve all three area airports, providing door-to-door service to Manhattan and points on Long Island every 15 to 30 minutes around the clock. As with Express Shuttle, you don't need to reserve your airport-to-Manhattan ride; just go to the ground-transportation desk or use the courtesy phone in baggage claim and ask for Super Shuttle. Hotel pickups for your return trip require 24 to 48 hours' notice; you can make your reservations online. Fares run $13 to $22 per person, depending on the airport, with discounts available for additional persons in the same party.

New York Airport Service (© **718/875-8200;** www.nyairport service.com) buses travel from JFK and LaGuardia to the Port Authority Bus Terminal (42nd St. and Eighth Ave.), Grand Central Terminal (Park Ave. between 41st and 42nd sts.), and to select Midtown hotels between 27th and 59th streets, plus the Jamaica LIRR Station in Queens, where you can pick up a train for Long Island. Follow the GROUND TRANSPORTATION signs to the curbside pickup, or look for the uniformed agent. Buses depart the airport every 20 to 70 minutes (depending on your departure point and destination) between 6am and midnight. Buses to JFK and LaGuardia depart the Port Authority and Grand Central Terminal on the Park Avenue side every 15 to 30 minutes, depending on the time of day and the day of the week. To request shuttle service from your hotel, call at least 24 hours in advance. One-way fare for JFK is $15, $27 round-trip; to LaGuardia it's $12 one-way and $21 round-trip.

BY CAR

From the **New Jersey Turnpike** (I-95) and points west, there are three Hudson River crossings to the city's West Side: the **Holland**

Tunnel (lower Manhattan), the **Lincoln Tunnel** (Midtown), and the **George Washington Bridge** (Upper Manhattan). From **upstate New York,** take the **New York State Thruway** (I-87), which crosses the Hudson River on the Tappan Zee Bridge and becomes the **Major Deegan Expressway** (I-87) through the Bronx. For the East Side, continue to the Triborough Bridge and then down the FDR Drive. For the West Side, take the Cross Bronx Expressway (I-95) to the Henry Hudson Parkway or the Taconic State Parkway to the Saw Mill River Parkway to the Henry Hudson Parkway south.

From **New England,** the **New England Thruway** (I-95) connects with the **Bruckner Expressway** (I-278), which leads to the Triborough Bridge (Robert F. Kennedy Bridge) and the FDR Drive on the East Side. For the West Side, take the Bruckner to the Cross Bronx Expressway (I-95) to the Henry Hudson Parkway south.

You'll pay tolls along some of these roads and at most crossings.

Once you arrive in Manhattan, park your car in a garage (expect to pay $20–$45 per day) and leave it there. Don't use your car for traveling within the city. Public transportation, taxis, and walking will easily get you where you want to go.

BY TRAIN

Amtrak (© 800/USA-RAIL; www.amtrak.com) runs frequent service to New York City's **Penn Station,** on Seventh Avenue between 31st and 33rd streets, where you can easily pick up a taxi, subway, or bus to your hotel. To get the best rates, book early (as much as 6 months in advance) and travel on weekends.

If you're traveling to New York from a city along Amtrak's Northeast Corridor—such as Boston, Philadelphia, Baltimore, or Washington, D.C.—Amtrak may be your best travel bet now that they've rolled out the high-speed Acela trains. The **Acela Express** trains cut travel time from D.C. down to 2½ hours, and travel time from Boston to a lightning-quick 3 hours. (If you book a seat on a Metroliner or regular unreserved service, the fares are cheaper, but expect to spend longer on the train).

MANHATTAN'S NEIGHBORHOODS IN BRIEF

Downtown

Lower Manhattan: South Street Seaport & the Financial District   At one time, this was New York—period. Established by the Dutch in 1625, New York's first settlements sprang up here, on the southern tip of Manhattan island; everything uptown was

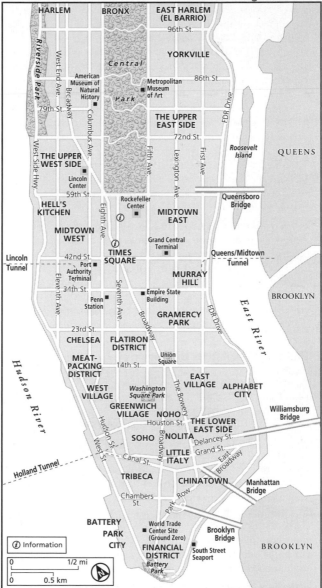

Manhattan's Neighborhoods

HARLEM

BRONX

EAST HARLEM
(EL BARRIO)

96th St.

YORKVILLE

Riverside Park

West End Ave.

Broadway

American
Museum of
Natural
History

Central

79th St.

Metropolitan
Museum
of Art

86th St.

Park

THE UPPER
EAST SIDE

72nd St.

FDR Drive

West Side Hwy.

THE UPPER
WEST SIDE

Columbus Ave.

Lincoln
Center

59th St.

Fifth Ave.

Lexington Ave.

First Ave.

*Roosevelt
Island*

QUEENS

HELL'S
KITCHEN

Rockefeller
Center

ⓘ

MIDTOWN
EAST

Queensboro
Bridge

MIDTOWN
WEST

Eighth Ave.

ⓘ

TIMES
SQUARE

Grand Central
Terminal

Lincoln
Tunnel

42nd St.
Port
Authority
Terminal

Eleventh Ave.

34th St.

Seventh Ave.

MURRAY
HILL

Queens/Midtown
Tunnel

BROOKLYN

Penn
Station

Empire State
Building

FDR Drive

East River

GRAMERCY
PARK

23rd St.

Broadway

CHELSEA

FLATIRON
DISTRICT

MEAT-
PACKING
DISTRICT

14th St.

Union
Square

WEST
VILLAGE

*Washington
Square Park*

EAST
VILLAGE

ALPHABET
CITY

GREENWICH
VILLAGE

The Bowery

NOHO

Williamsburg
Bridge

Hudson River

Houston St.

THE LOWER
EAST SIDE

SOHO

Hudson St.

Broadway

NOLITA

Delancey St.

West St.

Canal St.

LITTLE
ITALY

Grand St.

East Broadway

Holland Tunnel

TRIBECA

CHINATOWN

Manhattan
Bridge

Chambers
St.

Park Row

BATTERY
PARK
CITY

World Trade
Center Site
(Ground Zero)

Brooklyn
Bridge

BROOKLYN

FINANCIAL
DISTRICT

South Street
Seaport

*Battery
Park*

ⓘ Information

0   1/2 mi

0   0.5 km

21

farm country and wilderness. While all that's changed, this is still the best place in the city to search for the past.

Lower Manhattan constitutes everything south of Chambers Street. **Battery Park,** the point of departure for the Statue of Liberty, Ellis Island, and Staten Island, is on the far southern tip of the island. The **South Street Seaport,** now touristy but still a reminder of times when shipping was the lifeblood of the city, lies a bit north on the east side; it's just south of the Brooklyn Bridge.

The rest of the area is considered the **Financial District,** which contains **Ground Zero.** Until September 11, 2001, the Financial District was anchored by the **World Trade Center,** with the World Financial Center and Battery Park City to the west, and **Wall Street** running crosstown a little south and to the east.

Just about all of the major subway lines congregate here before they either end or head to Brooklyn.

TriBeCa   Bordered by the Hudson River to the west, the area north of Chambers Street, west of Broadway, and south of Canal Street is the *Tri*angle *Be*low *Ca*nal Street, or TriBeCa. Since the 1980s, as SoHo became saturated with chic, the spillover has been transforming TriBeCa into one of the city's hippest residential neighborhoods, where celebrities and families coexist in cast-iron warehouses converted into expensive apartments. Artists' lofts and galleries as well as hip antiques and design shops pepper the area, as do some of the city's best restaurants.

Chinatown   New York City's most famous ethnic enclave is bursting past its traditional boundaries and has encroached on Little Italy. The former marshlands northeast of City Hall and below Canal Street, from Broadway to the Bowery, are where Chinese immigrants were forced to live in the 1870s. This booming neighborhood is now a conglomeration of Asian populations. It offers tasty cheap eats in cuisines from Szechuan to Hunan to Cantonese to Vietnamese to Thai. Exotic shops offer strange foods, herbs, and souvenirs; bargains on clothing and leather are plentiful. It's a blast to walk down Canal Street, peering into the electronics and luggage stores and watching crabs cut loose from their handlers at the fish markets.

The Canal Street (J, M, Z, N, R, 6, Q, W) station will get you to the heart of the action. The streets are crowded during the day and empty out after around 9pm; they remain quite safe, but the neighborhood is more enjoyable during the bustle.

Little Italy   Little Italy, traditionally the area east of Broadway between Houston and north of Canal streets, is a shrinking community, due to the encroachment of thriving Chinatown. It's now limited mainly to **Mulberry Street,** where you'll find most restaurants and just a few offshoots. With rents going up in the increasingly trendy Lower East Side, a few chic spots are moving in, further intruding upon the old-world landscape. The best way to reach Little Italy is to walk east from the Spring Street station (on the no. 6 line) to Mulberry Street; turn south for Little Italy (you can't miss the year-round red, green, and white street decorations).

The Lower East Side   The Lower East Side boasts the best of both old and new New York: Witness the stretch of Houston between Forsyth and Allen streets, where Yonah Shimmel's Knish Shop sits shoulder-to-shoulder with the Sunshine Theater, an art house cinema —and both are thriving.

There are some remnants of what was once the largest Jewish population in America along **Orchard Street,** where you'll find great bargain-hunting in its many old-world fabric and clothing stores still thriving between the boutiques and lounges. Keep in mind that the old-world shops close early on Friday and all day on Saturday (the Jewish Sabbath). The expanding trendy set can be found in the blocks between Allen and Clinton streets south of Houston and north of Delancey, with more new shops, bars, and restaurants popping up in the blocks to the east every day.

This area is not well served by the subway system (one cause for its years of decline), so your best bet is to take the F train to Second Avenue (you can get off closer to First) and walk east on Houston; when you see Katz's Deli, you'll know you've arrived. You can also reach the LES from the Delancey Street station on the F line, and the Essex Street station on the J, M, or Z lines.

SoHo & Nolita   No relation to the London neighborhood, **SoHo** got its moniker as an abbreviation of "*So*uth of *Ho*uston Street." This fashionable neighborhood extends down to Canal Street, between Sixth Avenue to the west and Lafayette Street (1 block east of Broadway) to the east. It's easily accessible by subway: Take the N or R to the Prince Street station; the C, E, or 6 to Spring Street; or the F, B, D or V train to the Broadway-Lafayette stop (the Q train is not stopping at Broadway-Lafayette due to construction on the Manhattan Bridge).

An industrial zone during the 19th century, SoHo retains the cast-iron architecture of the era, and in many places, cobblestones peek out from beneath the asphalt. In the early 1960s, cutting-edge artists began occupying the drab and deteriorating buildings, soon turning it into the trendiest neighborhood in the city. SoHo is now a prime example of urban gentrification and a major New York attraction thanks to its impeccably restored buildings, fashionable restaurants and boutiques. On weekends the cobbled streets and narrow sidewalks are packed with shoppers, with the prime action between Broadway and Sullivan Street north of Grand Street.

In recent years SoHo has been crawling its way east, taking over Mott and Mulberry streets—and Elizabeth Street in particular— north of Kenmare Street, an area now known as **Nolita** for its *No*rth of *Li*ttle *Ita*ly location. Nolita is becoming increasingly well known for its hot shopping prospects, which include a number of pricey antiques and home-design stores. Taking the no. 6 train to Spring Street will get you closest by subway, but it's just a short walk east from SoHo proper.

The East Village & NoHo   The **East Village,** which extends between 14th Street and Houston Street, from Broadway east to First Avenue and beyond to Alphabet City—Avenues A, B, C, and D—is where what's left of Manhattan's bohemia is. The East Village is a fascinating mix of affordable ethnic and trendy restaurants, upstart clothing designers and kitschy boutiques, punk-rock clubs and cafes. Several Off- and Off-Off-Broadway theaters also call this place home.

The East Village isn't very accessible by subway; unless you're traveling along 14th Street (the L line will drop you off at Third or First aves.), your best bet is to take the 4, 5, 6, N, Q, R, or W to 14th Street/Union Square; the N or R to 8th Street; or the 6 to Astor Place and walk east.

The area around Broadway and Lafayette between Bleecker and 4th streets is called **NoHo** (for *No*rth of *Ho*uston), and has a completely different character. As you might have guessed, this area has developed much more like its neighbor to the south, SoHo. Here you'll find a crop of trendy lounges, stylish restaurants, cutting-edge designers, and upscale antiques shops. NoHo is fun to browse; the Bleecker Street stop on the no. 6 line will land you in the heart of it, and the Broadway-Lafayette stop on the B, D, F, or V lines will drop you at its southern edge.

Greenwich Village   Tree-lined streets crisscross and wind, following ancient streams and cow paths. Each block reveals yet another row of Greek Revival town houses, a well-preserved Federal-style house, or a peaceful courtyard or square. This is "the Village," from Broadway west to the Hudson River, bordered by Houston Street to the south and 14th Street to the north. It defies Manhattan's orderly grid system with streets that predate it, virtually every one chockablock with activity, and unless you live here, it may be impossible to master the lay of the land—so be sure to take a map along as you explore.

The Seventh Avenue line (1, 2, 3) is the area's main subway artery, while the West 4th Street station (where the A, C, or E lines meet the B, D, F or V lines) serves as its central hub.

The Village is probably the most chameleon-like of Manhattan's neighborhoods. Some of the highest-priced real estate in the city runs along lower Fifth Avenue, which dead-ends at **Washington Square Park.** Serpentine **Bleecker Street** stretches through most of the neighborhood and is emblematic of the area's historical bent. The anything-goes attitude in the Village has fostered a large gay community, which is still in evidence around **Christopher Street** and Sheridan Square (including the landmarked Stonewall Bar). The streets west of Seventh Avenue, known as the **West Village,** boast a more relaxed vibe and some charming historic brownstones. Three colleges—New York University, Parsons School of Design, and the New School for Social Research—keep the area thinking young.

Streets are often crowded with weekend warriors and teenagers, especially on Bleecker, West 4th, 8th, and surrounding streets, and have been known to become sketchy west of Seventh Avenue in the very late hours, especially on weekends.

Midtown

Chelsea & the Meatpacking District   **Chelsea** has come on strong in recent years as a hip address, especially for the gay community. A low-rise composite of town houses, tenements, lofts, and factories (with new high-rises popping up on seemingly every block), the neighborhood comprises roughly the area west of Sixth Avenue from 14th to 30th streets. (Sixth Ave. itself below 23rd St. is actually considered part of the Flatiron District; see below.) Its main arteries are Seventh and Eighth avenues, and it's primarily served by the C or E and 1 subway lines.

The **Chelsea Piers** sports complex to the far west and a host of shops (both unique boutiques and big names such as Williams-Sonoma), well-priced bistros, and thriving bars along the main drags have contributed to the area's rebirth. One of the most influential trends in Chelsea has been the establishment of far **West Chelsea** (from Ninth Ave. west) and the adjacent **Meatpacking District** (south of West Chelsea, roughly from 17th St. to Little W. 12th St.) as the style-setting neighborhoods for the 21st century. What SoHo was in the 1960s, this industrial west world (dubbed "the Lower West Side" by *New York* magazine) is today. New restaurants, cutting-edge shops, and hot bars pop up daily in the Meat-Packing District, while the area from West 22nd to West 29th streets between Tenth and Eleventh avenues is home to New

York's contemporary art scene. It's also the location for some of the city's hottest dance clubs. With galleries and bars in converted warehouses and former meat lockers, browsing can be frustrating, and the sometimes-desolate streets intimidating. Your best bet is to have a specific destination (and an exact address) in mind before you come.

The Flatiron District, Union Square & Gramercy Park These adjoining and, at places, overlapping neighborhoods are some of the city's most appealing. Their streets have been rediscovered by New Yorkers and visitors alike, thanks to the boom-to-bust dot-com revolution of the late 1990s; the Flatiron District served as its geographical heart and earned the nickname "Silicon Alley." These neighborhoods boast great shopping and dining and a central-to-everything location. A number of new hotels have been added to the mix over the last few years. The commercial spaces are often large, loftlike expanses with witty designs and graceful columns.

The **Flatiron District** lies south of 23rd Street to 14th Street, between Broadway and Sixth Avenue, and centers on the historic Flatiron Building on 23rd (so named for its triangular shape) and Park Avenue South, which has become a sophisticated, new Restaurant Row. Below 23rd Street along Sixth Avenue (once known as the Ladies' Mile shopping district), mass-market discounters such as Filene's Basement, Bed Bath & Beyond, and others have moved in. The shopping gets classier on Fifth Avenue, where you'll find a mix of national names and hip boutiques.

Union Square is the hub of the entire area; the N, Q, R, W, 4, 5, 6, or L trains stop here, making it easy to reach from most other neighborhoods. Long in the shadows of the more bustling (Times and Herald) and high-toned (Washington) city squares, Union Square has experienced a major renaissance. Local businesses joined forces with the city to rid the park of drug dealers, and now it's a delightful place to spend an afternoon. Union Square is best known as the setting for New York's premier greenmarket every Monday, Wednesday, Friday, and Saturday.

From about 16th to 23rd streets, east from Park Avenue South to about Second Avenue, is the leafy, largely residential district known as **Gramercy Park.**

Times Square & Midtown West **Midtown West,** the area from 34th to 59th streets west of Fifth Avenue to the Hudson River, encompasses several famous names: Madison Square Garden, the Garment District, Rockefeller Center, the Theater District, and Times Square. This is New York's tourism central, where you'll find the bright lights and bustle that draw people from all over. As such, this is the city's biggest hotel neighborhood, with options running from cheap to chic.

The 1, 2, 3 subway line serves the neon-lit station at the heart of Times Square, at 42nd Street between Broadway and Seventh Avenue, while the F, V, B, D line runs up Sixth Avenue to Rockefeller Center. The N, R, W line cuts diagonally across the neighborhood, following the path of Broadway before heading up Seventh Avenue at 42nd Street. The A, C, E line serves the West Side, running along Eighth Avenue.

If you know New York but haven't been here in a few years, you'll be surprised by the "new" **Times Square.** New Yorkers like to kvetch about the glory days of the old peep-show-and-porn-shop Times Square that this cleaned-up, Disneyfied version supplanted. And there really is not much here for the native. The revival, however, has been nothing short of an outstanding success for tourism. Expect dense crowds, though; it's often tough to make your way along the sidewalks.

To the west of the Theater District, in the 40s and 50s between Eighth and Tenth avenues, is **Hell's Kitchen,** also known as Clinton, an area that is much nicer than its ghoulish name and one of my favorites. The neighborhood resisted gentrification until the mid-1990s but has grown into a charming, less-touristy adjunct to the neighboring Theater District. Ninth Avenue, in particular, has blossomed into one of the city's finest dining avenues; stroll along and you'll have a world of dining to choose from, from American diner to sexy Mediterranean to traditional Thai.

Unlike Times Square, **Rockefeller Center** has needed no renovation. Situated between 46th and 50th streets from Sixth Avenue east to Fifth, this Art Deco complex contains some of the city's great architectural gems. If you can negotiate the crowds, holiday time is a great time to be here, as ice-skaters take over the central plaza and the Christmas tree twinkles against the night sky.

Between Seventh and Eighth avenues and 31st and 33rd streets, **Penn Station** sits beneath unsightly behemoth **Madison Square Garden,** where the Rangers, Liberty, and the Knicks play. Taking up all of 34th Street between Sixth and Seventh avenues is **Macy's,** the world's largest department store; exit Macy's at the southeast corner and you'll find more famous-label shopping around **Herald Square.** The blocks around 32nd Street just west of Fifth Avenue have developed into a thriving Koreatown, with mid-priced hotels and bright, bustling Asian restaurants offering some of the best-value stays and eats in Midtown.

Midtown East & Murray Hill   Midtown East, the area including Fifth Avenue and everything east from 34th to 59th streets, is the more upscale side of the Midtown map. This side of town is short of subway trains, served primarily by the Lexington Avenue 4, 5, 6 line.

Midtown East is where you'll find the city's finest collection of grand hotels, mostly along Lexington Avenue and near the park at the top of Fifth. The stretch of **Fifth Avenue** from Saks at 49th Street extending to the 24-hour Apple Store and F.A.O. Schwarz at 59th St. is home to the city's most high-profile haute shopping, including Tiffany & Co. Magnificent architectural highlights include the recently repolished **Chrysler Building,** with its stylized gargoyles glaring down on passersby; the Beaux Arts tour de force that is **Grand Central Terminal; St. Patrick's Cathedral;** and the glorious **Empire State Building.**

Far east, swank Sutton and Beekman places are enclaves of beautiful town houses, luxury living, and pocket parks that look out over the East River. Along this river is the **United Nations,** which isn't officially in New York City, or even the United States, but on a parcel of international land belonging to member nations.

Claiming the territory east from Madison Avenue, **Murray Hill** begins somewhere north of 23rd Street (the line between it and Gramercy Park is fuzzy), and is most clearly recognizable north of 30th Street to 42nd Street. This brownstone-lined quarter is largely a quiet residential neighborhood, most notable for its handful of good budget and mid-priced hotels.

Uptown

Upper West Side   North of 59th Street and encompassing everything west of Central Park, the Upper West Side contains **Lincoln Center,** one of the world's premier performing-arts venues; the **Time Warner Center** with its upscale shops; **Jazz at Lincoln Center;** the **Mandarin Oriental Hotel;** the **Whole Foods Market,** and possibly the most expensive food court in the world, with restaurants such as **Per Se** and **Masa.** You'll also find the **American Museum of Natural History** here.

Two major subway lines service the area: the 1, 2, 3 line runs up Broadway, while the B and C trains run up Central Park West, stopping at the historic Dakota apartments (where John Lennon was shot and Yoko Ono still lives) at 72nd Street, and at the Museum of Natural History at 81st Street.

Upper East Side   North of 59th Street and east of Central Park is some of the city's most expensive residential real estate. This is

New York at its most gentrified: Walk along Fifth and Park avenues, especially between 60th and 80th streets, and you're sure to encounter some of the wizened WASPs and Chanel-suited socialites that make up the most rarefied of the city's population. Madison Avenue from 60th Street well into the 80s is the money-eyed crowd's main shopping strip, recently vaunting ahead of Hong Kong's Causeway Bay to become the most expensive retail real estate *in the world*—so bring your platinum card.

The main attraction of this neighborhood is **Museum Mile,** the stretch of Fifth Avenue fronting Central Park that's home to no fewer than 10 terrific cultural institutions, including Frank Lloyd Wright's **Guggenheim,** and anchored by the mind-boggling **Metropolitan Museum of Art.** But the elegant rows of landmark town houses are worth a look alone: East 70th Street, from Madison east to Lexington, is one of the world's most charming residential streets. If you want to see where real people live, move east to Third Avenue and beyond; that's where affordable restaurants and active street life start popping up.

The Upper East Side is served by the packed Lexington Avenue line (4, 5, 6 trains), so wear walking shoes (or bring taxi fare) if you're heading here to explore.

Harlem   Harlem has benefited from a dramatic image makeover, and with new restaurants, clubs, and stores, is becoming a neighborhood in demand. Harlem is actually several areas. **Harlem proper** stretches from river to river, beginning at 125th Street on the West Side, 96th Street on the East Side, and 110th Street north of Central Park. East of Fifth Avenue, **Spanish Harlem (*El Barrio*)** runs between East 100th and East 125th streets. The neighborhood is benefiting greatly from the revitalization that has swept so much of the city, with national-brand retailers moving in, restaurants and hip nightspots opening everywhere, and visitors arriving to tour historic sites related to the golden age of African-American culture.

Washington Heights & Inwood   At the northern tip of Manhattan, Washington Heights (the area from 155th St. to Dyckman St., with adjacent Inwood running to the tip) is home to a large segment of Manhattan's Latino community, plus an increasing number of yuppies who don't mind trading a half-hour subway commute to Midtown for lower rents. **Fort Tryon Park** and **the Cloisters** are the two big reasons for visitors to come up this way. The Cloisters houses the Metropolitan Museum of Art's stunning medieval collection, in a building perched atop a hill, with excellent views across the Hudson to the Palisades. Committed off-the-beaten-path sight-seers might also want to visit the **Dyckman Farmhouse,** a historic jewel built in 1783 and the only remaining Dutch Colonial structure in Manhattan.

8 Getting Around

Frankly, Manhattan's transportation systems are a marvel. It's miraculous that so many people can gather on this little island and move around it. For the most part, you can get where you're going pretty quickly and easily using some combination of subways, buses, and cabs; this section will tell you how to do just that.

But between gridlock and subway delays, sometimes you just can't get there from here—unless you walk. Walking can be the fastest way to navigate the island. During rush hours, you'll easily beat car traffic while on foot, as taxis and buses stop and groan at gridlocked corners (don't even *try* going crosstown in a cab or bus in Midtown at midday). You'll also see a lot more by walking than you will if you ride beneath the street or fly by in a cab. So pack your most comfortable shoes and hit the pavement—it's the best, cheapest, and most appealing way to experience the city.

BY SUBWAY

Run by the **Metropolitan Transit Authority** (**MTA;** www.mta.info/nyct/subway), the subway system is the fastest way to travel around New York, especially during rush hours. Some 4.5 million people a day seem to agree with me, as it's their primary mode of transportation. The subway is quick, inexpensive, relatively safe, and efficient, as well as being a genuine New York experience.

The subway runs 24 hours a day, 7 days a week. The rush-hour crushes are roughly from 8 to 9:30am and from 5 to 6:30pm on weekdays; the rest of the time the trains are much more manageable.

Paying Your Way

The subway fare is $2 (half-price for seniors and those with disabilities); children under 44 inches ride free (up to three per adult).

Tokens are no longer available. People pay with the **MetroCard,** a magnetically encoded card that debits the fare when swiped through the turnstile (or the fare box on any city bus). Once you're in the system, you can transfer freely to any subway line that you can reach without exiting your station. MetroCards also allow you **free transfers** between the bus and subway within a 2-hour period.

MetroCards can be purchased from staffed token booths, where you can only pay with cash; at the ATM-style vending machines in every subway station, which accept cash, credit cards, and debit cards; from a MetroCard merchant, such as most Rite Aid drugstores; Hudson News, at Penn Station and Grand Central Terminal; or at the MTA information desk at the **Times Square Information Center,** 1560 Broadway, between 46th and 47th streets.

MetroCards come in a few different configurations:

Pay-Per-Ride MetroCards can be used for up to four people by swiping up to four times (bring the entire family). You can put any amount from $4 (two rides) to $80 on your card. Every time you put $7 or more on your Pay-Per-Ride MetroCard, it's automatically credited 15%—that's one free ride for every $15 you spend. You can buy Pay-Per-Ride MetroCards at any subway station; most stations have automated MetroCard vending machines, which allow you to buy MetroCards using your major credit card or debit card. MetroCards are also available from many shops and newsstands around town in $10 and $20 values. You can refill your card at any time until the expiration date on the card, usually about a year from the date of purchase, at any subway station.

Unlimited-Ride MetroCards, which can't be used for more than one person at a time or more frequently than 18-minute intervals, are available in four values: the **daily Fun Pass,** which allows you a day's worth of unlimited subway and bus rides for $7.50; the **7-Day MetroCard,** for $25; a **14-day MetroCard** for $47; and the **30-Day MetroCard,** for $81. Seven-, 14- and 30-day Unlimited-Ride Metro-Cards can be purchased at any subway station or from a MetroCard merchant. Fun Passes, however, cannot be purchased at token booths—you can only buy them at a MetroCard vending machine; from a MetroCard merchant; or at the MTA information desk at the Times Square Information Center. Unlimited-Ride MetroCards go into effect the first time you use them—so if you buy a card on Monday and don't begin to use it until Wednesday, Wednesday is when the clock starts ticking on your MetroCard.

A Fun Pass is good from the first time you use it until 3am the next day, while 7- and 30-day MetroCards run out at midnight on the last day. These MetroCards cannot be refilled. (At press time there were strong rumors that the 7-Day Metro Card and 30-Day Metro Card rates were going up).

Tips for using your MetroCard: The swiping mechanisms at turnstiles are the source of much grousing. If you swipe too fast or too slow, the turnstile will ask you to swipe again. If this happens, *do not move to a different turnstile,* or you may end up paying twice.

Subway Service Interruption Notes

Subway service is always subject to change, for reasons ranging from "a sick passenger" to regularly scheduled construction. Contact the **Metropolitan Transit Authority (MTA)** for
details at ℂ **718/330-1234** or **www.mta.nyc.ny.us**, where
you'll find system updates that are thorough, timely, and
clear. (You can also sign up online to receive service advisories
by e-mail.) Also read any posters that are taped up on the
platform or notices written on the token booth's whiteboard.

If you've tried repeatedly and really can't make your MetroCard
work, tell the token booth clerk; chances are good, though, that
you'll get the movement down after a couple of uses.

If you're not sure how much money you have left on your Metro-
Card, or what day it expires, use the station's MetroCard Reader,
usually located near the station entrance or the token booth (on
buses, the fare box will also provide you with this information).

To locate the nearest MetroCard merchant, or for any other Metro-
Card questions, call ℂ **800/METROCARD** (out of NYC only) or
212/METROCARD (212/638-7622) Monday through Friday
between 7am and 11pm, Saturday and Sunday from 9am to 5pm. Or
go online to **www.mta.nyc.ny.us/metrocard**, which can give you a
full rundown of MetroCard merchants in the tri-state area.

Using the System

As you can see from the subway map on the inside back cover of this
book, the subway system basically mimics the lay of the land above-
ground, with most lines in Manhattan running north and south, like
the avenues, and a few lines east and west, like the streets.

To go up and down the east side of Manhattan (and to the Bronx
and Brooklyn), take the 4, 5, or 6 train.

To travel up and down the West Side (and to the Bronx and
Brooklyn), take the 1, 2, or 3 line; the A, C, E, or F line; or the B or
D line.

The N, R, Q, and W lines first cut diagonally across town from
east to west and then snake under Seventh Avenue before shooting
out to Queens.

The crosstown S line, the Shuttle, runs back and forth between
Times Square and Grand Central Terminal. Farther downtown,
across 14th Street, the L line works its own crosstown magic.

Lines have assigned colors on subway maps and trains—red for the 1, 2, 3 line; green for the 4, 5, 6 trains; and so on—but nobody ever refers to them by color. Always refer to them by number or letter when asking questions. Within Manhattan, the distinction between different numbered trains that share the same line is usually that some are express and others are local. **Express trains** often skip about three stops for each one that they make; express stops are indicated on subway maps with a white (rather than solid) circle. Local stops are usually about 9 blocks apart.

Directions are almost always indicated using "uptown" (northbound) and "downtown" (southbound), so be sure to know what direction you want to head in. The outsides of some subway entrances are marked UPTOWN ONLY or DOWNTOWN ONLY; read carefully, as it's easy to head in the wrong direction. Once you're on the platform, check the signs overhead to make sure that the train you're waiting for will be traveling in the right direction. If you do make a mistake, it's a good idea to wait for an express station, such as 14th Street or 42nd Street, so you can get off and change to the other direction without paying again.

The days of graffiti-covered cars are gone, but the stations—and an increasing number of trains—are not as clean as they could be. Trains are air-conditioned (move to the next car if yours isn't),

---

Tips For More Bus & Subway Information

For additional transit information, call the Metropolitan Transit Authority's **MTA/New York City Transit's Travel Information Center** at ℰ **718/330-1234**. Extensive automated information is available at this number 24 hours a day, and travel agents are on hand to answer your questions and provide directions daily from 6am to 9pm. Customers who don't speak English can call ℰ **718/330-4847**. For online information that's always up-to-the-minute, visit **www.mta.nyc.ny.us**.

To request system maps, call the **Map Request Line** at ℰ **718/330-3322** (although realize that recent service changes may not yet be reflected on printed maps). Riders with disabilities should direct inquiries to ℰ **718/596-8585**; hearing-impaired riders can call ℰ **718/596-8273**. For MetroCard information, call ℰ **212/METROCARD** (638-7622) weekdays from 7am to 11pm, weekends 9am to 5pm, or go online to **www.mta.nyc.ny.us/metrocard**.

though during the dog days of summer the platforms can be sweltering. In theory, all subway cars have PA systems to allow you to hear the announcements, but they don't always work well. It's a good idea to move to a car with a working PA system in case sudden service changes are announced that you'll want to know about.

BY BUS

Less expensive than taxis and more pleasant than subways (they provide a mobile sightseeing window on Manhattan), MTA buses are a good transportation option. Their big drawback: They can get stuck in traffic, sometimes making it quicker to walk. They also stop every couple of blocks, rather than the 8 or 9 blocks that local subways traverse between stops. So for long distances, the subway is your best bet; but for short distances or traveling crosstown, try the bus.

Paying Your Way

Like the subway fare, **bus fare** is $2, half-price for seniors and riders with disabilities, and free for children under 44 inches (up to three per adult). The fare is payable with a **MetroCard** or **exact change.** Bus drivers don't make change, and fare boxes don't accept dollar bills or pennies. You can't purchase MetroCards on the bus, so you'll have to have them before you board; for details on where to get them, see "Paying Your Way," under "By Subway," above.

If you pay with a MetroCard, you can transfer to another bus or to the subway for free within 2 hours. If you pay cash, you must request a **free transfer** slip that allows you to change to an intersecting bus route only (transfer points are listed on the transfer paper) within 1 hour of issue. Transfer slips cannot be used to enter the subway.

Using the System

You can't flag a city bus down—you have to meet it at a bus stop. **Bus stops** are located every 2 or 3 blocks on the right-side corner of the street (facing the direction of traffic flow). They're marked by a curb painted yellow and a blue-and-white sign with a bus emblem *and the route number or numbers, and usually an ad-bedecked Plexi-*glass bus shelter. Guide-a-Ride boxes at most stops display a route map and a hysterically optimistic schedule.

Almost every major avenue has its own **bus route.** They run either north or south: downtown on Fifth, uptown on Madison, downtown on Lexington, uptown on Third, and so on. There are **crosstown buses** at strategic locations all around town: 8th Street (eastbound); 9th (westbound); 14th, 23rd, 34th, and 42nd (east- and westbound); 49th (eastbound); 50th (westbound); 57th (east- and westbound); 65th (eastbound across the West Side, through the

Tips **Take a Free Ride**

The Alliance for Downtown New York's **Downtown Connection** offers a free bus service that provides access to downtown destinations, including Battery Park City, the World Financial Center, and South Street Seaport. The buses, which run daily, every 10 minutes or so, from 10am to 7:30pm, make stops along a 5-mile route from Chambers Street on the west side to Beekman Street on the east side. For schedules and more information, call the Downtown Connection at © 212/ 566-6700, or visit **www.downtownny.com**.

park, and then north on Madison, continuing east on 68th to York Ave.); 67th (westbound on the East Side to Fifth Ave., and then south on Fifth, continuing west on 66th St., through the park and across the west side to West End Ave.); and 79th, 86th, 96th, 116th, and 125th (east- and westbound). Some bus routes, however, are erratic: The M104, for example, starts at the East River, then turns at Eighth Avenue and goes up Broadway. The buses of the Fifth Avenue line go up Madison or Sixth and follow various routes around the city.

Most routes operate 24 hours a day, but service is infrequent at night. During rush hour, main routes have "limited" buses, identifiable by the red card in the front window; they stop only at major cross streets.

To make sure that the bus you're boarding goes where you're going, check the map on the sign that's at every bus stop, get your hands on a route map, or **just ask.** The drivers are helpful, as long as you don't hold up the line too long.

While traveling, look out the window not only to take in the sights but also to keep track of cross streets so you know when to get off. Signal for a stop by pressing the tape strip above and beside the windows and along the metal straps, about 2 blocks before you want to stop. Exit through the pneumatic back doors (not the front door) by pushing on the yellow tape strip; the doors open automatically. Most city buses are equipped with wheelchair lifts. Buses also "kneel," lowering down to the curb to make boarding easier.

BY TAXI

If you don't want to deal with public transportation, finding an address that might be a few blocks from the subway station, or sharing your ride with 3.5 million other people, then take a taxi. The biggest advantages are, of course, that cabs can be hailed on any street (provided you find an empty one—often simple, yet at other times nearly impossible) and will take you right to your destination. I find they're best used at night when there's little traffic and when the subway may seem a little daunting. In Midtown at midday, you can usually walk to where you're going more quickly.

Official New York City taxis, licensed by the Taxi and Limousine Commission (TLC), are yellow, with the rates printed on the door and a light with a medallion number on the roof. You can hail a taxi on any street. *Never* accept a ride from any other car except an official city yellow cab (livery cars are not allowed to pick up fares on the street, despite what the driver tells you when he pulls over to see if he can pick up a fare).

The base fare on entering the cab is $2.50. The cost is 40¢ for every ⅕ mile or 40¢ per 60 seconds in stopped or slow-moving traffic (or for waiting time). There's no extra charge for each passenger or for luggage. However, you must pay bridge or tunnel tolls (sometimes the driver will front the toll and add it to your bill at the end; most times, however, you pay the driver before the toll). You'll pay a $1 surcharge between 4 and 8pm and a 50¢ surcharge after 8pm and before 6am. A 15% to 20% tip is customary.

Most taxis are now equipped with a device that allows you to pay by credit card, though some drivers will claim the machine is broken (there is a transaction fee for credit cards that cuts into their income) and ask you to pay in cash. You can choose to either add the tip to the credit card, or tip the driver in cash.

The TLC has posted a **Taxi Rider's Bill of Rights** sticker in every cab. Drivers are required to take you anywhere in the five boroughs, to Nassau or Westchester counties, or to Newark Airport. They are supposed to know how to get you to any address in Manhattan and all major points in the outer boroughs. They are also required to provide air-conditioning and turn off the radio on demand, and they cannot smoke while you're in the cab. They are required to be polite.

You are allowed to dictate the route. It's a good idea to look at a map before you get in a taxi. Taxi drivers have been known to jack up the fare on visitors who don't know better by taking a circuitous route between points A and B.

On the other hand, listen to drivers who propose an alternate route. These guys spend 8 or 10 hours a day on these streets, and they know where the worst traffic is, or where Con Ed has dug up an intersection that should be avoided. A knowledgeable driver will know how to get you to your destination quickly and efficiently.

Another important tip: **Always make sure the meter is turned on at the start of the ride.** You'll see the red LED readout register the initial $2.50 and start calculating the fare as you go. I've witnessed unscrupulous drivers buzzing unsuspecting visitors around the city with the meter off, and then overcharging them at drop-off time.

Always ask for the receipt—it comes in handy if you need to make a complaint or leave something behind.

A taxi driver is obligated to take you to your destination. If a taxi driver refuses to take you to your desired destination (which happens on occasion when you want to go to an outer borough or very far uptown), get the driver's name and medallion number (on his license in the divider between the front and back seats) and file a complaint with the Taxi and Limousine Commission.

For all driver complaints, including the one above, and to report lost property, call ℂ **311** or 212-NEWYORK (outside the metro area). For details on getting to and from the local airports by taxi, see "By Plane," under "Getting There," earlier in this chapter. For further taxi information—including a complete rundown of your rights as a taxi rider—point your Web browser to **www.ci.nyc.ny.us/taxi**.

BY CAR

Forget driving yourself around the city. It's not worth the headache. Traffic is horrendous, and you don't know the rules of the road (written or unwritten) or the arcane alternate-side-of-the-street parking regulations. You don't want to find out the price of parking violations or have to claim your car from the tow pound.

If you arrive in New York City by car, park it in a garage (expect to pay at least $25–$45 per day) and leave it there for the duration of your stay. (In our hotel chapter, we note if a hotel has a garage, or offers discounted parking, and the rate). If you drive a rental car in, return it as soon as you arrive and rent another when you leave.

2

Where to Stay

It's official: Hotel rates in New York are the most expensive in the U.S. That said, there are bargains out there at every price level; but a bargain in New York might be a king's ransom in St. Louis.

PRICE CATEGORIES & RACK RATES   The hotels listed below have provided us with their best rate estimates for 2009, and all quoted rates were correct at press time. Be aware, however, that **rates can change at any time.** Rates are always subject to availability, seasonal fluctuations, and plain-old rate hikes. It's smart to expect price shifts in both directions in late 2008 and 2009.

1 Financial District

VERY EXPENSIVE

Ritz-Carlton New York, Battery Park ✸✸✸   Perfect on almost every level, the only drawback to this Ritz-Carlton is its remote downtown location. But that location, on the southern tip of Manhattan, is also one of its strengths. Where else can you get, in most rooms anyway, magnificent views of New York Harbor from your bedroom—complete with telescope for close-ups of Lady Liberty? Where else can you have a cocktail in your hotel bar and watch the sun set over the harbor? And where else can you go for a morning jog around the Manhattan waterfront? This modern, Art Deco–influenced high-rise differs from the English-countryside look of most Ritz-Carlton properties, including its sister hotel on Central Park (p. 49). You'll find the full slate of comforts and services typical of Ritz-Carlton here, from Frette-dressed feather beds to the chain's signature Bath Butler, who will draw a scented bath for you in your own deep soaking tub. If you don't mind the location and the commute to Midtown, you won't find a more luxurious choice.

2 West St., New York, NY 10004. © **800/241-3333** or 212/344-0800. Fax 212/344-3801. www.ritzcarlton.com. 298 units. $350–$545 double; from $750 suite. Extra person 12 and over $30 (starting from $100 on club level). Check website for promotional weekend packages. AE, DC, DISC, MC, V. Valet parking $60. Subway: 4, 5 to Bowling Green. **Amenities:** Restaurant; lobby lounge (w/outdoor seating) for

Where to Stay Downtown

The Bowery Hotel **3**
Cosmopolitan Hotel **7**
Duane Street Hotel **6**
Exchange Hotel **8**
Hotel Gansevoort **1**
The Hotel on Rivington **5**
Larchmont Hotel **2**
The Mercer **4**
Ritz-Carlton New York
   Battery Park **10**
Wall Street Inn **9**

Ⓜ Subway stop
Ⓜ Closed indefinitely

afternoon tea and cocktails; 14th-floor cocktail bar w/light dining and outdoor seating; state-of-the-art health club w/views; spa treatments; 24-hr. concierge; well-equipped business center w/24-hr. secretarial services; 24-hr. room service; laundry service; dry cleaning; Ritz-Carlton Club Level w/5 food presentations daily; technology butler and bath butler services. *In room:* A/C, TV w/pay movies and video games, Wi-Fi, high-speed Internet, dataport, minibar, fridge, hair dryer, safe, CD player, DVD w/surround sound in suites and Club rooms.

EXPENSIVE/MODERATE

Exchange Hotel   This cozy hotel is a solid, midpriced choice if you are looking for a downtown location. A short walk from Wall Street, the South Street Seaport, Brooklyn Bridge, and Chinatown, the Exchange Hotel features personalized service and a few perks such as free wireless Internet and a complimentary continental breakfast. Recently renovated in a sleek, contemporary style, standard and deluxe guest rooms are on the small size, but are outfitted nicely with plasma televisions, minifridges, and microwaves. The suites are roomy with a separate living room, black leather furniture and a full-size kitchen. Bathrooms are tight in both the guest rooms and suites and sadly include those very fashionable marble bowl sinks that look good, but don't leave much space for any of your toiletries. That minor complaint aside, the Exchange is a welcome addition to an area much too lacking in lodging.

129 Front St. (btwn Wall and Pine sts.) New York, N.Y. 10005. © **212/742-0003**. Fax 212/742-0124. www.exchangehotel.com. 53 units. AE, DC, MC, V. $299–$389; suites $310–$469. Parking $25. Subway: 2, 3 to Wall St. **Amenities:** Lounge; free complimentary continental breakfast; access to nearby fitness club; laundry/valet service. *In room:* A/C, TV/VCR, free Wi-Fi, full-sized kitchens in suites, minifridge, iron/ironing board, safe, microwave.

The Wall Street Inn ★ *Finds*   This intimate hotel is the preferred choice for those working on the Street. But it's also a good choice for visitors who don't want to work. This intimate, seven-story hotel is ideal for those who want a lower Manhattan location without corporate blandness. The hotel is warm, comforting, and serene, and the friendly, professional staff offers the kind of personalized service you won't get from a chain. Rooms aren't huge, but the bedding is top-quality and all the conveniences are at hand. Rooms ending in "01" are smallest; seventh-floor rooms are best, as the bathrooms have extra counter space and whirlpool tubs.

9 S. William St. (at Broad St.), New York, NY 10004. © 800/747-1500 or **212/747-1500**. Fax 212/747-1900. www.thewallstreetinn.com. 46 units. $279–$450 double. Rates include continental breakfast. Ask about corporate, group, and/or deeply discounted weekend rates (as low as $265 at press time). AE, DC, DISC, MC, V. Parking $36 nearby. Subway: 2, 3 to Wall St.; 4, 5 to Bowling Green. **Amenities:** Well-outfitted

exercise room w/sauna and steam; concierge; business center; babysitting arranged; laundry service; dry cleaning; common guest kitchen w/microwave; video library. *In room:* A/C, TV/VCR, fax, high-speed Internet, fridge, hair dryer, iron, safe.

2 Lower East Side & TriBeCa
EXPENSIVE

The Hotel on Rivington ★★   The contrast of a 21-story, glass-tower luxury hotel in the midst of 19th- and early-20th-century Lower East Side tenement buildings is striking, but an accurate representation of what that neighborhood has become. From the floor-to-ceiling windows of your room, surrounded by amenities such as flatscreen televisions, Japanese soaking tubs in the bathrooms, and Tempur-Pedic mattresses, not only do you have incredible city views, but you can look down and spot ancient Lower East Side landmarks such as the sign for the Schapiro Kosher wine factory. You'll find yourself in a location where old-world customs and institutions coexist with the new and the super-cool. Along with the views, three-quarters of the rooms have terraces, the option of in-room spa services, and heated, tiled floors in the large bathrooms where you can enjoy your view of the city as you bathe—which also means someone with binoculars might just have a view of you, too.

107 Rivington St. (between Ludlow & Essex sts.), New York, NY 10002. (C) **212/475-2600.** Fax 212/475-5959. www.hotelonrivington.com. 110 units. From $395 double. AE, DC, MC, V. Parking $50. Subway: F to Delancey St. **Amenities:** Restaurant; fitness center; in-room spa services available; concierge; 24-hr. room service; laundry service; dry cleaning. *In room:* A/C, TV, Wi-Fi, dataport, fridge, hair dryer, CD players and JBL.

MODERATE

Duane Street Hotel ★ *(Finds)*   This cozy TriBeCa hotel opened with minimal fanfare in late 2007. But you don't need hype to sell solid goods and that's what they have. The rooms are on the small size and designed with IKEA-ish style furnishing, but like the loft apartments in the neighborhood, the walls are hardwood, the ceilings are high and the windows large, providing a sense of space. Bathrooms are spacious and well-outfitted with showers equipped with rain shower heads. Every room has a good-sized desk and a 32-inch plasma HDTV. Best of all is the personable, helpful staff that seems to enjoy doing the little extras. This is welcome addition to a vibrant neighborhood with limited midpriced hotel options.

130 Duane Street (at Church St.), New York, NY 10013. (C) **212/964-4600.** Fax 212/964-4800; www.duanestreethotel.com. 45 units. $259–$799 doubles. AE, DC, DISC,

MC, V. Subway: A, C, to Chambers Street. **Amenities:** Restaurant; concierge; business center; off-site fitness center; in-room spa services. *In room:* A/C, TV, free Wi-Fi, hair dryer, safe, CD player.

INEXPENSIVE

Cosmopolitan Hotel–Tribeca ★ *Value*   Behind a plain-vanilla TriBeCa awning is one of the best hotel deals in Manhattan for budget travelers who prefer a private bathroom. Everything is strictly budget but nice: The modern IKEA-ish furniture includes a work desk and an armoire (a few rooms have a dresser and hanging rack instead); for a few extra bucks, you can have a love seat, too. Beds are comfy, and sheets and towels are of good quality. Rooms are small but make the most of the limited space, and the whole place is pristine. The two-level minilofts have lots of character, but expect to duck on the second level. Management does a great job of keeping everything fresh. The TriBeCa location is safe, hip, and subway-convenient. Services are kept at a minimum to keep costs down.

95 W. Broadway (at Chambers St.), New York, NY 10007. ✆ **888/895-9400** or 212/566-1900. Fax 212/566-6909. www.cosmohotel.com. 105 units. $200–$270 double. AE, DC, MC, V. Subway: 1, 2, 3, A, C to Chambers St. *In room:* A/C, TV, dataport, ceiling fan.

3 SoHo

VERY EXPENSIVE

The Mercer ★★★   The best of the downtown, celebrity-crawling, trendy hotels, the Mercer is a place where even those who represent the antithesis of hip can feel at home. Though SoHo can be a bit over the top with its high-end boutiques, cutting-edge restaurants, and too-serious fashionistas on the streets, it is still an exciting place. And the corner of Mercer and Prince streets is probably the epicenter of SoHo. Still, once inside, there is a pronounced calm—from the postmodern library lounge and the Mizrahi-clad staff to the huge, soundproof loftlike guest rooms; the hotel is a perfect complement to the scene outside. The Mercer is one of the few New York hotels with ceiling fans. The tile-and-marble bathrooms have a steel cart for storage and an oversize shower stall or oversize two-person tub (state your preference when booking).

147 Mercer St. (at Prince St.), New York, NY 10012. ✆ **888/918-6060** or 212/966-6060. Fax 212/965-3838. www.mercerhotel.com. 75 units. $600–$700 double; $800–$900 studio; from $1,250 suite. AE, DC, DISC, MC, V. Parking $35 nearby. Subway: N, R to Prince St. **Amenities:** Restaurant; lounge; food and drink service in lobby; free access to nearby Crunch fitness center; 24-hr. concierge; secretarial services; 24-hr. room service; laundry service; dry cleaning; video, DVD, and CD libraries. *In room:* A/C, TV/DVD, Wi-Fi, dataport, minibar, safe, CD player, ceiling fan.

4 Greenwich Village, East Village & the Meatpacking District

To locate the hotels in this section, see the map on p. 39.

EXPENSIVE

The Bowery Hotel ☆☆   Despite the history associated with its name and location, the Bowery Hotel, opened in 2007, is about as far from a flophouse as you could imagine. Standing in the heart of NoHo, the hotel, though new, has that burnished, dark wood look inside, most evident in the expansive lobby with a fireplace, velvet draperies and furniture, vintage paneling, Moroccan tiles, and an adjoining outdoor area complete with plush lounge chairs. The rooms, and there are no two the same, are large and airy by New York standards with high ceilings, ceiling fans, many with terraces and all with spectacular views. As the Gansevoort Hotel did for the Meatpacking District, the Bowery Hotel is doing for the Bowery—making a once desolate area a hip destination.

335 Bowery (at 3rd St.), New York, N.Y. 10003. © **212/505-9100.** Fax 212/505-9700. www.theboweryhotel.com. 135 units. From $525 doubles; from $750 suites. AE, DISC, MC, V. Parking $31 self parking, $45 valet. **Amenities:** Restaurant; bar; concierge; 24-hour room service; laundry and dry cleaning service. *In room:* A/C, HDTV/DVD, Wi-Fi, minibar, hair dryer, iron, safe, iPod stereo and docking system.

Hotel Gansevoort ☆☆   Built from the ground up by hotelier Henry Kallan (of New York's Hotel Giraffe and The Library), the Gansevoort was the first major hotel in the Meatpacking District. And now, this 14-floor zinc-colored tower, with its open, sprawling lobby, popular restaurant **Ono,** and indoor/outdoor rooftop bar and pool is the symbolic anchor of the district. The Gansevoort offers excellent, personable service. Rooms are a good size with comfortable furnishings in soft tones and high-tech amenities such as plasma televisions and Wi-Fi. Suites have a living room and separate bedroom and some have small balconies and bay windows. Corner suites offer adjoining guest rooms. The generous-size bathrooms are done up in ceramic, stainless steel, and marble and are impeccably appointed. In all the guest rooms and throughout the hotel, original art by New York artists is on display.

18 Ninth Ave. (at 13th St.), New York, NY 10014. © **877/426-7386** or 212/206-6700. Fax 212/255-5858. www.hotelgansevoort.com. 187 units. From $435 double; from $675 suite. Parking $40. Subway: A, C, E to 14th St. Pet-friendly floors. **Amenities:** Restaurant; rooftop bar and lounge; indoor/outdoor pool; spa and fitness center; concierge; business center; 24-hr. room service; laundry service; dry cleaning; rooftop garden. *In room:* A/C, TV, Wi-Fi, high-speed Internet, dataport, minibar, hair dryer, iron, safe, 2-line telephones, voice mail.

Plenty of Room at the Inn

When you think of New York accommodations, you usually think big—tall monoliths with hundreds of rooms. You don't think of quaint guesthouses or inns where a home-cooked breakfast is served. But New York is a diverse city and that diversity can be found in its accommodations, too. So if you want an alternative to the quintessential New York hotel and prefer a taste of urban hominess, here are a few options.

On the high end, but worth it if you love authentic 19th-century Victorian romance, is the **Inn at Irving Place** ⚹⚹. Housed in a 170-year-old town house, their rates range from $445 to $645. The rooms are furnished in the style of Edith Wharton's Golden Age New York.

Complimentary breakfast is served each morning in Lady Mendl's parlor, where, if the weather is nippy, you'll find a comforting fire roaring.

Breakfast prepared by culinary students of the New School is one of the highlights of the **Inn on 23rd Street** ⚹⚹⚹. Each of the inn's 14 rooms, which range in price from $219 to $359 per night, were decorated by the owners, Annette and Barry Fisherman, with items they've collected from their travels. See p. 45 for a detailed review.

INEXPENSIVE

Larchmont Hotel ⚹⚹ *Value*   If you're willing to share a bathroom, it's hard to do better for the money at this wonderful European-style hotel. Each bright guest room is tastefully done in rattan and outfitted with a writing desk, a minilibrary of books, an alarm clock, a wash basin, and a few extras that you normally have to pay a lot more for, such as cotton bathrobes, slippers, and ceiling fans. Every floor has two shared bathrooms (with hair dryers) and a small, simple kitchen. The management is constantly renovating, so everything feels clean and fresh. What's more, those looking for a hip downtown base couldn't be better situated, because some of the city's best shopping, dining, and sightseeing—plus your choice of subway lines—are just a walk away. This hotel has devoted followers who recommend it to all their friends, so book *well* in advance (the management suggests 6–7 weeks' lead time).

The first home of the Gay Men's Health Crisis, an 1850 brownstone in Chelsea, is the **Colonial House Inn,** 318 W. 22nd St., between Eighth and Ninth avenues (© **800/689-3779** or 212/243-9669; www.colonialhouseinn.com). This 20-room four-story walk-up caters to a mostly GLBT clientele, but everybody is welcome. Some rooms have shared bathrooms; deluxe rooms have private bathrooms and some have working fireplaces. There's a roof deck with a clothing-optional area. Breakfast is included and rates range from $85 to $150 for a shared bathroom or $110 to $130 for a deluxe room with a private bathroom.

On the popular yet still residential Upper West Side is the aptly-named **Country Inn the City** ⓐ, 270 W. 77th St., between Broadway and West End Avenue (© **212/580-4183;** www.countryinnthecity.com). This 1891 town house has only four rooms, but all are spacious, quaintly decorated, and equipped with full kitchens. Rates range from $210 to $350 and include breakfast items in your refrigerator. But there is no resident innkeeper and a maid services your room only every few days.

27 W. 11th St. (btwn Fifth and Sixth aves.), New York, NY 10011. © **212/989-9333.** Fax 212/989-9496. www.larchmonthotel.com. 62 units, all with shared bathroom. $80–$99 single; $109–$120 double. Rates include continental breakfast. AE, MC, V. Parking $25 nearby. Subway: A, B, C, D, E, F, V to W. 4th St. (use 8th St. exit); F to 14th St. **Amenities:** Tour desk; room service (10am–6pm); common kitchenette. *In room:* A/C, TV, hair dryer, safe, ceiling fan.

5 Chelsea

MODERATE

Inn on 23rd Street ⓐⓐⓐ *(Finds)*   Behind an unassuming entrance in the middle of bustling 23rd Street is one of New York's lodging treasures: a real urban bed-and-breakfast with as personal a touch as you will find. All 14 guest rooms are spacious. Each has a king or queen bed outfitted with a pillow-top mattress and top-quality linens, satellite TV, a large private bathroom with Turkish towels, and a roomy closet. Rooms have themes based on how they are designed;

Where to Stay in Midtown, Chelsea & Gramercy Park

UPPER EAST SIDE

E. 67th St.
E. 66th St.
E. 65th St.
E. 64th St.
E. 63rd St.
E. 62nd St.
E. 61st St.
E. 60th St.
E. 59th St.
E. 58th St.
E. 57th St.
E. 56th St.
E. 55th St.
E. 54th St.
E. 53rd St.
E. 52nd St.
E. 51st St.
E. 50th St.
E. 49th St.
E. 48th St
E. 47th St.
E. 46th St.
E. 45th St.
E. 44th St.
E. 43rd St.
E. 42nd St.
E. 41st St.
E. 40th St.
E. 39th St.
E. 38th St.
E 37th St.
E 36th St.
E. 35th St.
E. 34th St.
E. 33rd St.
E. 32nd St.
E. 31st St.
E. 30th St.
E. 29th St.
E. 28th St.
E. 27th St.
E. 26th St.
E. 25th St.
E. 24th St.
E. 23rd St.
E. 22nd St.
E. 21st St.
E. 20th St.
E. 19th St.
E. 18th St.
E. 17th St.
E. 16th St.
E. 15th St.
E. 14th St.

1/4 mi
0.25 km

ROOSEVELT ISLAND

Transverse

PARK

The Pond

Central Park S.

East Drive

Fifth Ave.
Madison Ave.

MIDTOWN EAST

Rockefeller Center

Fifth Ave.
Madison Ave.
Vanderbilt Ave.
Park Ave.
Lexington Ave.
Third Ave.
Second Ave.
First Ave.

Room Lower Level
Roosevelt Island Tram
Queensboro Bridge
To Upper Level

York Ave.
Sutton Pl. South Sutton Pl.
Beekman Place
Mitchell Place

United Nations

Queens-Midtown Tunnel

FDR Drive

East River

Grand Central Terminal

New York Public Library

Bryant Park

Sixth Ave. (Ave. of the Americas)

MURRAY HILL

Queens-Midtown Tunnel

Tunnel Exit
Tunnel Entrance

Empire State Bldg.

W. 32nd St.
Broadway

Madison Ave.
Park Ave. S.

Fifth Ave.

Lexington Ave.

Second Ave.
First Ave.

Asser Levy Pl.
Ave. C.

Upper Manhattan

Uptown

Midtown

Downtown

Madison Square Park

Gramercy Park

FLATIRON DISTRICT

GRAMERCY PARK

Peter Cooper Village

Stuyvesant Town

Sixth Ave. (Ave. of the Americas)

Fifth Ave.

Union Sq. W.
Union Sq. E.

Union Square

Irving Pl.
Perlman Pl.

7
8
10
9
11
12
13 14
15
16
17
18
19
4
20
21
22
23
24
25
26
27
28
29
30
31

47

there's the Rosewood Room, with '60s built-ins; the Asian Bamboo Room; and Ken's Cabin, a lodgelike room with cushy, well-worn leather furnishings and Americana relics. I stayed in the Victorian suite where the decor included framed Victorian-era dental tools. The inn features a library where the complimentary breakfast is served and where there is also an honor bar. Other perks include free high-speed Internet access in the rooms, Wi-Fi in the library, and wine and cheese served on Friday and Saturday.

131 W. 23rd St. (btwn Sixth and Seventh aves.), New York, NY 10011. ℂ 877/387-2323 or 212/463-0330. Fax 212/463-0302. www.innon23rd.com. 14 units. $219–$259 double; $359 suite. Rates include continental breakfast. Extra person $25–$50. Children 12 and under stay free in parent's room. AE, DC, DISC, MC, V. Parking $20 nearby. Subway: F, 1 to 23rd St. **Amenities:** Fax and copy service; cozy library w/stereo and VCR. *In room:* A/C, TV, dataport, hair dryer, iron, high-speed Internet access.

6 Union Square, the Flatiron District & Gramercy Park

VERY EXPENSIVE

Gramercy Park Hotel ✿✿✿   This 1925-built legend bordering Gramercy Park has been redone stunningly by famed hotelier Ian Schrager. Start with the lobby, with its eclectic mix of art: Julian Schnabel-designed lamps, two 10-foot Italian fireplaces, Moroccan tiles, bronze tables, and a Venetian glass chandelier. What once was a 500-plus room hotel now features 185 rooms; where the former version had tiny rooms, now there is space. More than half of the rooms are suites, some with views overlooking Gramercy Park, and all have mahogany English cabinets where the minibar and DVD player are hidden, some variation of the overstuffed lounge chair, and a portrait of Schnabel's friend, the late Andy Warhol. Beds are velvet-upholstered, tables feature leather tops, and photos by world famous photojournalists adorn the walls. Bathrooms are large with wood-paneled walls. If you choose to leave your room, the hotel's magnificent **Rose Bar** is where you should venture first (p. 185).

2 Lexington Ave (at 21st St), New York, N.Y. 10010. ℂ 212/920-3300. Fax 212/673-5890. www.gramercyparkhotel.com. 185 units. From $595 double; from $700 suite. AE, DC, DISC, MC, V. Parking $55. Subway: 6 to 23rd St. **Amenities:** Restaurant; 2 bars, fitness center and spa, 24-hour room service, laundry service; dry cleaning; 24-hour concierge. *In room:* A/C, TV/DVD, Wi-Fi, high-speed Internet, dataport, minibar, hair dryer, safe, CD player, iPod and docking station.

EXPENSIVE

Carlton Hotel on Madison Avenue ✿✿   This 1904 Beaux Arts hotel was getting worn around the edges when it was rescued by architect David Rockwell and refurbished magnificently. The high-light of that $60-million renovation is the grand lobby complete with a marble curving staircase and a cathedral-like high ceiling. While the **Roger** (p. 60) a few blocks up, also recently renovated, went for a cool, sleek, modern-tropical look, the Hotel Carlton has tried to recapture the glory of the past blended with New Age nods such as contemporary furnishings in the lobby along with a bubbling, two-story waterfall. Rooms are a generous size and retain that Beaux Arts motif with the addition of modern amenities such as Wi-Fi and iPod clock radios. The marble bathrooms offer plenty of counter space; some rooms have bathtubs while others just have showers.

88 Madison Ave. (btwn 28th and 29th sts.), New York, NY 10016. (C) **800/601-8500** or 212/532-4100. Fax 212/889-8683. www.carltonhotelny.com. 316 units. $329 standard; from $450 suite. AE, DC, DISC, MC, V. Valet parking $40. Subway: 6 to 28th St./Lexington Ave. **Amenities:** Restaurant; concierge; business center; limited room service; laundry service; dry cleaning. *In room:* A/C, TV, Wi-Fi, iron/ironing board, safe, iPod clock radio.

Hotel Giraffe (★)(★)   In the increasingly fashionable Madison Park area, this hotel is a real charmer with a calm, intimate feel. Guest rooms are stylish, evoking an urban European character, with high ceilings, velveteen upholstered chairs, and black-and-white photographs from the 1920s and 1930s. All the rooms are good size, with high ceilings, while deluxe rooms and suites feature French doors that lead to small balconies with large windows and remote-controlled blackout shades. Bathrooms are spacious with plenty of marble counter space and glass-paneled doors, and all rooms have marble-topped desks. But what really separates this hotel from so many others are its services: A continental breakfast is included in the rate and served in the hotel's lobby, where coffee, cookies, and tea are available all afternoon, and wine, cheese, and piano music are offered each evening. There is also a lovely rooftop garden.

365 Park Ave. South (at 26th St.), New York, NY 10016. (C) **877/296-0009** or 212/685-7700. Fax 212/685-7771. www.hotelgiraffe.com. 73 units. $409–$559 from $650 1- or 2-bedroom suite; from $2,500 penthouse suite. Rates include continental breakfast and evening wine and cheese accompanied by piano music. Check website or ask about reduced rates (as low as $299 at press time). AE, DC, MC, V. Parking $28. Subway: 6 to 28th St. **Amenities:** Restaurant; 2 bars; complimentary access to nearby gym; concierge; business services; limited room service; laundry service; dry cleaning; rooftop garden; video and CD libraries. *In room:* A/C, TV/VCR, Wi-Fi, dataport, minibar, hair dryer, iron, safe, CD player.

INEXPENSIVE

Gershwin Hotel (★) (Kids)   This creative-minded, Warholesque hotel caters to up-and-coming artistic types—and well-established names with an eye for good value—with its bold modern art collection and wild style. The lobby was recently renovated, and along with a new bar, **Gallery at the Gershwin,** much of the original art remains. The standard rooms are clean and bright, with Picasso style wall murals and Philippe Starck–ish takes on motel furnishings. Superior rooms are best, as they're newly renovated, and well worth the extra $10; all have a queen bed, two twins, or two doubles, plus a newish private bathroom with cute, colorful tile. If you're bringing the brood, two-room suites, or Family Rooms, are a good option. For the *very* low budget traveler, the Gershwin also offers hostel-style accommodations at $33 a night in multibed rooms.

7 E. 27th St. (btwn Fifth and Madison aves.), New York, NY 10016. ℰ **212/545-8000.** Fax 212/684-5546. www.gershwinhotel.com. 150 units. $109–$285 double; $239–$385 family room. Extra person $20. Check website for discounts or other value-added packages. For hostel rooms, use this website: www.gershwinhostel.com. AE, MC, V. Parking $25 3 blocks away. Subway: N, R, 6 to 28th St. **Amenities:** Bar; tour desk; babysitting; laundry service; dry cleaning; Internet access. *In room:* A/C, TV, Wi-Fi, dataport, hair dryer, iron.

7 Times Square & Midtown West

VERY EXPENSIVE

Ritz-Carlton New York, Central Park ★★★ *Kids*   There's a lot to like about this hotel—from its location overlooking Central Park to the impeccable service—but what I like best is that this luxury hotel manages to maintain a homey elegance and does not intimidate you with an overabundance of style. Rooms are spacious and decorated in English-country style. Suites are larger than most New York apartments. Rooms facing Central Park come with telescopes, and all have flatscreen TVs with DVD players; the hotel even has a library of Academy Award–winning films for you to borrow. The marble bathrooms are oversize and feature a choice of bathrobes. For families who can afford the steep prices, the hotel is extremely kid-friendly. Suites have sofa beds, and cribs and rollaway beds can be brought in. Children are given in-room cookies and milk. Adults can get pampered at the Switzerland-based La Prairie spa or dine at the hotel's restaurant, **BLT Market** (p. 89).

50 Central Park South (at Sixth Ave.), New York, NY 10019. ℰ **212/308-9100.** Fax 212/207-8831. www.ritzcarlton.com. 259 units. $650–$1,295 double; from $995 suite. Package and weekend rates available. AE, DC, DISC, MC, V. Parking $50. Subway: N, R, W to 5th Ave and F to 57th St. Pets under 60 lbs. accepted. **Amenities:** Restaurant; bar; lobby lounge for tea and cocktails; fitness center; La Prairie spa and facial center; concierge; complimentary Bentley limousine service; business center; 24-hr. room service; babysitting; overnight laundry; dry cleaning; technology butler

and bath butler services. *In room:* A/C, TV/DVD, high-speed Internet, dataport, mini-bar, hair dryer, iron, safe, telescopes in rooms w/park view.

EXPENSIVE

AKA Central Park ⚐   In 2007, AKA opened four extended-stay residences with hotel-like amenities in Times Square, Sutton Place, the United Nations-area and Central Park. Since the AKA properties operate like a combination apartment/hotel; your stay can be as brief as 1 night. The rooms, all of them spacious studios to two bedrooms, feature full modern kitchens, marble bathrooms, two televisions, and services such as a concierge, fitness center, wireless Internet, and a complimentary weekday breakfast. I found the Central Park location, 1 block from Central Park South, the homiest. It's an attractive and calming alternative to the nearby hotel hysteria.

42 W. 58th St. (btwn 5th–6th Aves.) New York, NY, 10019. 🕻 **212/753-3500.** Fax 646/744-3120; www.stayaka.com. 134 units. Rates from $395. AE, DC, MC, V. Parking $50 per day. Subway: N, R, Q, W to 57th St. **Amenities:** Complimentary breakfast (weekdays), health club and spa services, concierge, business center, room service, laundry service, dry cleaning. *In room:* A/C, 2 TVs, Wi-Fi, full kitchen, hair dryer/ironing board, safe, 2-line cordless phone w/complimentary local telephone services, CD/DVD player.

The Algonquin ⚐⚐   The atmosphere in this 1902 landmark building is so steeped in writers' lore you'll feel guilty turning on the television instead of reading the latest issue of the *New Yorker* that's provided in the guest rooms. Rooms can be cramped, but they are equipped with possibly the most comfortable, inviting beds in the city as well as 21st-century technology such as high-speed Internet and flatscreen televisions. If you have a tendency toward claustrophobia, head to the plush lobby, where you can sit in cushy chairs, sip exquisite (and expensive) cocktails, have a snack, or just read or play on your laptop (the lobby is Wi-Fi-equipped). For a splurge, stay in one of the roomy one-bedroom suites, where all that is missing to get you going on that novel you've been toying with is a manual Smith Corona typewriter.

Meals are served in the celebrated **Round Table Room,** while the **Oak Room** (p. 182) is one of the city's top cabaret rooms, featuring such esteemed talents as Andrea Marcovicci and Julie Wilson.

59 W. 44th St. (btwn Fifth and Sixth aves.), New York, NY 10036. 🕻 **888/304-2047** or 212/840-6800. Fax 212/944-1419. www.algonquinhotel.com. 174 units. $399–$699 double; from $349 suite. Check website or inquire about discounted rates or special package deals. AE, DC, DISC, MC, V. Parking $28 across the street. Subway: B, D, F, V to 42nd St. **Amenities:** 2 restaurants; lounge; bar; exercise room; concierge; limited room service; laundry service; dry cleaning. *In room:* A/C, TV w/pay movies, high-speed Internet, dataport, hair dryer, iron, safe.

Doubletree Guest Suites Times Square ๕ (Kids)   For many, this 43-story Doubletree, in the heart of darkness known as Times Square, where the streets are gridlocked, the neon burns holes into your eyes, and the noise is ear-splitting, might offer a more Vegaslike experience than a true New York one. But at times we all must make sacrifices for our children, and this Doubletree is perfect for the kids. From the fresh-baked chocolate-chip cookies served upon arrival, the spacious, affordable suites big enough for two 5-year-olds to play hide-and-seek (as mine did), and the all-day children's room-service menu to the proximity to the gargantuan Toys "R" Us and other kid-friendly Times Square offerings, this Doubletree is hard to beat for families. Bathrooms have two entrances so the kids don't have to traipse through the parent's rooms.

1568 Broadway (at 47th St. & Seventh Ave.), New York, NY 10036. © **800/222-TREE** or 212/719-1600. Fax 212/921-5212. www.doubletree.com. 460 units. From $349 suite. Extra person $20. Children under 18 stay free in parent's suite. Ask about senior, corporate, and AAA discounts and special promotions. AE, DC, DISC, MC, V. Parking $35. Subway: N, R to 49th St. **Amenities:** Restaurant; lounge; fitness center; concierge; limited room service; babysitting; laundry service; dry cleaning. *In room:* A/C, 2 TVs w/pay movies and video games, high-speed Internet, dataport, minibar, fridge, wet bar w/coffeemaker, hair dryer, iron, safe, microwave.

Flatotel ๕๕ (Kids) (Finds)   In the heart of midtown and surrounded by Sheratons and other brand name hotels, the Flatotel (Flat, like an apartment in London combined with hotel amenities) offers something those brands do not: space. All the hotel's sleek, apartmentlike rooms, especially the suites, are large by New York standards and all feature refrigerators and microwaves, while suites have kitchenettes or full kitchens, two flatscreen televisions, and generous desks. The marble bathrooms are spacious and well-equipped. The hotel features 60 one- to three-bedroom family suites with dining areas and full kitchens in each. In some suites on higher floors—the hotel is 47 stories—you have spectacular, river-to-river views. Though the hotel has the appearance of a corporate refuge, with its dark marble and metal tones, its services are personable and more like a boutique than the Midtown monolith it appears to be.

132 West 52nd St (btwn Sixth and Seventh aves.), New York, NY 10019. © **800/ FLATOTEL** or 212/887-9400. Fax 212/887-9795. www.flatotel.com. 288 units. From $399 doubles; from $549 suites. AE, DC, DISC, MC, V. Parking $30 self parking, $47 valet. Subway: B,D,E to Seventh Ave. **Amenities:** Restaurant; bar; fitness center; business center; concierge; room service; dry cleaning. *In room:* A/C, TV, high-speed Internet, dataport, fridge, microwave, coffee/tea maker, iron/ironing board, hair dryer, safe, CD player.

Jumeirah Essex House ★★★   In 2006, the Dubai-based hotel group Jumeirah took over managing the landmark 76-year old hotel overlooking Central Park, which had become worn around the edges. After a $90-million renovation, the hotel was unveiled, and the results are sparkling. The lobby has been spruced up but retains the Art Deco look with its black-and-white marble floor, white banquettes where afternoon tea is now served, and historic photos of New York lining the corridors. The rooms have been updated with neat wall-to-wall wooden cabinetry, leather-framed mirrors, and window blinds that mirror the leaf patterns you might see across the street in the park. State-of-the art technology, such as "stumble lights" underneath nightstands, has been added as part of the renovations. You won't find tiny rooms here, nor should you; suites are magnificent, especially those overlooking the park.

160 Central Park South (btwn Sixth and Seventh aves.), New York, NY, 10019. © 888/645-5697 or 212/247-0300. Fax 212/315-1839. www.jumeirahessexhouse.com. 515 units. From $709 doubles; from $959 suites. Valet parking $55. AE, DC, DISC, MC, V. Subway: N, R, W, Q to 57th St. **Amenities:** Restaurant; bar; lobby lounge; afternoon tea; fitness center; spa; concierge; room service; business center; dry cleaning. *In room:* A/C, TV, Wi-Fi, minibar, hair dryer, iron, safe, speaker phones.

Le Parker Meridien ★★ *Kids*   Not many hotels in New York can rival the attributes of this hotel: Its location on 57th Street, not too far from Times Square and a close walk from Central Park and Fifth Avenue shopping, is practically perfect; the 17,000-square-foot fitness center, called Gravity, features basketball and racquetball courts, a spa, and a rooftop pool; three excellent restaurants, including **Norma's** (p. 92), for breakfast, and the aptly-named **Burger Joint,** rated by many as the best burger in the city; a gorgeous lobby; and elevators with televisions that show *Tom and Jerry* and Charlie Chaplin shorts. The spacious hotel rooms, though a bit on the IKEA side, have a fun feel to them, with hidden drawers and swirling television platforms, inventively exploiting an economical use of space. Rooms have wood platform beds with feather beds, built-ins that include large work desks, stylish Aeron chairs, free high-speed Internet, and 32-inch flatscreen televisions with VCR, CD, and DVD players. The slate-and-limestone bathrooms are large but unfortunately come with shower only.

118 W. 57th St. (btwn Sixth and Seventh aves.), New York, NY 10019. © 800/543-4300 or 212/245-5000. Fax 212/307-1776. www.parkermeridien.com. 731 units. $600–$800 double; from $780 suite. Extra person $30. Excellent packages and weekend rates often available (as low as $225 at press time). AE, DC, DISC, MC, V. Parking $45. Subway: F, N, Q, R to 57th St. Pets accepted. **Amenities:** 3 restaurants; rooftop pool; fantastic fitness center and spa; concierge (2 w/Clefs d'Or distinction); weekday

morning courtesy car to Wall St.; full-service business center; 24-hr. room service; laundry service; dry cleaning. *In room:* A/C, 32-in. TV w/DVD/CD player, high-speed Internet, dataport, minibar, hair dryer, iron, safe, nightly complimentary shoeshine.

Sofitel New York ★★★ *(Finds* There are many fine hotels on 44th Street between Fifth and Sixth avenues, but the best, in my estimation, is the soaring Sofitel. Upon entering the hotel and the warm, inviting lobby with check-in tucked off to the side, you wouldn't think you were entering a hotel that is this new, which is one of the reasons why the hotel is so special. The designers have melded modern, new-world amenities with European old-world elegance. The rooms are spacious and comfortable, adorned with art. The lighting is soft and romantic, the walls and windows soundproof. Suites are equipped with king beds, two televisions, and pocket doors separating the bedroom from a sitting room. Bathrooms in all rooms are magnificent, with separate showers and soaking tubs.

45 W. 44th St. (btwn Fifth and Sixth aves.), New York, NY 10036. (C) **212/354-8844.** Fax 212/354-2480. www.sofitel.com. 398 units. $299–$599 double; from $439 suite. 1 child stays free in parent's room. AE, DC, MC, V. Parking $45. Subway: B, D, F, V to 42nd St. Pets accepted. **Amenities:** Restaurant; bar; exercise room; concierge; 24-hr. room service; laundry service; dry cleaning. *In room:* A/C, TV w/pay movies and Internet access, high-speed Internet, dataport, minibar, hair dryer, iron, safe, CD player.

MODERATE

Casablanca Hotel ★★ *(Value* Just off Broadway in the middle of Times Square, the Casablanca Hotel is an oasis. Where, in **Rick's Café,** the Casablanca's homey guest lounge, you can sit by a fire, read a paper, check your e-mail, watch TV on the huge screen, or sip a cappuccino from the serve-yourself machine. If the days or nights are balmy, you can lounge on the rooftop deck or second-floor courtyard. The rooms might not be the biggest around, but they are well outfitted with ceiling fans, free bottles of water, and beautifully tiled bathrooms where, if you wish, you can open the window and let sounds outside remind you where you really are. The Casablanca is an HK Hotels property and like their other hotels, service is top-notch. Because of its location, moderate prices, and size (only 48 rooms), the Casablanca is in high demand, so book early.

147 W. 43rd St. (just east of Broadway), New York, NY 10036. (C) **888/922-7225** or 212/869-1212. Fax 212/391-7585. www.casablancahotel.com. 48 units. $249–$299 double; from $399 suite. Rates include continental breakfast, all-day cappuccino, and weekday wine and cheese. Check website for Internet rates and other special deals. AE, DC, MC, V. Parking $25 next door. Subway: N, R, 1, 2, 3 to 42nd St./Times Sq. **Amenities:** Cyber lounge; free access to New York Sports Club; concierge; business center; limited room service; laundry service; dry cleaning; video library. *In room:* A/C, TV/VCR, dataport, minibar, hair dryer, CD player, ceiling fan.

414 Hotel ☆ *Finds*   A block from Times Square and close to exciting Hell's Kitchen, this place offers 37-inch flatscreen televisions in every room, spacious, well-equipped bathrooms; complimentary bottled water, continental breakfast, and Wi-Fi; in-room refrigerators; and a lovely courtyard. It all sounds too good for a budget hotel. But if you want all that and don't want to pay anything close to what hotels offering much less are asking, then you also have to endure the 414's thin walls; if stomping above you is a problem ask for a top floor room, which would mean you would have to walk the four floors: the hotel does not have an elevator. Despite these inconveniences, the 414 Hotel has comfortable, clean rooms and the perks make it a good Midtown moderate choice.

414 W. 46th St. (btwn Ninth and Tenth aves.) New York, NY 10036. ℂ **866/ 414-HOTEL** or 212/399-0006. Fax 212/957-8710. www.hotel414.com. 22 units. $169–$259 double. Subway: A, C, E, 7, 42nd Street. **Amenities:** Complimentary continental breakfast; comp coffee, juice, tea; concierge; dry cleaning (upon request); business services (upon request). *In room:* A/C, TV, Wi-Fi, dataport, fridge, hair dryer, safe.

Hotel Metro ☆☆ *Kids*   The Metro is the choice in Midtown for those who don't want to sacrifice style or comfort for affordability. This Art Deco–style jewel has larger rooms than you'd expect for the price. They're outfitted with retro furnishings, playful fabrics, fluffy pillows, smallish but well appointed marble bathrooms, and alarm clocks. Only about half the bathrooms have tubs, but the others have shower stalls big enough for two (junior suites have whirlpool tubs). The "family room" is a two-room suite that has a second bedroom in lieu of a sitting area. The comfy library/lounge area off the lobby, where complimentary buffet breakfast is laid out and the coffeepot's on all day, is a popular hangout. Service is attentive; and the rooftop terrace boasts a breathtaking view of the Empire State Building and makes a great place to order up room service from the **Metro Grill.**

45 W. 35th St. (btwn Fifth and Sixth aves.), New York, NY 10001. ℂ **800/356-3870** or 212/947-2500. Fax 212/279-1310. www.hotelmetronyc.com. 179 units. $250–$365 double; $245–$420 triple or quad; $255–$425 family room; $275–$475 suite. Extra person $25. 1 child under 13 stays free in parent's room. Rates include continental breakfast. Check with airlines and other package operators for great-value package deals. AE, DC, MC, V. Parking $20 nearby. Subway: B, D, F, V, N, R to 34th St. **Amenities:** Restaurant; alfresco rooftop bar in summer; good fitness room; salon; limited room service; laundry service; dry cleaning. *In room:* A/C, TV, high-speed Internet, dataport, fridge, hair dryer, iron.

Hotel QT ☆☆ *Value*   Owned by Andre Balazs, of the **Mercer** (p. 42), Hotel QT offers much of the Mercer's style without the hefty rates. From its enviable Midtown location to its extras such as a swimming pool in the lobby, steam room and sauna, free high-speed

Internet, complimentary continental breakfast, and good-size rooms, including a number with bunk beds, Hotel QT is one of the best moderate options in the Times Square area. You check in at a kiosk/front desk where you pick up periodicals or essentials to stock your minibar. Making your way to the elevators, you might see guests swimming in the lobby pool or having a drink at the pool's swim-up bar, an unusual site in the Big Apple. The rooms are sparse in tone, but the queen- and king-size platform beds are plush and dressed with Egyptian cotton sheets. The biggest drawback is the bathrooms: There are no doors on the bathrooms—sliding doors conceal the shower (none of the rooms have tubs) and the toilet.

125 W. 45th St. (btwn Sixth Ave. and Broadway), New York, NY 10036. © 212/354-2323. Fax 212/302-8585. www.hotelqt.com. 140 units. $199–$350 double. AE, DC, MC, V. Parking nearby $25. Subway: B, D, F, V to 47th–50th St./Rockefeller Center. **Amenities:** Bar; swimming pool; gym; sauna; steam room; complimentary continental breakfast. *In room:* A/C, TV, free Wi-Fi, free high-speed Internet, minifridge, hair dryer, iron/ironing board, safe, CD player, DVD player, 2-line phones w/free local calls.

INEXPENSIVE

Red Roof Inn ✿ (*Value*)   Manhattan's first and only Red Roof Inn offers relief from Midtown's high-priced hotel scene. The hotel occupies a former office building that was gutted and laid out fresh, allowing for more spacious rooms and bathrooms than you'll usually find in this price category. The lobby feels smart, and elevators are quiet and efficient. In-room amenities—including coffeemakers and TVs with on-screen Web access—are better than most competitors', and furnishings are new and comfortable. Wi-Fi is available throughout the property. The location—on a block lined with nice hotels and affordable Korean restaurants, a stone's throw from the Empire State Building—is excellent. Be sure to compare the rates offered by Apple Core Hotel's reservation line and those quoted on Red Roof's national reservation line and website, as they can vary significantly. Complimentary continental breakfast adds to the value.

6 W. 32nd St. (btwn Broadway and Fifth Ave.), New York, NY 10001. © 800/755-3194, 800/RED-ROOF, or 212/643-7100. Fax 212/643-7101. www.applecorehotels. com or www.redroof.com. 171 units. $89–$329 double (usually less than $189). Rates include continental breakfast. Children under 13 stay free in parent's room. AE, DC, DISC, MC, V. Parking $26. Subway: B, D, F, N, R, V to 34th St. **Amenities:** Breakfast room; wine-and-beer lounge; exercise room; concierge; laundry service; dry cleaning. *In room:* A/C, TV w/pay movies and Internet access, Wi-Fi, dataport, fridge, coffeemaker, hair dryer, iron, video games.

Travel Inn (*Kids*) (*Value*)   Extras such as a huge outdoor pool and sun deck, a sunny, up-to-date fitness room, and *free* parking (with in and out privileges!) make the Travel Inn a terrific deal. The Travel Inn may not be loaded with personality, but it does offer the clean, bright regularity of a good chain hotel—an attractive trait in a city where "quirky" is the catchword at most affordable hotels. Rooms are over-size and comfortably furnished, with extra-firm beds and work desks; even the smallest double is sizable and has a roomy bathroom, and double/doubles make great affordable shares for families. A total renovation over the last couple of years has made everything feel like new, even the nicely tiled bathrooms. Though a bit off the track, Off-Broadway theaters and affordable restaurants are at hand, and it's a 10-minute walk to the Theater District.

515 W. 42nd St. (just west of Tenth Ave.), New York, NY 10036. ℂ 888/HOTEL58, 800/869-4630, or 212/695-7171. Fax 212/967-5025. www.thetravelinnhotelcom. 160 units. $105–$250 double. Extra person $10. Children under 16 stay free in parent's room. AAA discounts available; check website for special Internet deals. AE, DC, DISC, MC, V. Free self-parking. Subway: A, C, E to 42nd St./Port Authority. **Amenities:** Coffee shop; terrific outdoor pool w/deck chairs and lifeguard in season; fitness center; Gray Line tour desk; 24-hr. room service. *In room:* A/C, TV, dataport, hair dryer, iron.

8 Midtown East & Murray Hill

To find the hotels in this section, see the map on p. 46 and 47. Also consider the grandest of dames, the **Plaza,** at Fifth Avenue and Central Park South (ℂ **212/759-3000;** www.fairmont.com/thePlaza) which, at press time, was just re-opening. After a $400 million, 2-year renovation, the Plaza is now part condo, and part hotel. There are 282 guest rooms ranging from a roomy 482-square feet guest room to suites of almost 1,500 square feet, some with terraces, and all feature butler service. The famous **Palm Court** is open once again for high (expensive) tea, and the **Oak Room** and Oak Bar for cocktails and dinner. New at the Plaza are the lobby's **Champagne Bar** and the **Rose Club** overlooking the lobby and a fitness club helmed by trainer to the stars, Radu. Rates start at (gulp) $1,000 per night. What would Eloise think?

VERY EXPENSIVE

The Peninsula-New York ✶✶✶   Housed in a beauty of a landmark Beaux Arts building, the Peninsula is the perfect combination of old-world charm and state-of-the-art technology. Rooms are huge, with plenty of closet and storage space, but best of all is the bedside control panel that allows you to regulate lighting, television, stereo, air-conditioning, and the DO NOT DISTURB sign on your door. Even though you don't have to leave the comfort of your bed, eventually you will need to go to the bathroom, and when you do, you'll find huge marble bathrooms with spacious soaking tubs and yet another control panel at your fingertips, including the controls for, in most rooms, a television so you can watch while taking your bubble bath (now that's happy excess). The Peninsula also features one of the best and biggest New York hotel health clubs and spas, the rooftop **Pen-Top Bar,** and a faultless concierge desk.

700 Fifth Ave. (at 55th St.), New York, NY 10019. © **800/262-9467** or 212/956-2888. Fax 212/903-3949. www.peninsula.com. 239 units. $775–$1125 double; from $1,275 suite. Extra person $50. Children under 12 stay free in parent's room. Winter weekend package rates from $585 at press time. AE, DC, DISC, MC, V. Valet parking $55. Subway: E, V to Fifth Ave. Pets accepted. **Amenities:** Restaurant; rooftop bar; library-style lounge for afternoon tea and cocktails; tri-level rooftop health club and spa w/treatment rooms; pool; exercise classes; whirlpool; sauna; and sun deck; 24-hr. concierge; business center; 24-hr. room service; in-room massage; babysitting; laundry service; dry cleaning. *In room:* A/C, TV w/pay movies, fax, Wi-Fi, high-speed Internet, minibar, hair dryer, safe, complimentary "water bar" w/5 choices of bottled water.

St. Regis ✷✷✷   When John Jacob Astor built the St. Regis in 1904, he set out to create a hotel that would reflect the elegance and luxury of grand hotels in Europe. Over a hundred years later, the St. Regis, a New York landmark, still reflects that splendor. This Beaux Arts classic is a marvel: antique furniture, crystal chandeliers, silk wall coverings, and marble floors adorn the public spaces and the high-ceilinged, airy guest rooms. The suites are particularly ornate, some with French doors, four-poster beds, and decorative fireplaces. The marble bathrooms are spacious and feature separate showers and tubs. In a nod to the future, plasma televisions were recently added in all the rooms, along with LCD screens in the bathrooms. Service is efficiently white-gloved and every guest is assigned a tuxedoed butler, on call 24 hours to answer any reasonable requests. **Afternoon tea** is served daily in the Astor Court and Chef Alain Ducasse claimed the former Lespinasse space for his new **Adour.**

2 E. 55th St. (at Fifth Ave.), New York, NY 10022. © **212/753-4500.** Fax 212/787-3447. www.stregis.com. 256 units. $695–$995 double; from $1,150 suite. Check Internet for specials as low as $400 at press time. AE, DC, DISC, MC, V. Parking $55. Subway: E, V to Fifth Ave. **Amenities:** Restaurant; historic bar; tea lounge; fitness center and spa; concierge; 24-hr. room service; babysitting; laundry service; 24-hr. butler service; valet service. *In room:* A/C, TV, high-speed Internet, minibar, hair dryer, safe, DVD/CD player.

EXPENSIVE

The Benjamin ✷✷✷   From the retro sign and clock on Lexington Avenue to the high-ceilinged marble lobby, when you enter The Benjamin, it's as if you've stepped into Jazz Age New York. But once you get to your spacious room and notice the high-tech amenities, such as Bose Wave radios, browsers and video games for the TVs, high-speed Internet access, fax machines, ergonomic chairs and moveable workstations, you'll know you're in the 21st century. All rooms are airy, but the deluxe studios and one-bedroom suites are extra large. How many hotels can claim a "sleep concierge" or *guarantee* a good night's sleep? And don't forget the pillow menu featuring 11 options, including buckwheat and Swedish Memory, in which foam designed by NASA reacts to your body temperature. If you are a light sleeper, book a room away from Lexington Avenue, which can get busy (that is, noisy) most weeknights and mornings. Bathrooms feature Frette robes, TV speakers, and water pressure from the showerhead strong enough to make you think you've just experienced a deep-tissue massage.

125 E. 50th St. (at Lexington Ave.), New York, NY 10022. © **888/4-BENJAMIN,** 212/320-8002, or 212/715-2500. Fax 212/715-2525. www.thebenjamin.com. 209 units. From $459 superior double; from $499 deluxe studio; from $559 suite. Call or check website for special weekend-stay offers. AE, DC, DISC, MC, V. Parking $45. Subway: 6 to 51st St.; E, F to Lexington Ave. Pets accepted. **Amenities:** Restaurant; cocktail lounge; state-of-the-art exercise room; full-service spa; concierge; sleep concierge; business services; 24-hr. room service; dry cleaning; valet service. *In room:* A/C, TV w/pay movies/video games/Internet access, fax/copier/printer, dataport, kitchenette, minibar, coffeemaker, laptop-size safe, china, high-speed Internet connection, microwave.

Hotel Elysée ★★   This romantic gem of a hotel in the heart of Midtown might be easy to miss: It's dwarfed by modern glass towers. But that it is so inconspicuous is part of the Elysée's romantic appeal. Built in 1926, the hotel has a storied past as the preferred address for artists and writers including Tennessee Williams, Jimmy Breslin, Maria Callas and Vladimir Horowitz (who donated a Steinway, which still resides in the Piano Suite), John Barrymore, and Marlon Brando. The hotel retains that sexy, discreet feel and now is run by HK Hotels (The Giraffe, The Gansevoort, and The Library). Rooms were recently renovated and have many quirky features; some have fireplaces, others have kitchens or solariums, and all are decorated in country-French furnishings. Good-size bathrooms are done in Italian marble and well outfitted. Off the gorgeous black-and-white marble-floored lobby is the **Monkey Bar.** On the second floor is the Club Room, where a free continental breakfast is offered daily along with complimentary wine and cheese weekday evenings.

60 E. 54th St. (btwn Park and Madison aves.), New York, NY 10022. © **800/535-9733** or 212/753-1066. Fax 212/980-9278. www.elyseehotel.com. 101 units. From $295 double; from $425 suite. Check the website for seasonal specials. Rates include continental breakfast and weekday evening wine and cheese. AE, DC, DISC, MC, V. Parking $30. Subway: E, V to Fifth Ave. **Amenities:** Restaurant; bar; free access to

nearby gym; concierge; limited room service; laundry service; dry cleaning. *In room:* A/C, TV/VCR, dataport, minibar, hair dryer, iron, safe, Wi-Fi.

The Kitano New York ⭐⭐⭐ *Finds*   Owned by the Kitano Group of Japan, this elegant Murray Hill gem offers a unique mix of East and West sensibilities. The marble and mahogany lobby, with its Y-shaped staircase and Botero bronze *Dog,* is one of the most attractive in New York. The hotel was first opened in 1973; in the mid-1990s, along with acquiring an 1896 landmark town house next door, the Kitano was fully renovated. If you're a lucky (and wealthy) individual, you'll get the opportunity to stay in one of three one-bedroom town house suites, each with sunken living room, bay windows, and original, eclectic art. The hotel also offers a Tatami suite, with tatami mats, rice paper screens, and a Japanese Tea Ceremony room. Most rooms are not quite that luxurious or unique, but all include tasteful mahogany furniture, soundproof windows, and, for a real taste of Japan, green tea upon arrival; marble bathrooms are large and have heated towel racks and removable shower heads. On the mezzanine-level is a bar, which on Wednesday through Saturday evenings offers the acclaimed **Jazz at the Kitano.**

66 Park Ave. (at 38th St.), New York, NY 10016. ℂ 800/548-2666 or **212/885-7000.** Fax 212/885-7100. www.kitano.com. 149 units. $480–$605 double; from $715 suite. Check website for specials (as low as $239 at press time). AE, DC, DISC, MC, V. Parking $40. Subway: 4, 5, 6, 7, S to Grand Central. **Amenities:** 2 restaurants; bar w/live jazz; access to a nearby health club; concierge; complimentary limo service to Wall St. on weekdays; limited room service; laundry service; dry cleaning. *In room:* A/C, TV, fax, high-speed Internet, dataport, hair dryer, iron, complimentary tea.

The Library Hotel ⭐⭐ *Finds*   Just a block from the New York Public Library, each of the Library Hotel's 10 guest-room floors is dedicated to 1 of the 10 major categories of the Dewey Decimal System. When I visited the hotel, I was appropriately booked into a "Geography and Travel" room. Overall, the hotel has a pleasing, informal feel. Guest rooms, which come in three categories—petite (really small), deluxe, and junior suites—feature mahogany built-ins, generous desks, and immaculate marble bathrooms; all are extremely comfortable. The Library's public spaces—a reading room where weekday wine and cheese and a complimentary daily breakfast are served, a writer's den with a fireplace and flatscreen television, and a rooftop terrace—all help make the Library a welcome refuge in the heart of the city.

299 Madison Ave. (at 41st St.), New York, NY 10017. ℂ **877/793-7323** or 212/ 983-4500. Fax 212/499-9099. www.libraryhotel.com. 60 units. $345–$435 double; $525 Love Room or junior suite; $960 2-room family suite. Rates include continental breakfast buffet, all-day snacks, and weekday wine and cheese. Inquire about corporate, promotional, and weekend rates (as low as $329 at press time). AE, DC,

MC, V. Parking $30 nearby. Subway: 4, 5, 6, 7, S to 42nd St./Grand Central. **Amenities:** Restaurant; free access to nearby health club; business center; 24-hr. room service; laundry service; dry cleaning; video library of American Film Institute's Top 100 films. *In room:* A/C, TV/VCR, high-speed Internet, dataport, minibar, hair dryer, iron, laptop-size safe, CD player.

The Roger 🏵🏵   The hotel's namesake, Roger Williams, in time abandoned his puritanical roots to become a secular leader. Starting from the welcoming lobby with its odd assortment of mod yet comfortable seating, where jazz combos entertain 3 nights a week, to the different varieties of rooms—some small, some generous, some with landscaped terraces, others with views of the Empire State building; all with impressive amenities such as quilts, flatscreen televisions, complimentary high-speed and wireless Internet, and marble bathrooms—the Roger is one of the top choices in a quiet-yet-convenient location. A floating granite staircase leads from the lobby to a mezzanine lounge, where you can have breakfast in the morning and drink cocktails by candlelight at night.

131 Madison Ave. (at E. 31st St.), New York, NY 10016. ℂ **888/448-7788** or 212/448-7000. Fax 212/448-7007. www.hotelrogerwilliams.com. 200 units. From $289 a night at press time. AE, DC, DISC, MC, V. Subway: 6 to 28th St./Lexington Ave. **Amenities:** Lounge; fitness center; concierge; laundry service; dry cleaning; complimentary Wi-Fi; conference suite. *In room:* A/C, flatscreen TV, Wi-Fi, high-speed Internet, minibar, iron/ironing board, safe.

Waldorf=Astoria and the Waldorf Towers 🏵🏵   If you are looking for the epitome of old-school elegance, you can't do better than the Waldorf=Astoria. This massive 1-square-block Art Deco masterpiece is not only a hotel icon, it's a genuine New York City landmark. Here you'll find a lobby so big and grand, it's reminiscent of Grand Central Station, including having its own signature clock. With over 1,000 rooms, the pace can be hectic, and at times the lines for checking in might remind you of the post office. And what rooms they are; no two the same, yet all are airy, with high ceilings, traditional decor, comfortable linens and beds, and spacious marble bathrooms, along with fax machines and high-speed Internet access. For even more opulence, try a suite in the **Waldorf Towers,** where most rooms are bigger than most New York City apartments.

   Peacock Alley, off the main lobby, is also open for breakfast, lunch and dinner, but famous for the sumptuous Sunday brunch.

301 Park Ave. (btwn 49th and 50th sts.), New York, NY 10022. ℂ **800/WALDORF,** 800/774-1500, or 212/355-3000. Fax 212/872-7272 (Astoria) or 212/872-4875 (Towers). www.waldorfastoria.com or www.waldorf-towers.com. 1,245 units (180 in the Towers). Waldorf=Astoria $229–$585 double; from $549 suite. Waldorf Towers $549–$959 double; from $799 suite. Extra person $35. Children under 18 stay free

in parent's room. Corporate, senior, seasonal, and weekend discounts may be available (as low as $189 at press time), as well as attractive package deals. AE, DC, DISC, MC, V. Parking $55. Subway: 6 to 51st St. **Amenities:** 4 restaurants; 4 bars; 3,000-sq.-ft. fitness center and spa; concierge and theater desk; 24-hr. business center; salon; 24-hr. room service; laundry service; dry cleaning; executive-level rooms. Tower rooms include butler service, Clefs d'Or concierge. *In room:* A/C, TV w/pay movies, high-speed Internet (in executive-level rooms and suites), dataport, minibar, coffeemaker, hair dryer, iron. Waldorf Towers suites include kitchenette or wet bar w/fridge, safe.

INEXPENSIVE

Hotel Grand Union *Value* This centrally located hotel is big with budget-minded international travelers. A white-on-white lobby leads to clean and spacious rooms with nice extras uncommon in this price category, such as hair dryers and free HBO. Fluorescent overhead lighting, unattractive colonial-style furniture, and an utter lack of natural light dampen the mood—but considering the roominess, low rates, and central-to-everything location, the Grand Union is a good deal. Room no. 309, a nicely configured quad with two twins and a queen in a separate alcove, is great for families. Most bathrooms have been outfitted in granite or tile; ask for a newly renovated one. The staff is helpful, and there's a pleasant sitting room off the lobby and an adjacent coffee shop for morning coffee or a quick burger.

34 E. 32nd St. (btwn Madison and Park aves.), New York, NY 10016. ✆ **212/683-5890.** Fax 212/689-7397. www.hotelgrandunion.com. 95 units. $175–$300 single or double; $215–$325 twin or triple; $255–375 quad. Call or check website for special rates (as low as $90 at press time). AE, DC, DISC, MC, V. Parking $22 nearby. Subway: 6 to 33rd St. **Amenities:** Coffee shop; tour desk; fax service; Wi-Fi. *In room:* A/C, TV, dataport, fridge, hair dryer.

Hotel Thirty Thirty ★ *Value* Thirty Thirty is just right for bargain-hunting travelers looking for a splash of style with an affordable price tag. The design-conscious tone is set in the loftlike industrial-modern lobby. Rooms are on the smallish side but do the trick for those who intend to spend their days out on the town rather than holed up here. Configurations are split between twin/twins (great for friends), queens, and queen/queens (great for triples, budget-minded quads, or shares that want more spreading-out room). Nice features include cushioned headboards; firm mattresses; two-line phones; built-in wardrobes; and spacious, nicely tiled bathrooms. A few larger units have kitchenettes, great if you're staying for a while, as you'll appreciate the extra room and the fridge. There's no room service, but delivery is available from nearby restaurants.

30 E. 30th St. (btwn Madison and Park aves.), New York, NY 10016. ✆ **800/804-4480** or 212/689-1900. Fax 212/689-0023. www.thirtythirty-nyc.com. 243 units.

$249–$349 double; $279–$399 double with kitchenette; $399–$499 quad. Call for last-minute deals, or check website for special promotions (as low as $99 at press time). AE, DC, DISC, MC, V. Parking $30 1 block away. Subway: 6 to 28th St. Pets accepted with advance approval. **Amenities:** Restaurant; concierge; laundry service; dry cleaning. *In room:* A/C, TV, dataport, hair dryer.

9 Upper West Side

VERY EXPENSIVE

Trump International Hotel & Tower ★★★   From the outside, it's a another tall, dark monolith, hovering over Columbus Circle and lower Central Park. But go inside and spend a night or two, experience services such as your own "Trump Attaché," a personal concierge who will provide comprehensive services; take advantage of such first-class facilities as the 6,000-square-foot health club with lap pool and a full-service spa; or order room service from the hotel's signature restaurant, the four-star **Jean-Georges.**

Guest rooms are surprisingly understated, with high ceilings and floor-to-ceiling windows, some with incredible views of Central Park and all with telescopes for taking in the view, and marble bathrooms with Jacuzzi tubs. But if that's not enough—it certainly was for me—you also get two complimentary bottles of Trump water, complete with a picture of the Donald on each one. For a hotel this well run, you can forgive the man for his excesses.

1 Central Park West (at 60th St.), New York, NY 10023. ℂ **212/299-1000.** Fax 212/299-1150. www.trumpintl.com. 167 units. From $765 double; from $1,200 1- or 2-bedroom suite. Children stay free in parent's room. Check website for special rates and packages; also check www.travelweb.com for discounted rates. AE, DC, DISC, MC, V. Parking $48. Subway: A, B, C, D, 1 to 59th St./Columbus Circle. **Amenities:** Restaurant; spa and health club w/steam, sauna, and pool; Clefs d'Or concierge; staffed business center w/secretarial services; 24-hr. room service; in-room massage; babysitting; laundry service; dry cleaning; butler (personal attaché); CD library. *In room:* A/C, TV/VCR w/pay movies and video games, fax/copier/printer, high-speed Internet, dataport, minibar, coffeemaker, hair dryer, iron, laptop-size safe, DVD/CD player.

MODERATE

Hotel Beacon ★★ (Kids) (Value)   For families, you won't find a better location—or value. Close to Central Park and Riverside Park, the Museum of Natural History and major subway lines, the Beacon's location is ideal. Rooms are generously sized and feature a kitchenette, a roomy closet, and a marble bathroom. Nearly all standard rooms feature two double beds, and they're big enough to sleep a family on a budget. The one- and two-bedroom suites are some of the best bargains in the city; each has two closets and a pullout sofa in the living room. The two-bedrooms have a second bathroom,

Where to Stay Uptown

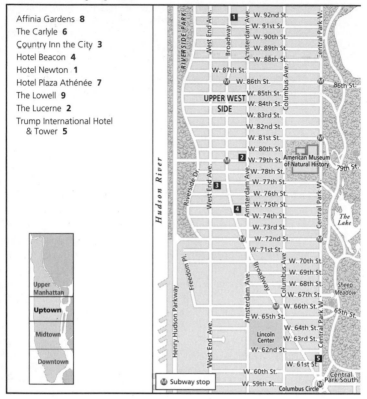

Affinia Gardens **8**
The Carlyle **6**
Country Inn the City **3**
Hotel Beacon **4**
Hotel Newton **1**
Hotel Plaza Athénée **7**
The Lowell **9**
The Lucerne **2**
Trump International Hotel & Tower **5**

making them well outfitted enough to house a small army—including my own. There's no room service, but a wealth of budget dining options that deliver, along with some excellent markets make the Beacon even more of a home away from home.

2130 Broadway (at 75th St.), New York, NY 10023. © **800/572-4969** or 212/787-1100. Fax 212/724-0839. www.beaconhotel.com. 236 units. $210–$325 single or double; from $295 1- or 2-bedroom suite. Extra person $15. Children under 17 stay free in parent's room. Check website for special deals (doubles from $145; 1-bedroom suites as low as $195 at press time). AE, DC, DISC, MC, V. Parking $41 1 block away. Subway: 1, 2, 3 to 72nd St. **Amenities:** Coffee shop adjacent; access to health club in the building; concierge; laundry service; dry cleaning; coin-op laundry; fax and copy service; Internet center. *In room:* A/C, TV w/pay movies, kitchenette, hair dryer, iron, laptop-size safe.

The Lucerne 𝒞𝒞 *Finds*   As a longtime resident of the Upper West Side, I can easily say the Lucerne, in a magnificent 1903 landmark

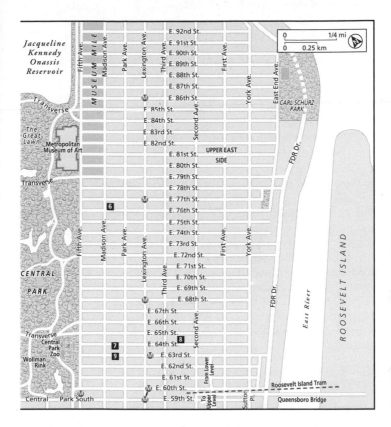

building, best captures the feel of that neighborhood. Service is impeccable, especially for a moderately priced hotel, and everything is fresh and immaculate. The rooms are comfortable and big enough for kings, queens, or two doubles, with attractive bathrooms. Some of the rooms have views of the Hudson River. The suites are extra-special and include kitchenettes, stocked minifridges, microwaves, and sitting rooms with sofas and extra TVs. The highly-rated **Nice Matin** offers room service for breakfast, lunch, and dinner. But if you don't want to dine there, you can sample some of the neighborhood food at nearby Zabar's or H&H Bagels.

201 W. 79th St. (at Amsterdam Ave.), New York, NY 10024. © **800/492-8122** or 212/875-1000. Fax 212/579-2408. www.thelucernehotel.com. 216 units. $330–$460 double or queen; $380–$500 king or junior suite; $420–$710 1-bedroom suite (check website for Internet specials and packages). Extra person $20. Children under

16 stay free in parent's room. AAA discounts offered; check website for Internet specials. AE, DC, DISC, MC, V. Parking $29 nearby. Subway: 1 to 79th St. **Amenities:** Restaurant; fitness center; business center; limited room service; laundry service; dry cleaning. *In room:* A/C, TV w/Nintendo and Internet access, dataport, coffeemaker, hair dryer, iron.

INEXPENSIVE

Hotel Newton ★ *Value*   On the northern extreme of the Upper West Side, the Newton, unlike many of its peers, doesn't scream "budget" at every turn. As you enter the pretty lobby, you're greeted by a uniformed staff who are attentive and professional. The rooms are large, with good, firm beds, a desk, and a new bathroom, plus roomy closets in most (a few of the cheapest have wall racks only). Some are big enough to accommodate families, with two doubles or two queen-sized beds. The suites feature two queens in the bedroom, a sofa in the sitting room, plus niceties such as a microwave, mini-fridge, and iron that make them well worth the few extra dollars. The bigger rooms and suites have been upgraded with cherrywood furnishings, but even the older laminated furniture is much nicer than I usually see in this price range. The AAA-approved hotel is impeccably kept. The 96th Street express subway stop is just a block away, providing convenient access to the rest of the city, and the Key West Diner next door is a favorite for huge, cheap breakfasts.

2528 Broadway (btwn 94th and 95th sts.), New York, NY 10025. © **888/HOTEL58** or 212/678-6500. Fax 212/678-6758. www.hotelnewtoncom. 110 units. $95–$175 double or junior suite. Extra person $25. Children under 15 stay free in parent's room. AAA, corporate, senior, and group rates available; check website for special Internet deals. AE, DC, DISC, MC, V. Parking $27 nearby. Subway: 1, 2, 3 to 96th St. **Amenities:** 24-hr. room service. *In room:* A/C, TV, Wi-Fi, hair dryer.

10 Upper East Side

To find the hotels described in this section, see p. 64.

VERY EXPENSIVE

The Carlyle, A Rosewood Hotel ★★★   This 34-story *grande dame* towers over Madison Avenue majestically, perfectly epitomizing the old-world, moneyed neighborhood. Service is white-glove (literally) and doormen wear bowler hats; many celebrities and dignitaries, some with faces obscured by silk scarves, sip tea in the hotel's cozy Gallery. Guest rooms range from singles to seven-room suites, some with terraces and full dining rooms. All have marble bathrooms with whirlpool tubs and all the amenities you'd expect from a hotel of this caliber. The English manor–style decor is luxurious but not excessive, creating the comfortably elegant ambience of an Upper East Side apartment. Many suites have views of either downtown or the West Side and Central Park.

The marble-floored lobby with Piranesi prints and murals is a beauty. The hotel's supper club **Cafe Carlyle** (p. 182) is the place for first-rate cabaret. Charming **Bemelmans Bar,** named after illustrator Ludwig Bemelmans, who created the Madeline books and painted the mural here, is a great spot for cocktails.

35 E. 76th St. (at Madison Ave.), New York, NY 10021. © **800/227-5737** or 212/744-1600. Fax 212/717-4682. www.thecarlyle.com. 180 units. $650–$950 double; from $950 1- or 2-bedroom suite. AE, DC, DISC, MC, V. Parking $48. Subway: 6 to 77th St. Pets under 25 lbs accepted. **Amenities:** 3 restaurants (including one of the city's best cabaret rooms); tearoom; bar; high-tech fitness room w/sauna, Jacuzzi, and spa services; concierge; 24-hr. room service; laundry service; dry cleaning; video library. *In room:* A/C, TV/VCR, fax/copier/printer, high-speed Internet, dataport, pantry kitchenette or full kitchen w/minibar, hair dryer, safe, CD player.

Hotel Plaza Athénée 𝕮𝕮𝕮   This hideaway in New York's most elegant neighborhood (the stretch of Madison Ave. in the 60s) is elegant, luxurious, and oozing with sophistication. With antique furniture, hand-painted murals, and the Italian-marble floor that adorns the lobby, the Plaza Athénée has a European feel. In that tradition, service here is as good as it gets, with personalized check-in and attentive staff. The rooms come in a variety of shapes and sizes, and are all high-ceilinged and spacious; entrance foyers give them a residential feel. They are designed in rich fabrics and warm colors that help set a tone that makes you want to lounge in your room longer than you should. Many of the suites have terraces large enough to dine on. The Portuguese-marble bathrooms are outfitted with thick robes made for the hotel. The leather-floored lounge is called **Bar Seine** and is a welcome spot for a predinner cocktail. The restaurant, **Arabelle,** receives high praise for its weekend brunch.

37 E. 64th St. (btwn Madison and Park aves.), New York, NY 10021. © **800/447-8800** or 212/734-9100. Fax 212/772-0958. www.plaza-athenee.com. 149 units. $755–$825 double; from $1,620 suite. Check for packages and seasonal specials (as low as $495 at press time). AE, DC, DISC, MC, V. Parking $53. Subway: F to Lexington Ave. **Amenities:** Restaurant; bar; fitness center; Clefs d'Or concierge; business center; 24-hr. room service; laundry service; dry cleaning. *In room:* A/C, TV, fax, high-speed Internet, dataport, minibar, hair dryer, safe.

The Lowell 𝕮𝕮𝕮 *(Kids)*   The Lowell's style of luxury is best described as elegant, sophisticated 20th-century opulence. It has the feel of a residential dwelling; the lobby is small and clubby with first-rate European, old-world service. The rooms are the real treasures; each unique and all a good size. About two-thirds are suites with kitchenettes or full kitchens; some have terraces and most have working fireplaces. In the rooms you'll also find nice big, cushy arm-chairs, lots of leather, interesting artwork, and porcelain figurines scattered about. Bathrooms are Italian marble and outfitted with Bulgari amenities. On a quiet, tree-lined street 1 block from Central Park and right in the middle of Madison Avenue shopping, the Low-ell's location is ideal for those who want (and can afford) an urban retreat away from the Midtown madness.

28 E. 63rd St. (btwn Madison and Park aves.), New York, NY 10021. ℂ **212/838-1400.** Fax 212/319-4230. www.lowellhotel.com. 70 units. From $735 doubles; from $935 suites. Ask about packages and weekend and seasonal rates. AE, DC, DISC, MC, V. Parking $49. Subway: F to Lexington Ave. Pets under 15 lb. accepted. **Amenities:** 2 restaurants; tearoom; well-outfitted fitness room; 24-hr. concierge; limousine service; secretarial services; 24-hr. room service; babysitting; laundry service; dry cleaning; video library. *In room:* A/C, TV/VCR/DVD, fax/copier, Wi-Fi, dataport, mini-bar, hair dryer, CD player.

EXPENSIVE

Affinia Gardens ⓡ *Finds*   One of the newest members of the Affinia hospitality group (the Benjamin, p. 58, Dumont, Affinia Manhattan), this Upper East Side property has a residential feel that is true to the neighborhood. Affinia has transformed the hotel into an oasis of tranquility. Off the lobby is the lounge, appropriately called "Serenity," a 24-hour quiet zone where you can sit in comfort, sip tea, and unwind. If you choose to relax in your room, you can order, free of charge, a "tranquility kit." Or you can just lay back on the very comfortable Affinia bed and snooze to the calming sound of the ocean, brook, wind, or forest that come with the clock radio/CD player. This is an all-suite hotel and rooms range from junior suites to two-bedrooms; all are generously sized and come with full kitchens. Bathrooms, proportionally, are on the smallish side but well outfitted. Though it's in a highly desirable New York neighbor-hood, the hotel is a bit out of the way from the center of things. But that can be a plus if tranquility is what you seek.

215 E. 64th St. (btwn Second and Third aves.), New York, NY 10021. ℂ **866/AFFINIA** or 212/355-1230. Fax 212/758-7858. www.affinia.com. 136 units. Rates from $399, all suites. Check website for specials and Internet rates. Valet parking $32. AE, DC, DISC, MC, V. Subway: 6 to 68th St.–Lexington Ave. Fitness club; small business center; limited room service; coin-operated laundry. *In room:* A/C, TV/DVD, high-speed Internet, dataport, kitchen, iron, safe, CD player/clock radio.

3

Where to Dine

Attention, foodies: Welcome to your mecca. New York is the best restaurant town in the country, and one of the finest in the world. Other cities might have particular specialties, but no other culinary capital spans the globe as successfully as the Big Apple.

RESERVATIONS

Reservations are always a good idea, and a virtual necessity if your party is bigger than two. Do yourself a favor and call ahead so you won't be disappointed. If you're booking dinner on a weekend night, it's a good idea to call a few days in advance if you can.

But what if they don't *take* reservations?   Lots of restaurants, especially at the affordable end of the price range, don't take reservations. One of the ways they keep prices down is by packing people in as quickly as possible. Thus, the best cheap and mid-price restaurants often have a wait. Your best bet is to go early. Often you can get in more quickly on a weeknight. Or just go, knowing that you're going to have to wait if you head to a popular spot; hunker down with a cocktail at the bar and enjoy the festivities around you.

1 Financial District & TriBeCa

VERY EXPENSIVE

Chanterelle ★★★ CONTEMPORARY FRENCH   One of New York's best "special occasion" restaurants mainly because, well, they treat you so special. The dining room is a charmer with floral displays and an interesting modern art collection. Tables are far enough apart to give diners plenty of intimacy, something rare in many New York restaurants these days. Your server will work with you on your choices, pairing items that go best together. The French-themed menu is seasonal and changes every few weeks, but one signature dish appears on almost every menu: a marvelous grilled seafood sausage. The wine list is superlative but expensive. Still, you don't come to Chanterelle on the cheap—you come to celebrate.

2 Harrison St. (at Hudson St.). © 212/966-6960. www.chanterellenyc.com. Reservations recommended well in advance. Fixed-price lunch $42; a la carte lunch

Where to Dine Downtown

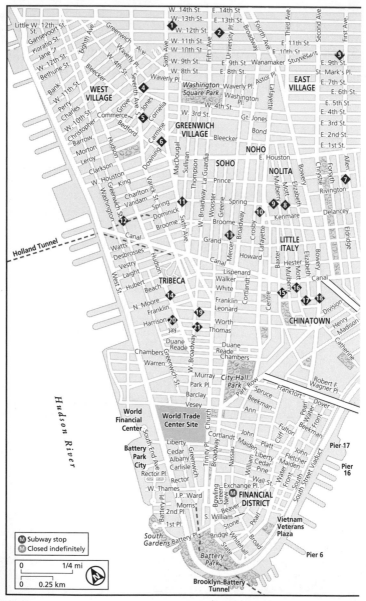

W. 14th St.   E. 14th St
W. 13th St.   E. 13th St
W. 12th St.   E. 12th St.
W. 11th St.   E. 11th St.
W. 10th St.   E. 10th St.
W. 9th St.   Wanamaker   E. 9th St.
W. 8th St.   E. 8th St.   St. Mark's Pl.

Little W. 12th St.
Gansevoort St.
Horatio St.
Jane St.
W. 12th St.
Bethune St.

EAST
VILLAGE
E. 7th St.
E. 6th St.
E. 5th St.
E. 4th St.
E. 3rd St.
E. 2nd St.
E. 1st St.

WEST
VILLAGE

Bank
Perry
Charles
W. 10th St.
Christopher
Barrow
Morton
Leroy
Clarkson
W. Houston
Charlton
Vandam
Spring
Dominick
Broome

Greenwich Ave
Waverly Pl.
Waverly Pl.

Washington
Square Park
Waverly Pl.
Washington
W. 4th St.
W. 3rd St.

GREENWICH
VILLAGE

Gt. Jones
Bond

NOHO

SOHO
Prince
Spring

NOLITA

LITTLE
ITALY
Hester
Canal

Holland Tunnel

Canal
Watts
Desbrosses
Vestry
Laight
Hubert
Beach

TRIBECA
N. Moore
Franklin
Harrison
Jay

Lispenard
Walker
White
Franklin
Leonard
Worth
Thomas

CHINATOWN

Duane
Reade
Chambers

Murray
Park Pl.
Barclay
Vesey

City Hall
Park

Spruce
Beekman
Ann

Robert F.
Wagner Pl.

Hudson River

World
Financial
Center

Battery
Park
City

World Trade
Center Site

Liberty
Cedar
Albany
Carlisle
Rector
W. Thames
J.P. Ward
Morris
2nd Pl.
1st Pl.

Cortlandt
John
Maiden
Liberty
Cedar
Pine
Wall St.
Exchange Pl.
Beaver
S. William
Stone

Pier 17
Pier 16

FINANCIAL
DISTRICT

Bowling
Green

Vietnam
Veterans
Plaza

South
Gardens
Battery Pl.
Bridge
Whitehall
State
Battery
Park

Pier 6

Brooklyn-Battery
Tunnel

Ⓜ Subway stop
Ⓜ Closed indefinitely

0   1/4 mi
0   0.25 km

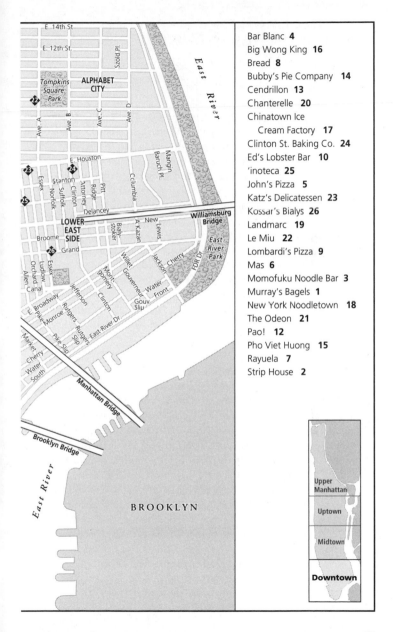

Bar Blanc **4**
Big Wong King **16**
Bread **8**
Bubby's Pie Company **14**
Cendrillon **13**
Chanterelle **20**
Chinatown Ice
 Cream Factory **17**
Clinton St. Baking Co. **24**
Ed's Lobster Bar **10**
'inoteca **25**
John's Pizza **5**
Katz's Delicatessen **23**
Kossar's Bialys **26**
Landmarc **19**
Le Miu **22**
Lombardi's Pizza **9**
Mas **6**
Momofuku Noodle Bar **3**
Murray's Bagels **1**
New York Noodletown **18**
The Odeon **21**
Pao! **12**
Pho Viet Huong **15**
Rayuela **7**
Strip House **2**

$22–$30; 3-course fixed-price dinner $95; tasting menu $125. AE, DISC, MC, V. Mon–Wed 5:30–10:30pm; Mon–Sat noon–2:30pm; Thurs–Sat 5:30–11pm; Sun 5–10pm. Subway: 1 to Franklin St.

EXPENSIVE

Landmarc *Finds* MEDITERRANEAN   This cozy, intimate TriBeCa restaurant is too good to be considered a neighborhood joint. Chef/owner Marc Murphy has put his own spin on this Italian/French rendition of a bistro. You'll find excellent smoked mozzarella and ricotta fritters alongside escargots bordelaise. It will be up to you to decide whether you imagine yourself in a Tuscan trattoria or a Provençal bistro. Or you can mix and match. Try the pasta of the day accompanied by mussels with a choice of sauce—Provençal, Dijonnaise, or a blend of shallots, parsley, and white wine. Steaks and chops are cooked over an open fire and steaks are offered with a variety of sauces; I had the hangar with a shallot bordelaise that complemented the meat perfectly. What keeps the neighbors pouring in, along with the food, are the affordable wines sold, not by the glass, but by the bottle or half bottle. Desserts are simple, small, and priced that way, with none more than $3.

179 W. Broadway (btwn Leonard and Worth sts.). *(C)* 212/343-3883. www.anvilny. com. Reservations recommended. Main courses $15–$34. AE, DC, DISC, MC, V. Mon–Fri noon–2am; Sat, Sun 9am–4pm and 5:30pm–2am. Subway: 1 to Franklin St.

MODERATE

Bubby's Pie Company *AMERICAN   You might have to wait in line to eat at Bubby's. You might get squeezed in at a table perilously close to another couple. And you might have to talk loudly to maintain a conversation with your dining companion. But your level of discomfort will subside as you begin to eat Bubby's comfort food. Whether it is the slow-cooked pulled barbecue pork, the lighter-than-air meatloaf, or the buttermilk-fried half chicken, with sides such as collard greens, sautéed spinach, mac 'n' cheese, or baked beans, Bubby's dishes define comfort. Take Bubby's advice and save room for dessert, especially the homemade pies; one taste of the chocolate peanut-butter pie brought on happy childhood flashbacks. Breakfast is big here and lasts well into the middle of the day. On weekends, though, the wait for brunch can be long. Bubby's also has a branch across the river in the DUMBO neighborhood of Brooklyn.

120 Hudson St. (at N. Moore St.). *(C)* 212/219-0666. www.bubbys.com. Reservations recommended for dinner (not accepted for brunch). Main courses $10–$15 breakfast, brunch, and lunch; $10–$21 dinner. DC, DISC, MC, V. Mon–Thurs 8am–11pm; Fri 8am–midnight; Sat 9am–4:30pm and 6pm–midnight; Sun

9am–10pm. Subway: 1 to Franklin St. Bubby's Brooklyn: 1 Main St. (at Water St.).
© 718/222-0666. Subway: A, C to High St.; F to York St.

The Odeon ⭐ AMERICAN BRASSERIE   For over 2 decades The Odeon has been a symbol of the TriBeCa sensibility; in fact, the restaurant can claim credit for the neighborhood's cachet—it was the first to lure artists, actors, writers, and models to the area below Canal Street before it was given its moniker. They came to drink, schmooze, and enjoy the hearty no-frills brasserie grub such as the country frisee salad with bacon, Roquefort cheese, and pear vinaigrette; truffled poached egg; grilled skirt steak; *moules frites* (mussels with fries); and sautéed cod. Though the restaurant is not the celebrity magnet it was in its heyday in the '80s, the food, drink, and that inviting, open, Deco-ish room has withstood the test of time and has surpassed trendy to claim New York establishment status.

145 W. Broadway (at Thomas St.). © 212/233-0507. www.theodeonrestaurant.com. Reservations recommended. Main courses $13–$35 at lunch; $19–$35 at dinner (most less than $21); fixed-price lunch $27. AE, DC, DISC, MC, V. Mon–Fri noon–11pm; Sat 10am–midnight; Sun 10am–11pm. Subway: 1, 2, 3 to Chambers St.

2 Chinatown

To find the restaurants reviewed below, see the map on p. 71.

INEXPENSIVE

Big Wong King ⭐ CANTONESE   For over 30 years, Big Wong has been an institution for workers from the nearby courthouses and Chinese families who come to feast on *congee* (rice porridge) and fried crullers for breakfast. They also come for the superb roasted meats, the pork and duck seen hanging in the window, the comforting noodle soups, and the terrific barbecued ribs. This is simple, down-home Cantonese food—lo mein, chow fun, bok choy in oyster sauce—cooked lovingly, and so cheap. If you don't mind sharing a table, Big Wong is a must at any time of day.

67 Mott St. (btwn Canal and Bayard sts.). © 212/964-0540. Appetizers $1.50–$5; congee $1.50–$6; soups $3–$5; Cantonese noodles $5.25–$11. No credit cards. Daily 8:30am–9pm. Subway: N, R.

New York Noodletown ⭐⭐ CHINESE/SEAFOOD   So what if the restaurant has the ambience of a school cafeteria? I'm wary of an overadorned dining room in Chinatown; the simpler the better. And New York Noodletown is simple, but the food is the real thing. Seafood-based noodle soups are spectacular, as is the platter of chopped roast pork. Those two items alone would make me happy.

Tips **A Chinatown Sweet Treat**

When in Chinatown, after a dim sum banquet or a noodle joint, skip the feeble dessert offerings and head to one of my favorite ice cream shops in the city, the **Chinatown Ice Cream Factory** *(Finds)*, 65 Bayard St., between Mott and Elizabeth streets (**© 212/608-4170**). The ice cream here features Asian flavors such as almond cookie, litchi, and an incredible green tea.

But I'm greedy and wouldn't leave the restaurant without one of its shrimp dishes, especially the salt-baked shrimp. If your hotel has a good-size refrigerator, take the leftovers home—they'll make a great snack the next day. New York Noodletown keeps long hours, which makes it one of the best late-night bets in the neighborhood, too.

28½ Bowery (at Bayard St.). **©** 212/349-0923. Reservations accepted. Main courses $4–$15. No credit cards. Daily 9am–3:30am. Subway: N, R, 6 to Canal St.

Pho Viet Huong *(Finds)* *(Value)* VIETNAMESE   Chinatown has its own enclave of Vietnamese restaurants, and the best is Pho Viet Huong. The menu is vast and needs intense perusing, but your waiter will help you pare it down. The Vietnamese know soup, and *pho,* a beef-based soup served with many ingredients, is the most famous, but the hot-and-sour *canh* soup, with either shrimp or fish, is the real deal. The small version is more than enough for two to share while the large is more than enough for a family. The odd pairing of barbecued beef wrapped in grape leaves is another of the restaurant's specialties and should not be missed, while the *bun,* various meats and vegetables served over rice vermicelli, are simple, hearty, and inexpensive. You'll even find Vietnamese sandwiches here: French bread filled with ham, chicken, eggs, lamb, and even pâté. All of the above is best washed down with an icy cold Saigon beer.

73 Mulberry St. (btwn Bayard and Canal sts.). **©** 212/233-8988. Appetizers $3–$8.50; soups $6–$7; main courses $10–$25. AE, MC, V. Sun–Thurs 10am–10pm; Fri–Sat 10am–11pm. Subway: 6, N, R, Q to Canal St.

3 Lower East Side

EXPENSIVE

Rayuela *(Finds Finds)* NUEVO LATINO   Rayuela bills its cuisine as *estilo libre Latino,* meaning "freestyle Latino." So the menu features a hodgepodge of Latino foods; a little Peruvian here, a dash of Mexican there, maybe a dollop of Cuba with a scoop of Spain. Like so many restaurants, you can make your meal from various small plates and Rayuela is no exception; the appetizer of *camarones con chorizo*, shrimp in a spicy salsa with *fufu*, a root vegetable, and thin yucca fries is a worthy nod to the cuisine of the Dominican Republic and a worthy complement to the ceviche. Despite the abundance of small plates, it's hard to ignore Rayuela's entrees, especially the *surena*, an Ecuadorian seafood stew of mussels, clams, shrimp, octopus, and scallops in a broth flavored with coconut and garlic. In the now foodie neighborhood of the Lower East Side, Rayuela offers two levels: a bustling downstairs lounge and small bites scene where a live olive tree grows and a more intimate dining room upstairs. On either floor, Rayuela's food will not disappoint.

165 Allen St. (btwn Rivington and Stanton sts.). ℂ **212/253-8840.** www.rayuela nyc.com. Reservations recommended. Ceviches $12–$17; main courses: $22–$31. AE, DC, DISC, MC, V. Sun–Thurs 5:30–11pm; Fri–Sat 5:30pm–midnight; brunch Sat–Sun 10am–5pm. Subway: F, V to Second Avenue.

MODERATE

'inoteca *Finds* ITALIAN SMALL PLATES   The Lower East Side was once the home to many Kosher wine factories, but you'll find only Italian wines at cozy 'inoteca. The list is over 250 bottles long, but even better are the exquisitely prepared small plates that complement the wines. Though the Italian-language menu is a challenge, servers are helpful. The panini stand out in their freshness and their delicacy, with the *coppa* (a spicy cured ham) with hot peppers and *rucola* (arugula) being the standout. The *tramezzini*, a crustless sandwich, is nothing like the crustless sandwiches served at high tea. Here, among other things, you can have yours stuffed with tuna and chick peas or with *pollo alla diavola*, spicy shredded pieces of dark-meat chicken. The "Fritto" section includes a wonderful mozzarella *in corroza*, breaded mozzarella stuffed with a juicy anchovy sauce and lightly fried. Whatever you order, don't rush; 'inoteca is a place to go slow, to savor both wine and food.

98 Rivington St. (at Ludlow St.). ℂ **212/614-0473.** www.inotecanyc.com. Reservations accepted for parties of 6 or more. Panini $8–$17; *piatti* (small plates) $8–$11. AE, MC, V. Daily noon–3am; brunch Sat–Sun 10am–4pm. Subway: F, J, M, Z to Delancey St.

INEXPENSIVE

Clinton St. Baking Company *Finds* AMERICAN   Though they are open all day, breakfast and desserts are the best offerings here. The blueberry pancakes with maple butter and the buttermilk-biscuit egg sandwich are worth braving the lines for, while the desserts, all homemade and topped with a scoop or two of ice cream from the Brooklyn Ice Cream Factory, are good any time of day.

4 Clinton St. (at Houston St.). ✆ 646/602-6263. Main courses $8–$14. No credit cards. Mon–Fri 8am–11pm (closed 4–6pm); Sat 10am–11pm; Sun 10am–4pm. Subway: F or V to Second Ave.

Katz's Delicatessen ⭐⭐ *Value* JEWISH DELI   This is arguably the city's best Jewish deli. The motto is "There's Nothing More New York Than Katz's," and it's spot-on. Founded in 1888, this cavernous, brightly lit place is suitably Noo Yawk, with dill pickles, Dr. Brown's cream soda, and old-world attitude to spare. But one word of caution: Katz's has become a serious tourist destination so if you see a tour bus parked in front, you might be in for a long wait. (And remember to tip your carver, who gives you a plate with a sample of pastrami or corned beef as he prepares your sandwich!)

205 E. Houston St. (at Ludlow St.). ✆ 212/254-2246. Reservations not accepted. Sandwiches $3–$10; other main courses $5–$18. AE, DC, DISC, MC, V. ($20 minimum). Sun–Tues 8am–10pm; Wed 8am–11pm; Thurs 8am–midnight; Fri–Sat 8am–3am. Subway: F to Second Ave.

4 SoHo & Nolita

To locate the restaurants reviewed below, see the map on p. 70.

EXPENSIVE

Fiamma ⭐ MODERN ITALIAN   From Stephen Hanson (Blue Water Grill, Ruby Foo's, Dos Caminos), the Steven Spielberg of restaurateurs, comes his art-house effort, and this one wins all the awards. The restaurant is beautifully designed in a modern northern-Italian style with mirrors, red walls, leather chairs, and a glass elevator that can deposit you on any of the four floors. New chef Fabio Trabocchi has installed some fanciful and unique creations to the menu such as spicy grilled calamari with scallops, an onion compote appetizer, and striped bass with fennel, oysters and clams. Some of his creations are on the fussy side, but the flavors always interesting. The Fiamma, under Trabocchi's lead, is now anything but traditional Italian. Dinner is a scene, so don't expect intimacy; but lunch, with a similar menu, is a much more relaxed option.

206 Spring St. (btwn Sixth Ave. and Sullivan St.). ✆ 212/653-0100. www.brguest restaurants.com. Reservations recommended. Pasta $22–$26; main courses $29–$44. AE, DISC, MC, V.; Tues–Thurs 6–11pm; Fri 6pm–midnight; Sat 5:30pm–midnight. Subway: C, E to Spring St.

MODERATE

Cendrillon ☆☆ *Finds* FILIPINO/ASIAN   Cendrillon features authentic yet innovative Filipino food in a comfortable setting with exposed brick, a skylight in the main dining room, and cozy booths up front. How authentic? Try a shot of *lambagong,* also known as "coconut grappa." It's a potent drink distilled from the coconut flower sap and blended with sugar-cane sap, and as far as I know, Cendrillon is the only restaurant in New York to serve it. The drink will ignite your appetite for the flavors to follow, like the squash soup with crab dumplings or the fresh *lumpia* with tamarind and peanut sauce (Asian vegetables wrapped in a purple-yam-and-rice wrapper). Cendrillon's chicken adobo (chicken braised in a marinade of vinegar, soy, chiles, and garlic) renders the bird tender and tasty as you could imagine, while Romy's (the chef/owner) spareribs, marinated in rice wine and garlic, rubbed with spices, and cooked in a Chinese smokehouse, are as good as any I've had cooked in a Texas smokehouse. Save room for the exotic desserts like the Buko pie, made with coconut and topped with vanilla-bean ice cream, or the *halo halo,* a parfait stuffed with ice creams and sorbets with flavors like avocado, jackfruit, and purple yam.

45 Mercer St. (btwn Broome and Grand sts.). ✆ **212/343-9012.** www.cendrillon. com. Main courses $15–$24. AE, DISC, MC, V. Sun 11am–10pm; Tues–Sat 11am–10pm. Subway: N/R to Prince St.; 6 to Spring St.; 1, A, C, E to Canal St.

Ed's Lobster Bar ☆☆ SEAFOOD   You may be a long way in distance (and price) from a roadside shack in Maine when dining at Ed's, but take a seat at the white marble counter and sink your teeth into Ed's signature lobster roll (prepared cold with mayonnaise) and you might just think that it's the rocky Atlantic coast outside the window rather than bustling Lafayette Street in the middle of NoHo. After you've tried the overstuffed lobster roll, if you still have room, try the oysters, raw or delicately fried. Or the fried Ipswich clams . . . or the steamers . . . or the chowder . . . really there's not much you won't want to try. Thankfully unpretentious, Ed's is straight-ahead New England seafood served in a casual, laid-back dining room and whitewashed bar. They even have paper bibs, homemade pickles, and Belfast Bay lobster ale on tap. What more, really, could you want in a seafood "shack" in downtown New York city?

222 Lafayette St. (btwn Spring and Kenmare sts.). ✆ **212/343-3236.** www.lobster barnyc.com. Main courses: $15–$30. (Lobster and oysters at market price). Tues–Fri noon–3pm; Sat noon–4pm; Sun noon–9pm; Tues–Thurs 5–11pm; Fri–Sat 5pm–midnight. Subway: 6 to Spring St.

Pao! *&* PORTUGUESE   New York has multiple restaurants of almost every ethnicity, yet there is a scarcity of Portuguese eateries. Of the few, this cozy charmer is the best. Pao!, which translates to "bread," keeps it simple, and the results are pure and authentic. Start with *caldo verde,* Portuguese soup, made with kale, potatoes, and smoky *linguica* (Portuguese sausage). The baked-octopus salad, tender and soaked in a garlic/cilantro vinaigrette, rivals any I've had in numerous Greek restaurants, while the cod cakes, another Portuguese standard, are light and not too salty. The combination of pork and seafood might seem odd, but it's common in Portugal; Pao!'s pairing of pork and clams is an acquired taste—one I've acquired. Salt cod is to Portugal what hamburgers are to the United States, and I'll take Pao!'s hearty *bacalhau a braz*—salt cod with egg, onion, and straw potatoes—over hamburger most any day. To complement the food, stick with a delicious Portuguese wine, from which there are many to choose. Desserts are egg-based and delicate; the soft pound cake with lemon egg custard filling is heavenly.

322 Spring St. (at Greenwich St.). *℄* 212/334-5464. Reservations recommended. AE, DC, MC, V. Lunch $12–$14; dinner $17–$20. Mon–Fri noon–2:30pm; daily 6–11pm. Subway: C, E to Spring St.

INEXPENSIVE

Lombardi's Pizza is at 32 Spring St., between Mott and Mulberry streets (*℄* **212/941-7994;** see "Pizza, New York–Style," p. 94).

Bread *&* ITALIAN   The bread at Bread comes from Balthazar Bakery down the street, but it's what they do with it that makes this eatery so special. For example, they take a rustic ciabatta loaf, slather it with Sicilian sardines, Thai mayonnaise, tomato, and lettuce, and then turn it over to their panini press. The result is a gooey convergence of flavors that you will attempt to gobble down gracefully. It *will* fall apart, but that's okay; someone will be along shortly with more napkins. Besides the spectacular sardine sandwich, the Italian tuna with mesclun greens and tomatoes in a lemon dressing, and the fontina with grilled zucchini, eggplant, arugula, and tomato in a balsamic vinaigrette are also standouts. Really, there are no losers on the bread side of Bread's menu, which also includes salads, pastas, and "plates."

20 Spring St. (btwn Mott and Elizabeth sts.). *℄* **212/334-1015.** Reservations not accepted. Breads $7–$9.50; plates $6–$16. AE, DC, DISC, MC, V. Sun–Thurs 10:30am–midnight; Fri–Sat 10:30am–1am. Subway: 6 to Spring St.

5 The East Village & NoHo

To locate the restaurants reviewed below, see the map on p. 70.

EXPENSIVE

Le Miu ★★ *Finds* JAPANESE   What happens when four celebrated Japanese chefs from notable restaurants (Nobu 57 and Megu to name two) open their own joint? In some cases, the result could be chaos, but in the case of Le Miu, good things happened. The restaurant, a slim, austere space tucked away on a bustling East Village block, is a refuge for those seeking fresh, delicately prepared sushi standards along with some interesting innovations. The Le Miu tartar: tuna, yellowtail, and salmon topped with caviar is a welcoming beginning, followed by sardine with ginger ceviche. The Saikyo miso marinated black cod in a phyllo jacket and the king crab leg with a curry milk sauce are revelations. The prices, for sushi this good, are hard to beat. Le Miu also has an impressive hot- and cold-sake list.

107 Ave. A (btwn 6th and 7th sts.). © 212/473-3100. www.lemiusushi.com. Reservations recommended. Prix-fixe $55–$75; main courses $14–$28. AE, DC, MC, V. Tues–Sun 5:30pm–midnight. Subway: F, V to Second Ave.

MODERATE

Momofuku Noodle Bar ★ ASIAN   In 2007, this popular East Village noodle slurping destination moved from a tiny space to still small, but sleek confines a few blocks up the street. Now there are a few communal tables along with a larger bar. With the move came an expanded menu. Instead of just noodles, at the practically unclassifiable Momofuku, you will find such items on the menu as fried veal sweetbreads, spicy honeycomb tripe, grilled beef tongue, country ham and hash browns, and grits and shrimp—this in a supposed Asian noodle bar. But despite the seemingly contradictory menu, the Southern-style Asian noodle combo works. Still, unless you have a craving for offal, come to Momofuku for the noodles; the ramen in particular. And in the Momofuku Ramen, a big bowl brimming with rich broth, noodles, shredded smoky pulled pork, and a poached egg, you actually can get a taste of the South and of Asia all in one bowl. Of the hot items, the roasted brussel sprouts with a kimchee puree, bacon, and carrots is a revelation, while the steamed pork bun is stuffed with a side of pork belly. Service is brisk, but try to get to Momofuku early or for lunch, before the lines begin to form.

171 First Ave. (btwn 10th and 11th sts.) © 212/777-7773. Reservations not accepted. Main courses: $10–$17. AE, DISC, MC, V. Daily noon–4pm; Sun–Thurs 5:30–11pm; Fri–Sat 5:30pm–midnight. Subway: L at Third Ave.

6 Greenwich Village & the Meatpacking District

EXPENSIVE

Bar Blanc 𝕽 CONTEMPORARY AMERICAN   I'm not sure the three owners, who are all alumni of David Bouley restaurants, really mean to say that Bar Blanc is a bar before it is a restaurant. The narrow space and the whitewashed look lends itself perfectly to the name, and the *caipiroska*, the vodka version of the caipirinha, was as good as I've had in any bar, but there is no doubt that the food is foremost here. The menu is as sparse as the decor, and in neither case is that a bad thing. It's not about quantity, it's about quality. An appetizer of two pan-seared jumbo scallops wrapped in a fatty piece of smoked pork belly might not seem like much, but each bite was memorable. The entrees are not much more formidable than the appetizers, but just as delicious: the juicy, milk-fed porcelet (an elegant way of describing pork), flavored with chanterelles and roasted brussels sprouts, and the strip steak, grilled over Japanese charcoal and accompanied by a bone marrow sauce. If you can, ask for a table in the back, away from the bar where you might be able to have a quiet conversation.

142 W. 10th St (at Waverly Pl.). © 212/255-2330. www.barblanc.com. Reservations recommended. Main courses: $29–$36; AE, DISC, MC, V. Tues–Sun 5:30–11pm. Subway: A, B, C, D, E, F, V to W. 4th St.

Mas 𝕽𝕽 *Finds* FRENCH   I've never had the pleasure of dining in a French country farmhouse, but if the experience at Mas is anything like it, now I know what I've been missing. This "farmhouse" is in the West Village, and though there are nods to the rustic in the decor, there is also an atmosphere of sophistication. A glass-enclosed wine cellar is visible from the small dining room, the restaurant stays open late, and you'll find hipsters in jeans and T-shirts as well as folks in power suits eating here. And it's that combination, along with the creative menu, that makes Mas so special. The dishes are innovative and the ingredients are fresh, many of them supplied by upstate New York farms. The tender, perfectly prepared braised pork belly, from Flying Pig Farm, is served with polenta and a stew of escargot and lima beans; and the duck breast, from Stone Church Farm, melds magically with apple puree, sautéed Brussels sprouts. Service is low-key but attentive, and the seating, though somewhat cramped, is not enough to dim the romantic aura.

39 Downing St. (btwn Bedford and Varick sts.). © 212/255-1790. www.masfarm house.com. Reservations recommended. 4-course tasting menu $68; 6-course $95; main courses $32–$36. AE, DC, DISC, MC, V. Mon–Sat 6pm–4am (small-plate tasting menu after 11:30pm). Subway: 1 to Houston St.

Strip House ✰✰ STEAK   With a photo gallery of seminude bur-
lesque performers decorating the red velvet walls, burgundy banquettes, and a steady flow of lounge music, you may, as I once did,
mistakenly refer to the Strip House as the Strip Club. But despite the
faux-*Playboy* look, the decadence here is in the titanic portions of
perfectly charred and seasoned red meat, specifically, the strip steak.
I had the strip on the bone that I still remember with fondness. The
filet mignon is simply and impeccably prepared and the porterhouse
for two, carved at your table, is in the Peter Luger league. The sides
are variations on the standards: creamed spinach with black truffles,
french fries with herbs and garlic, and, best of all, the crisp goose-fat
potatoes. Is goose fat a good fat or a bad fat? Only your dietician
knows for sure. Desserts are monumental, especially the multilayered
chocolate cake, so ask for extra forks. With the exception of the banquettes, seating is tight.

13 E. 12th St. (btwn University Place and Fifth Ave.). ✆ **212/328-0000.** www.strip
house.net Reservations recommended. Main courses $28–$51. AE, DC, DISC, MC, V.
Mon–Thurs & Sun 5–11pm; Fri–Sat 5pm–midnight. Subway: L, N, R, Q, 4, 5, 6 to 14th
St./Union Sq.

INEXPENSIVE

The original **John's Pizzeria** is at 278 Bleecker St., near Seventh
Avenue (✆ **212/243-1680;** see "Pizza, New York–Style," on p. 94).
Also, you'll find **Murray's Bagels** at 500 Sixth Ave., between 12th
and 13th streets (✆ **212/466-2830;** see "The Hole Truth: N.Y.'s
Best Bagels," on p. 88).

7 Chelsea

To locate the restaurants in this section, see the map on p. 82.

EXPENSIVE

Buddakan ✰ ASIAN   My expectations of Buddakan were of a
loud, dance club scene in a 16,000-square-feet bi-level space where
the food would be showy, but flavorless. I was right about the loud,
scene, but wrong about the food. The "Brasserie" is the main dining
room on the lower level and the steps can seem steep after a few cocktails in the upstairs lounge such as the signature *Heat,* a combination
of tequila, Cointreau, and chilled cucumbers. To fortify yourself after
those cocktails, don't hesitate to order some of Buddakan's superb
appetizers like the edamame dumplings, the crab and corn fritters,
and the crispy calamari salad. In fact, you can make your meal out of
appetizers—the extensive menu works best for large parties and has

Where to Dine in Midtown

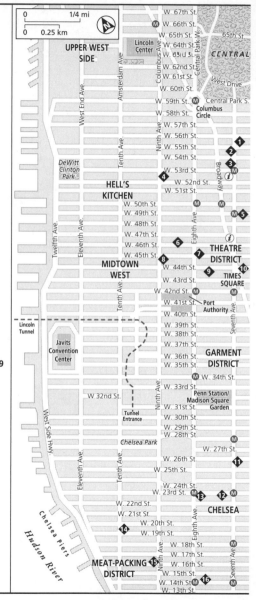

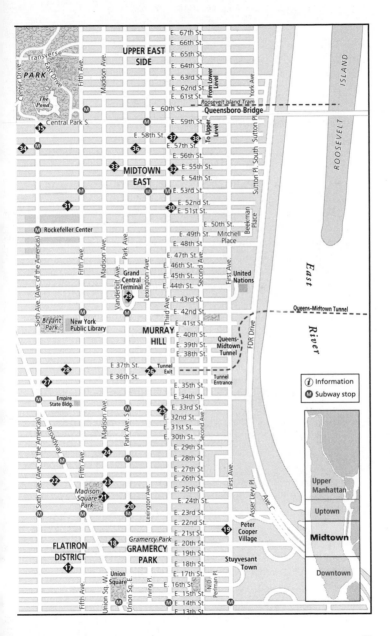

UPPER EAST SIDE

Central Park S.

E. 67th St.
E. 66th St.
E. 65th St.
E. 64th St.
E. 63rd St.
E. 62nd St.
E. 61st St.

From Lower Level

Roosevelt Island Tram
Queensboro Bridge

E. 60th St.
E. 59th St.

To Upper Level

E. 58th St.
E. 57th St.
E. 56th St.

MIDTOWN EAST

E. 55th St.
E. 54th St.
E. 53rd St.
E. 52nd St.
E. 51st St.
E. 50th St.

Mitchell Place

Rockefeller Center

E. 49th St.
E. 48th St.
E. 47th St.
E. 46th St.
E. 45th St.
E. 44th St.
E. 43rd St.
E. 42nd St.
E. 41st St.
E. 40th St.
E. 39th St.
E. 38th St.

Grand Central Terminal

United Nations

MURRAY HILL

Queens–Midtown Tunnel

Bryant Park
New York Public Library

E. 37th St. Tunnel Exit
E. 36th St.

Empire State Bldg.

E. 35th St.
E. 34th St.
E. 33rd St.
E. 32nd St.
E. 31st St.
E. 30th St.
E. 29th St.
E. 28th St.
E. 27th St.
E. 26th St.
E. 25th St.
E. 24th St.
E. 23rd St.
E. 22nd St.
E. 21st St.
E. 20th St.
E. 19th St.
E. 18th St.
E. 17th St.
E. 16th St.
E. 15th St.
E. 14th St.
E. 13th St.

Tunnel Entrance

Madison Square Park

Peter Cooper Village

Stuyvesant Town

FLATIRON DISTRICT

Gramercy Park
GRAMERCY PARK

Union Square

Madison Ave.
Fifth Ave.
Madison Ave.
Fifth Ave.
Park Ave.
Vanderbilt Ave.
Lexington Ave.
Third Ave.
Second Ave.
First Ave.
Sutton Pl.
Sutton Pl. South
York Ave.
Beekman Place
FDR Drive

Sixth Ave. (Ave. of the Americas)
Fifth Ave.
Broadway
Sixth Ave. (Ave. of the Americas)
Madison Ave.
Park Ave. S.
Lexington Ave.
Second Ave.
First Ave.
Asser Levy Pl.
Ave. C

Union Sq. W.
Union Sq. E.
Irving Pl.
N.I.D.
Perlman Pl.

Transverse

Center Drive

PARK

East Drive

The Pond

ROOSEVELT ISLAND

East River

Queens–Midtown Tunnel

(i) Information
(M) Subway stop

Upper Manhattan

Uptown

Midtown

Downtown

83

the now-obligatory "communal" table. But if you order one entrée, make sure it's the sizzling short rib; tender and removed from the bone on top of a bed of mushroom chow fun.

75 Ninth Ave (at 16th St.). ℂ 212/989-6699. www.buddakannyc.com. Dim Sum—appetizers $9–$13; main courses $17–$35. AE, DC, MC, V. Hours: Sun–Wed 5:30pm–midnight; Thurs–Sat 5:30pm–1am. Subway: A, C, E to 14th St.

Cookshop 𝒦𝒦 AMERICAN   On far-west Tenth Avenue, with a prime view of a garage across the street, Cookshop is brawny and boisterous with food to match. Seating can be tight and you would hear your neighbor's conversation if it weren't so loud in the restaurant. But never mind, enjoy the chef's creations. A pizza with shaved king oyster mushrooms and stracchino cheese or the grilled Montauk squid in a salsa verde make good starters to complement the restaurant's innovative cocktails. Or combine a few of the snacks such as the fried spiced hominy or the smoked pork tacos as starters for the table. Cookshop offers entrée options in four categories: sauté, grill, wood oven, and rotisserie. The whole roasted porgy, head and all, cooked in the wood oven is moist and full of flavor, while the chile-braised beef short ribs served over cheddar grits from the sauté section are tender to the bone. Service is efficient and helpful.

156 Tenth Ave. (at 20th St.). ℂ 212/924-4440. www.cookshopny.com. Reservations recommended. Main courses $21–$36. AE, DC, MC, V. Mon–Sat 5:30pm–midnight; Sun 11:30am–3pm and 5:30–10pm. Subway: C, E to 23rd St.

MODERATE

La Nacional 𝒦𝒦 (Finds) SPANISH/TAPAS   It's not easy finding the oldest Spanish restaurant in New York; in fact, the search for this unmarked restaurant on West 14th Street might get you a bit frustrated. Once you find it, though, you will be rewarded. Founded in 1868 as a gathering spot for the Benevolent Spanish Society, La Nacional, a social club, is a hidden treat. At one time food was secondary to the company of Spanish expats who congregated here, filling the room with smoke and loud talk of Spanish politics and football. It was here where Gabriel Garcia Lorca spent countless hours documenting his New York City experience. The cigarette smoke has been replaced by the smoke of the grill, which turns out tasty tapas like sardines, octopus, and shrimp. There is a somewhat formal dining room in the front, while in the back, next to the open kitchen, there are a few tables and TVs usually tuned to soccer matches. Come and share a bottle of Spanish wine and make a meal out of the tapas—the *albondigas* (Spanish meatballs), *boquerones* (white anchovy filets), and the aforementioned octopus are my favorites—or you can order the excellent paella. Tapas range from $4 to $9 while no entree is more than $18. In a ballroom on the second level, the club sponsors flamenco performances and dance lessons.

239 W. 14th St. (btwn Seventh and Eighth aves.). ⒸⒸ 212/243-9308. www.lanacional tapas.com. Tapas $7–$9; main courses $16–$18. AE, DC, DISC, MC, V. Sun–Wed noon–11pm; Thurs–Sat noon–11pm. Subway: A, C, E, 1, 2, 3 to 14th St.

RUB ⒸⒸ BARBECUE   RUB is short for Righteous Urban Barbecue—a contradiction in terms if there ever was one. Co-owned by Kansas City pit master Paul Kirk, who has won seven World Barbecue Championships and is a member of the Barbecue Hall of Fame, the arrival of RUB in New York was eagerly anticipated by those barbecue fanatics who are aware there is a Barbecue Hall of Fame. Could chef Kirk replicate his cuisine in New York where pollutant-inducing smokers are illegal? The answer is no. You will never get that true smoked taste without creating some serious smoke, but that doesn't mean what you get at RUB is bad. On the contrary, the smoked turkey and barbecued chicken are the best I've had; moist inside with a distinctive smoked flavor, and the ribs, St. Louis–style, were delicate and crispy, yet tender and meaty. The "burnt ends," the fatty part of the brisket, however, were a bit tough. The restaurant is cramped and loud and the prices urban (meaning high) but the food at RUB will provide all the comfort you need.

208 W. 23rd St. (btwn Seventh and Eighth aves.). ⒸⒸ 212/524-4300. www.rubbbq. net. Sandwiches $9–$12; platters $15–$23; Taste of the Baron $46. AE, MC, V. Tues–Thurs noon–11pm; Fri–Sat noon–midnight. Subway: 1 to 23rd St.

8 Union Square, the Flatiron District & Gramercy Park

EXPENSIVE

A Voce ⒸⒸ MODERN ITALIAN   The kind of food that is served at A Voce, rustic Italian for the most part with exceptional nods to innovation, seems somewhat out of place in the loud, postmodern dining room in a sleek highrise just off Madison Park. At A Voce you can start with something peasant-pleasing like Sardinian Sample the hip, wild *branzini tartara* (Mediterranean sea bass)—something no peasant would ever eat. And though my grandmother never made meat ravioli—the chef's meat ravioli is so good it certainly was *not* from a can, or, continuing on that rustic theme, the "country-style Tuscan tripe," with barlotti beans, tomato, fried duck egg, and grilled ciabatta bread, which (minus the duck egg) would have made my normally dour Calabrese grandfather happy. A Voce offers daily specials called "*del mercato*" which feature the chef's more unusual creations like, a "rabbit terrina" with salt-cured *foie gras*. You won't go wrong whether you try the rustic or the modern. The palate-cleansing citrus tiramisu is the perfect conclusion.

41 Madison Avenue (at 26th St.). ℂ 212/545-8555. www.avocerestaurant.com. AE, DC, MC, V. Main courses: $18–$39. Mon–Fri 11:45am–2:30pm; 5:30–11pm; Sat–Sun 5:30–11pm. Subway: N, R, W to 23rd St.

Primehouse ⋒ STEAKHOUSE   There are many meanings of the word "prime," and in the case of Primehouse, the newest (2007) from restaurateur Stephen Hanson (Fiamma, Dos Caminos, Ocean Grill, and so on), it means top-of-the-line meat, of which there are many cuts at Primehouse. The space is gargantuan; and, at times, I felt service would have been a bit more prompt if the waiters could have used skateboards to traverse the long walk from kitchen to table. Once the food did arrive, all was forgiven. The combination of raw seafood and steak has traditionally been a natural one. At Primehouse, the oysters, from either the East or West Coast (or you can try a sampler of both) were fresh and briny. The romaine, tomato, onion and Maytag blue cheese salad was crisp, even when smothered by the rich blue cheese dressing, but do not attempt to tackle it yourself—it will finish you before your steak arrives, and that would be a mistake, especially if you've splurged and ordered one of the special cuts aged in the restaurant's "Himalayan Salt Room." I sampled the 35-day aged Kansas City sirloin along with the 40-day aged rib-eye; and whatever they do for all those days, it works.

381 Park Ave. S. (at 27th St.). ℂ 212/824-2600. www.brguestrestaurants.com. Reservations Recommended. Main courses: $24–$62. AE, DC, DISC, MC, V. Mon–Fri 11:30am–4pm; Sat–Sun 11am–4pm; Mon–Wed 5–11pm; Thurs–Sat 5pm–midnight; Sun 5–10pm. Subway: N,R,Q, 6 to 28th St.

MODERATE

Hill Country ⋒ BARBECUE   In a competitive market, and the world of barbecue is *very* competitive, everyone needs an edge. Hill Country's is Texas-style barbecue. And in Texas, beef reigns, so it's not surprising that the standouts are the barbecued beef items, specifically the brisket, served moist or lean (go for the moist) and the gargantuan beef ribs, coated with a spicy dry rub. If you can't go without your dose of the pig, the Kruez market sausage, shipped from Texas, is the real deal. At Hill Country, once you are seated at one of the picnic tables in the Texas-sized, loud dining room, you are given a card. Then you proceed to the meat and/or sides counter where you place your order: by the pound for the meat or by the size container for the sides. Whatever you ordered, drinks and desserts included, are checked off, and on your way out, your card is added up by a cashier. The system is a bit gimmicky and awkward, but all is forgiven once you dig in and the grease begins to spread on the brown butcher paper beneath your food. Hill Country is a mecca for meat lovers, but don't ignore those sides: the cheddar mac and cheese, beer braised cowboy pinto beans, and the white corn pudding are musts.

30 W. 26th St (btwn Broadway–6th Ave.). © 212/255-4544. www.hillcountryny. com. Meat $6.50–$20 per pound; sides $4.50–$16. AE, DISC, MC, V. Sun–Wed noon–10pm; Thurs–Sat noon–11pm. Subway: F, V to 23rd St.

La Pizza Fresca Ristorante ★★ *Finds* PIZZA/ITALIAN   When comparing the top pizzerias in New York, you rarely hear La Pizza Fresca Ristorante mentioned. And that's a mistake. Those who have sampled the genuine Neapolitan pizza (one of only two New York pizzerias certified for authenticity by the Italian organization, *Associazione Vera Pizza Napoletana*) swear by La Pizza Fresca's quality. To achieve certification there are a number of qualifications; a wood burning oven, San Marzano tomatoes, bufala mozzarella, hand-pressed dough, and all the ingredients must be cooked with the pizza in the oven. The result is a pizza as good (almost) as you might find in Naples and as good as just about any other in New York. You can have your pizza many different ways, including the delicious *Quattro formaggi,* a combination of four cheeses and a hint of pancetta (Italian bacon); but for the unadulterated Neapolitan flavor, try the simple, tomato, bufala mozzarella, and basil pie. Also impressive is La Pizza Fresca's 800-plus wine list. The restaurant is comfortable and cozy with low-lighting, exposed brick, and the constant glow from the pizza oven.

31 E. 20th St (btwn Park Ave and Broadway). © 212/598-0141. www.lapizza fresca.com. Reservations not accepted. Pizza $9–$19; main courses: $12–$28. AE, DC, DISC, MC, V. Mon–Sat noon–3:30pm; Mon–Sat 5:30–11pm; Sun 5–11pm. Subway: 6 to 23rd St.

INEXPENSIVE

Also consider Danny Meyer's **Shake Shack,** in Madison Square Park (© **212/889-6600**). For healthy burgers, try either outlet of the **New York Burger Co.,** 303 Park Ave. South, between 23rd and 24th streets (© **212/254-2727**), and 678 Sixth Ave., between 21st and 22nd streets (© **212/229-1404**). For a burger with boutique quality meat, try **Brgr,** 287 Seventh Ave., at 26th St. (© **212/488-7500**).

The Hole Truth: N.Y.'s Best Bagels

Not many things are more New York than a bagel, and New Yorkers are loyal to their favorite purveyors, who include:

Absolute Bagels, 2708 Broadway, between 107th and 108th streets (℅ **212/932-2052**). Their egg bagels, hot out of the oven, melt in your mouth, and their whitefish salad is perfectly smoky, though not overpowering.

Ess-A-Bagel, 359 First Ave., at 21st Street (℅ **212/260-2252**; www.ess-a-bagel.com). When it comes to size, Ess-a-Bagel's are the best of the biggest; plump, chewy, and oh-so-satisfying. Also at 831 Third Ave., between 50th and 51st streets (℅ **212/980-1010**).

H&H Bagels, 2239 Broadway, at 80th Street (℅ **212/595-8003**; www.handhbagel.com). H&H makes what has long been reputed as the best bagel in New York—at a pricey $1 a bagel. The bagels are always fresh and warm, the bagel aficionado's prerequisite. Also at 639 W. 46th St., at Twelfth Avenue (℅ **212/595-8000**). Takeout only.

Kossar's Bialys, 367 Grand St., at Essex Street (℅ **877/4-BIALYS**; www.kossarsbialys.com). We know about their bialys, but don't forget the bagels. Also hand-rolled, the result is a slightly crunchy exterior with a tender, moist middle. You came for the bialys, but you'll leave with both.

Murray's Bagels, 500 Sixth Ave., between 12th and 13th streets (℅ **212/462-2830**), and 242 Eighth Ave., at 23rd Street (℅ **646/638-1334**). There's nothing like a soft, warm bagel to begin your day, and Murray's does them beautifully. Their smoked fish goes perfectly on their bagels.

City Bakery *♐ Kids* ORGANIC AMERICAN   City Bakery offers comfort food that manages to be delicious, nutritious, *and* eco-friendly. Its salad bar is unlike any other in the city, where the integrity of the ingredients is as important as the taste. This is health food, all right—roasted beets with walnuts, sautéed greens, lavender eggplant tossed in miso—but with heart and soul, offering such classic favorites as French toast with artisanal bacon, mac 'n' cheese, fried chicken, tortilla pie, even smoked salmon with all the trimmings on Sunday. There is a plethora of sinful desserts; kids love the spinning wheel of chocolate and the homemade marshmallows. *One caveat:* It's a bit pricey for a salad bar, but oh, what good eats.

3 W. 18th St. (btwn Fifth & Sixth aves.). © **212/366-1414.** Salad bar $12 per lb.; soups $4–$7; sandwiches $5–$10. AE, MC, V. Mon–Fri 7:30am–7pm; Sat 7:30am–6:30pm; Sun 9am–6pm. Subway: N, R, Q, 4, 5, 6 to Union Sq

9 Times Square & Midtown West

To locate the restaurants in this section, see the map on p. 82.

VERY EXPENSIVE

Anthos ☆☆ INNOVATIVE GREEK   With hostess and co-owner Donatella Arpaia (Mia Dona p. 101), chef Michael Psilakis (Kefi p. 105) has a grand, albeit slick stage in which to showcase his immense talents. The only nods here to Greek traditional cuisine are the grilled octopus, Greek salad, and the side order of moussaka that comes with the perfectly prepared lamb chop loin. Psilakis's signature Greek "crudo," or raw *mezes,* yellowtail, diver scallops, and tuna are a popular starter. The sardine escabeche, a row of properly briny, fresh from the sea, sardines, each on a sliver of cucumber along with the potato and garlic *skorkalia* soup, not really a soup at all, and the above-mentioned octopus are more than enough to make your meal. But if you made a meal of only the mezes, you would miss out on such entrees as the whole, simply grilled, *loup de mer,* served boned but with the head included, or the tantalizing crispy turbot with eggplant puree. Desserts are irresistible; don't miss the sesame ice cream encased in a halvah shell. Service is first rate, and it better be considering the location and the price you are paying.

36 W. 52nd St. (btwn Fifth and Sixth aves.). © **212/582-6900.** www.anthosnyc. com. Reservations recommended. Main course: $26–$45. AE, DC, DISC, MC, V. Mon–Fri noon–2:45pm; Mon–Thurs 5–10:30pm; Fri–Sat 5–11pm. Subway: B, D, F, V to 47, 50, Rockefeller Center.

BLT Market ☆☆ AMERICAN   The newest (in 2007) in the BLT (Bistro Laurent Tourondel) restaurant empire calls the Ritz-Carlton Central Park home. And it's the perfect setting, across from the greenery of Central Park, for the "market" cuisine served here. Other restaurants have chimed in on market-fresh food, but few can do it as well as the people at BLT. The ingredients change seasonally, sometimes daily, depending on what's fresh at the market. Each month, the menu lists what is peak in that particular season. When I visited in November, sunchokes, pumpkin, black cod, bosc pear, chestnut, and a variety of mushrooms were some of the fresh items used in the dishes prepared that day. Matsutake mushroom and sunchokes, for example could be found in the roasted langoustine appetizer, while the amazingly flaky and moist entree of black cod sat atop a delicious celeriac puree. The bosc pear was used in a perfectly made tart tatin for dessert, while chestnuts were found in a floating island accompanied by orange blossom madeleines. Service, as it is at all the BLT restaurants, is professional and helpful, and the room tries to recreate a rustic, farmhouselike ambience with water served in milk bottles and an old plow at the restaurant's entrance.

1430 Avenue of the Americas (at 59th St., in the Ritz-Carlton Central Park). ℂ 212/521-6125. www.bltmarket.com. Reservations recommended. Main courses: $32–$45. AE, DC, DISC, MC, V. Daily 11:45am–2pm and 5:30–10pm. Subway: N, Q, R, W to 57th St.

EXPENSIVE

Frankie & Johnnie's ★★ STEAKHOUSE   When restaurants open other branches, red flags go up. Does that mean they have become a chain and their quality has eroded to chain-food status? In the case of Frankie & Johnnie's, the legendary Theater District former-speakeasy-turned-steakhouse, which opened another outlet in the two-story townhouse once owned by John Barrymore, those fears were allayed after one bite of their signature sirloin. It also helps that the dining room on the second floor of the town house is gorgeous, especially the Barrymore room, the actor's former study with stained-glass ceiling panels, dark wood walls, and a working fireplace. Not only are Frankie & Johnnie's steaks underrated in the competitive world of New York steakhouses, but the other options are superb as well. The crabcake appetizer had an overwhelmingly high crab-to-cake ratio—and that's a good thing in my book—while the side of hash browns was the best I've had. Service is old-school, and if you are staying in Midtown, the restaurant provides complimentary limo service to and from the restaurant.

32 W. 37th St. (btwn Fifth and Sixth aves.). ℂ 212/997-8940. www.frankieand johnnies.com. Reservations recommended. Main courses $25–$36. Mon–Fri noon–2:30pm; Mon–Thurs 4–10:30pm; Fri–Sat 4–11pm. Subway: B, C, D, N, R, Q, W, V to 34th St./Herald Sq. Also at 269 W. 45th St. (at Eighth Ave.). ℂ 212/997-9494. Subway: 1, 2, 3, 7, A, C, E, N, R, Q, S, W to 42nd St.

Keens Steakhouse ★★★ STEAKHOUSE   Up until the latter part of the 20th century, Keens, which was established in 1885, referred to itself as a "chop house." They are now known as a steak-house, but I wish they had remained true to their roots. To their credit, they are a steakhouse in name only. They not only serve the basics of a steakhouse—the porterhouse for two, aged, T-Bone, and filet mignon with the requisite sides such as creamed spinach and hash browns—they serve chops: lamb chops, prime rib, short ribs, and most notably, mutton chops. It is the mutton chop that has made Keens the original that it is. The monstrous cut has two flaps of long, thick, rich, subtly gamy meat on either side of the bone that look kind of like muttonchop sideburns. Keens is the real thing, from the thousands of ceramic pipes on the ceiling (regulars were given their own personal pipes, including celebrities like Babe Ruth, George M. Cohan, and Albert Einstein) to the series of rooms on two floors with wood paneling, leather banquettes, a bar with a three-page menu of single malts, and the framed playbill Lincoln was reading at Ford's Theater that infamous evening in 1865.

72 W. 36th St. (at Sixth Ave.). ℂ 212/947-3636. www.keens.com. Reservations recommended. Main courses $26–$45. AE, DC, DISC, MC, V. Mon–Fri 11:45am–10:30pm; Sat 5–10:30pm; Sun 5–9pm. Subway: B, D, F, N, R, W, Q, V to 34th St./Herald Sq.

Molyvos 𝄫𝄫 GREEK   When Molyvos opened in 1997 it was her-alded as a trailblazer of innovative Greek cuisine. A decade later, upscale, innovative Greek is the current "in vogue" cuisine in Man-hattan. Molyvos's success is based on its ability to please those who want simple, traditional Greek food as well as exciting, Greek-accented creations. For those who like their Greek unadulterated, you won't go wrong with cold *mezedes,* such as the spreads *tzatziki, melitzanosalata,* and *taramosalata,* and hot *mezedes* like spinach pie or grilled octopus. For Greek food with an edge there's ouzo-cured salmon on a chickpea fritter or the terrific seafood Cretan bread salad. Just a sampling of the *mezedes* should be enough for anyone's hearty appetite but with entrees as good as grilled *garides,* wild head-on prawns barbecued "souvlaki-style" and the *chios* pork and *gigante* bean stew, not ordering one would be a mistake. The sommelier will pair your choices with a Greek wine, of which there are many. Or, skip the wine and sample one or two of the dozens of ouzos, but don't skip the desserts. Sure you've had baklava before, but have you ever had chocolate baklava? It's as good as it sounds.

871 Seventh Ave. (btwn 55th and 56th sts.). ℂ 212/582-7500. www.molyvos.com. Reservations recommended. Main courses $17–$29 at lunch (most less than $20); $20–$36 at dinner (most less than $25); fixed-price lunch $24; pretheater 3-course dinner $36 (5:30–6:45pm). AE, DC, DISC, MC, V. Mon–Thurs noon–11:30pm; Fri–Sat

noon–midnight; Sun noon–11pm. Subway: N, R to 57th St.; B, D, E to Seventh Ave.

MODERATE

The family-style Italian restaurant **Carmine's** has a Times Square branch at 200 W. 44th St., between Broadway and Eighth Avenue (© **212/221-3800**).

Becco ⓕ *Finds* ITALIAN   If you're a fan of Lidia Bastianich's PBS cooking shows, you'll be happy to know you can sample her simple, hearty Italian cooking here. Becco, on Restaurant Row, is designed to serve her meals "at a different price point" (read: cheaper) than her East Side restaurant, Felidia. The prices are not rock-bottom, but in terms of service, portions, and quality, you get tremendous bang for your buck at Becco (which means to "peck, nibble, or savor something in a discriminating way"). The main courses can head north of the $20 mark, but take a look at the prix-fixe "Sinfonia de Pasta" menu ($17.95 at lunch, $22.95 at dinner), which includes a Caesar salad or an antipasto plate, followed by unlimited servings of the three fresh-made daily pastas. There's also an excellent selection of Italian wines at $25 a bottle. If you can't make up your mind about dessert, have them all: A tasting plate includes gelato, cheesecake, and whatever else the dessert chef has whipped up that day. Lidia herself does turn up at Becco and Felidia; you can even dine with her (see website for details).

355 W. 46th St. (btwn Eighth and Ninth aves.). © **212/397-7597**. www.becconyc. com. Reservations recommended. Main courses lunch $13–$25; dinner $19–$35. AE, DC, DISC, MC, V. Mon noon–3pm and 5–10pm; Tues noon–3pm and 5pm–midnight; Wed 11:30am–2:30pm and 4pm–midnight; Thurs–Fri noon–3pm and 5pm–midnight; Sat 11:30am–2:30pm and 4pm–midnight; Sun noon–10pm. Subway: C, E to 50th St.

Norma's ⓕⓕ *Finds* CREATIVE AMERICAN BREAKFAST Nowhere is breakfast treated with such reverence, and decadence, as at Norma's, a soaring, ultramodern ode to the ultimate comfort food. There's something for everyone on the huge menu. Classics come in styles both simple and haute: Blueberry pancakes come piled high with fresh Maine berries and Devonshire cream, while buttermilks are topped with fresh Georgia peaches and chopped walnuts. Even oatmeal is special: genuine Irish McCann's, dressed with sautéed green apples and red pears and brûléed for a flash of sugary sweetness. Don't pass on the applewood-smoked bacon, so good it's worth blowing any diet for. Norma's can even win over breakfast foes with creative sandwiches, a generous Cobb with seared ahi, and a terrific chicken potpie. It's not cheap for breakfast, but definitely worth the splurge.

At Le Parker Meridien Hotel, 118 W. 57th St. (btwn Sixth and Seventh aves.). © **212/**

708-7460. www.normasnyc.com. Reservations accepted. Main courses $8–$23 (most $13–$18). AE, DC, DISC, MC, V. Mon–Fri 6:30am–3pm; Sat–Sun 7am–3pm. Subway: B, N, Q, R, W to 57th St.

Virgil's Real BBQ *(Kids)* BARBECUE/SOUTHERN   In the heart of the theme-restaurant wasteland known as Times Square is a theme restaurant that actually has good food. The "theme" is Southern barbecue and the restaurant, sprawling over two levels, is made to look and feel like a Southern roadhouse with good-ol'-boy decorations on the walls and blues on the soundtrack. Virgil's does an admirable job in re-creating that authentic flavor so hard to find north of the Mason-Dixon Line. The spice-rubbed ribs are slow-cooked and meaty, but it's the Owensboro lamb (smoked slices of lamb) and the Texas beef brisket that are the standouts. Both are melt-in-your-mouth tender; the lamb is sprinkled with a flavorful mustard sauce, while the brisket is perfect with a few dabs of Virgil's homemade spicy barbecue sauce. For starters, the corn dogs with poblano mustard are something New Yorkers rarely have the pleasure of experiencing, while the BBQ nachos—tortilla chips slathered with melted cheese and barbecued pulled pork—are a meal in themselves. Desserts are what you would expect from a restaurant emulating a Southern theme: big and sweet. Try the homemade ice-cream sandwich made with the cookie of the day. Virgil's is a great place to bring the kids; if they're noisy, no one will notice.

At Le Parker Meridien Hotel, 118 W. 57th St. (btwn Sixth and Seventh aves.). © 212/ 708-7460. www.normasnyc.com. Reservations accepted. Main courses $8–$23 (most $13–$18). AE, DC, DISC, MC, V. Mon–Fri 6:30am–3pm; Sat–Sun 7am–3pm. Subway: B, N, Q, R, W to 57th St.

INEXPENSIVE

If you're looking for the quintessential New York deli, you have a choice between the **Stage Deli,** 834 Seventh Ave., between 53rd and 54th streets (© **212/245-7850**), known for its huge celebrity-named sandwiches, and the **Carnegie Deli,** 854 Seventh Ave., at 55th Street (© **800/334-5606**), the place to go for the best pastrami, corned beef, and cheesecake in town. For more, see the sidebar "The New York Deli News," on p. 96.

There's a **John's Pizzeria** in Times Square, 260 W. 44th St., between Broadway and Eighth Avenue (© **212/391-7560;** subway: 1, 2, 3, 7, A, B, C, E, N, R, W, Q, S to 42nd Street/Times Square; see the box "Pizza, New York–Style," on p. 94). Also consider the **Burger Joint**, in the lobby of Le Parker Meridien Hotel, 118 W. 57th St. (© **212/708-7460**), for cheap yet excellent burgers.

Pizza, New York Style

Once the domain of countless first-rate pizzerias, Manhattan's pizza offerings have noticeably dropped in quality. The proliferation of national chains into the market has lowered standards. Still, there is plenty of good pizza to be found. Don't be tempted by imitations; when it comes to pizza, search out the real deal. Here are some of the best:

DiFara Pizza 𝕱, 1424 Avenue J, Brooklyn, at E. 15th St. (𝄢 **718/258-1367**). DiFara's is ballyhooed in local publications as the best pizza in the city. And though the exterior is nondescript, looking like your basic neighborhood pizzeria and the interior is cramped, and to be kind, somewhat unkempt with bits of congealed cheese, olive oil, sauce, and crust from a generation of diners still on the tables, DiFara's lives up to its reputation thanks to the zeal of owner Dominic DeMarco, who, for over 40 years, has made every pizza himself. Stooped but determined, DeMarco, in his own deliberate way and using top ingredients, crafts each pizza finishing with hand-grated Parmesan cheese, a few dollops of extra-virgin olive oil, and then, using scissors, hand cutting fresh basil onto the pie. The result is a work of art, but one that might test your patience. Expect to wait an hour for a pie, maybe a bit less for a slice. But after one taste, you will know it was worth it.

Grimaldi's Pizzeria, 19 Old Fulton St., between Front and Water streets (𝄢 **718/858-4300;** www.grimaldis.com). If you need incentive to walk across the Brooklyn Bridge, Grimaldi's, in Brooklyn Heights, provides it. In fact, the pizza is so good, made in a coal oven with a rich sauce and homemade mozzarella, you might run across the bridge to get to it. *Be warned:* It can get very crowded at dinnertime.

John's Pizzeria, 278 Bleecker St., near Seventh Avenue South (𝄢 **212/243-1680**). Since it has expanded from this original location—there are now three—the once-gleaming luster of John's has faded slightly, but the pizza is still a cut above the rest. Thin-crusted and out of a coal oven with the proper ratio of tomato sauce to cheese, John's pizza has a loyal following. Though the quality at all the locations is good, the original Bleecker Street location is the most old-world romantic and my favorite. Also at 260 W. 44th St., between Broadway and Eighth Avenue (✆ 212/391-7560), and 408 E. 64th St., between York and First avenues (✆ 212/935-2895).

Lombardi's, 32 Spring St., between Mulberry and Mott streets (✆ 212/941-7994; www.lombardispizza.com). Claiming to be New York's first "licensed" pizzeria, Lombardi's opened in 1905 and still uses a generations-old Neapolitan family pizza recipe. The coal oven kicks out perfectly cooked pies, some topped with ingredients such as pancetta, homemade sausage, and even fresh-shucked clams. A garden in the back makes it even more inviting during warm weather.

Patsy's Pizzeria ⭐⭐, 2287 First Ave., between 117th and 118th streets (✆ 212/534-9783). My favorite, and also the favorite of Frank Sinatra, who liked it so much he had pies flown out to Las Vegas. The coal oven has been burning since 1932, and though its neighborhood in east Harlem has had its ups and downs, the quality of pizza has never wavered. Try the marinara pizza, a pie with fresh marinara sauce—but no cheese—that's so good you won't miss the mozzarella. Unlike the other pizzerias mentioned, you can order by the slice at Patsy's. Don't be fooled by imitators using Patsy's name; this is the original and the best.

Totonno's Pizzeria Napolitano, 1524 Neptune Ave., between West 15th and West 16th streets, Coney Island, Brooklyn (✆ 718/372-8606). This unassuming pizzeria has been at the same spot since 1924 and it makes pizzas almost exactly as it did 80 years ago—thin crust, fresh sauce, and mozzarella, and that's about it. Don't even think about asking for an exotic topping on these pies (and why would you?). Enjoy it in its simple unadorned glory. Totonno's second branch is on the Upper East Side, 1544 Second Ave., between 80th and 81st streets (✆ 212/327-2800). Go ahead and order the exotic toppings there, but for the real deal, go to Coney Island.

The New York Deli News

There's nothing more *Noo Yawk* than hunkering down over a mammoth pastrami on rye at an authentic Jewish deli, where anything you order comes with a bowl of lip-smacking sour dills and a side of attitude. Here are some of the best.

Artie's New York Delicatessen, 2290 Broadway, between 82nd and 83rd streets (✆ **212/579-5959;** www.arties.com). Compared to the legends below, Arties, which has been around since 1999, is the new kid on the deli block but can hold its own on the playground with the big boys, thank you very much (especially in the wiener department).

Barney Greengrass, the Sturgeon King, 541 Amsterdam Ave., between 86th and 87th streets on the Upper West Side (✆ **212/724-4707**). This unassuming, daytime-only deli has become legendary for its high-quality salmon (sable, gravlax, Nova Scotia, kippered, lox, pastrami—you choose), whitefish, and sturgeon (of course).

Carnegie Deli, 854 Seventh Ave., at 55th Street (✆ **800/334-5606** or 212/757-2245; www.carnegiedeli.com). It's worth subjecting yourself to surly service, tourist-targeted overpricing, and elbow-to-elbow seating for some of the best pastrami and corned beef in town. Even big eaters may be challenged by mammoth sandwiches with such names as "Fifty Ways to Love Your Liver" (chopped liver, hard-boiled egg, lettuce, tomato, and onion).

Nizza ★★ *Value* FRENCH/ITALIAN   You won't do much better for pre- or post-theater dining than Nizza. New in 2007, Nizza offers the cuisine of the French Mediterranean, the city of Nice specifically, and its Ligurian-Italian influence. It's a restaurant where you can fill up on appetizers and salads, starting with the tangy tapenade of black olives served with light, freshly baked focaccia chips and *socca*, a chickpea pancake cooked in a brick oven and sprinkled with fresh herbs. Or savor a glass of wine with a plate of *salumi*, a selection of cured meats such as *coppa, mortadella*, prosciutto, and a variety of salamis, including duck. The romaine salad I had in a garlic vinaigrette with anchovies and shaved pecorino cheese made me swear off

Katz's Delicatessen ✿✿, the city's best deli. remains fabulously old-world despite its hipster-hot Lower East Side location at 205 E. Houston St., at Ludlow Street (✆ 212/254-2246). For more on Katz's, see p. 76.

2nd Avenue Deli ✿ 162 E. 33rd St., between Lexington and Third avenues (✆ 212/689-9000). After a hiatus of more than 2 years, the Second Avenue Deli has returned, but now it's just off Third Avenue, about 20 blocks north of its former East Village location. That East Village feel is gone, but not the quality Kosher deli specialties. The standards: corned beef, pastrami and brisket are as good as you'll get, while such guilty pleasures as *gribenes* (fried chicken skin) and chicken liver, despite their artery-clogging qualities, are almost impossible to resist. Unlike other delis, you might even get a smile from your waiter!

Stage Deli, 834 Seventh Ave., between 53rd and 54th streets (✆ 212/245-7850; www.stagedeli.com). Noisy and crowded and packed with tourists, it's still as authentic as they come. The celebrity sandwiches, ostensibly created by the personalities themselves, are jaw-distending mountains of top-quality fixings: The Tom Hanks is roast beef, chopped liver, onion, and chicken fat, while the Dolly Parton is (drumroll, please) twin rolls of corned beef and pastrami.

Caesar salad forever—well almost. From the brick oven come pizzas, including a Provencal pie with ratatouille, goat cheese, and pesto; entrees such as the delicate *polpette* (meatballs), served on a bed of polenta and garnished with a hot green pepper; and wild boar lasagna that is much less ferocious than it sounds. The restaurant is loud and seating is on the tight side, but you easily forgive Nizza these faults once you sample the memorable food and, especially, the easy-on-your-wallet prices.

630 Ninth Ave (at 45th St.). ✆ 212/956-1800. $8–$12. AE, MC, V. Tues–Sat 11:30am–2am; Sun–Mon 11:30am–midnight. Subway: A, C, E, 7 to 42nd Street.

Sapporo ★ *Value* JAPANESE NOODLES Peruse the community bulletin board as you enter Sapporo and you might find yourself a deal on an apartment—if you can read Japanese. Thankfully, the menu is in English in this Theater District Japanese noodle shop. If the mostly Japanese clientele doesn't convince you of Sapporo's authenticity, the din of satisfied diners slurping huge bowls of steaming ramen (noodle soup with meat and vegetables) will. And though the ramen is Sapporo's specialty, the *gyoza* (Japanese dumplings) and the *donburi* (pork or chicken over rice with soy-flavored sauce) are also terrific. Best of all, nothing on the menu is over $10 and that's not easy to find in the Theater District.

152 W. 49th St. (btwn Sixth & Seventh aves.). ℂ **212/869-8972.** Reservations not accepted. Main courses $6–$9. No credit cards. Mon–Sat 11am–11pm; Sun 11am–10pm. Subway: N, R to 49th St.

Wondee Siam ★ *Finds* THAI Hell's Kitchen offers countless ethnic culinary variations and one of the most prevalent is Thai—there are at least six Thai restaurants in a 5-block radius. My favorite is the tiny, zero-ambience Wondee Siam. I don't need colorful decorations or a big fish tank to enjoy authentic, uncompromisingly spicy Thai food and that's what I get at Wondee Siam. Here you don't have to worry that your waiter will assume you want a milder form of Thai. If there is a little red asterisk next to your item, you can be sure it is appropriately spicy. The soups are terrific, especially the sinus-clearing *tom yum.* In fact, there is a whole section of yum (chiles) dishes on the menu; my favorite being the *larb gai,* minced ground chicken with ground toasted rice. The curries are also first-rate as are the noodles, including the mild pad Thai. This is strictly BYOB and you'll want to do so to complement the spicy food.

792 Ninth Ave. (btwn 52nd and 53rd sts.). ℂ **212/459-9057.** Reservations not accepted. Main courses $8.50–$18 (most under $10). No credit cards. Mon–Sat 11am–11pm; Sun 11am–10:30pm. Subway: C, E to 50th St. Wondee Siam II, 813 Ninth Ave. (btwn 53rd and 54th sts.). ℂ **917/286-1726.**

10 Midtown East & Murray Hill

To locate the restaurants in this section, see the map on p. 82.

EXPENSIVE

Aquavit ★★★ SCANDINAVIAN I'll miss the waterfall and the intimate setting that Aquavit vacated in 2005. Thankfully, however, the food and staff had no trouble adjusting to the transition. Everything remains first-rate. The restaurant is now in the bottom of a glass tower on East 55th Street, designed in sleek Scandinavian style with modernist furniture. In the front is an informal and less-expensive cafe, while past a long bar is the dining room.

After the move, if anything, the food has improved. The smoked fish—really all the fish—is prepared perfectly. I often daydream about the herring plate: four types of herring accompanied by a tiny glass of Aquavit, distilled liquor not unlike vodka flavored with fruit and spices, and a frosty Carlsberg beer. The hot smoked Arctic char on the main a la carte menu, served with clams and bean puree in a mustard green broth, is also a winner. Most fixed-price menus offer a well-chosen beverage accompaniment option.

65 E. 55th St. (btwn Park and Madison aves.). © 212/307-7311. www.aquavit.org. Reservations recommended. Cafe main courses $9–$32; 3-course fixed-price meal $24 at lunch, $35 at dinner; main dining room fixed-price meal $39 at lunch, $82 at dinner ($39 for vegetarians); 3-course pre-theater dinner (5:30–6:15pm) $55; tasting menus $58 at lunch, $115 at dinner ($90 for vegetarians); supplement for paired wines $30 at lunch, $80 at dinner. AE, DC, MC, V. Mon–Fri noon–2:30pm; Sun–Thurs 5:30–10:30pm; Fri–Sat 5:15–10:30pm. Subway: E, F to Fifth Ave.

BLT Steak ✶✶✶ STEAKHOUSE/BISTRO   Steakhouses are often stereotyped as bastions of male bonding; testosterone-fueled with red meat and hearty drinks. But BLT (Bistro Laurent Tourendel) Steak breaks that mold in a big way; on the night I visited, I noticed more women—slinky and model-like—chomping on thick cuts of beef than men. That doesn't mean men can't also enjoy the beef here; served in cast-iron pots and finished in steak butter with a choice of sauces—béarnaise, red wine, horseradish, and bleu cheese, to name a few. The signature is the porterhouse for two (at $70!), but I recommend the New York strip or the short ribs braised in red wine. Both can be shared, which may be a good idea, especially after devouring the complimentary popovers and sampling an appetizer such as the tuna tartare or a side of onion rings or creamy spinach. Even after sharing one of the meats, you might not have room for the chestnut-chocolate sundae or peanut-butter chocolate mousse, and that would be a shame. This is not a restaurant for intimate conversation; even the music was muffled by the din of the diners.

106 E. 57th St. (btwn Park and Lexington aves.). © 212/752-7470. www.bltsteak. com. Reservations highly recommended. Main courses $24–$39. AE, DC, MC, V. Mon–Fri 11:45am–2:30pm; Mon–Thurs 5:30–11pm; Fri–Sat 5:30–11:30pm. Subway: 4, 5, 6, N, R, W to 59th St.

Country ✶✶ FRENCH/AMERICAN   Stunningly elegant and urbane, there is really nothing country about Country. And that's not a knock. Gorgeously designed by David Rockwell, the restaurant's centerpiece is the 200-square-foot Tiffany skylight dome that was hidden over the years by a dropped ceiling. The prix-fixe menu changes every 2 weeks and matches the decor's sophisticated style. When I visited in early spring, warm asparagus in a light lemon vinaigrette was an outstanding first-course option while the lamb cannelloni (tender pieces of shredded lamb in a wonton-thin dumpling) made the perfect second-course accompaniment. Of the third-course options, the striped bass with crushed herbs, potatoes, and clams was the standout. A selection of cheeses is offered as a dessert option and it's hard to resist. Downstairs are the more countrified, darker, wood-paneled booths of Café at Country.

90 Madison Ave. (at 29th St.). 𝒞 212/889-7100. Reservations required. Prix-fixe $105; 5-course tasting menu $110; 4-course tasting menu $105; 6-course $135. AE, DC, DISC, MC, V. Sun–Thurs 5:30–10pm; Fri–Sat 5:30–11pm. Café at Country main courses $15–$27. Mon–Sat 11:30am–3pm and 5:30–11pm; Sun 10:30am–3pm. Subway: N/R to 28th St.; 6 to 28th St.

MODERATE

Also consider **P.J. Clarke's** 𝓰, 915 Third Ave., at 55th Street (𝒞 **212/ 317-1616;** www.pjclarkes.com), for their old-world charm and legendary hamburger. For a more innovative, experimental hamburger, try **Rare Bar & Grill,** 303 Lexington Ave., between 37th and 38th streets (𝒞 **212/481-1999**).

Chola 𝓰𝓰 𝓕𝓲𝓷𝓭𝓼 INDIAN   Don't let the nondescript, neighborhood Chinese restaurant look fool you, the food of Chola is as good as you will find just about anywhere in Manhattan. The menu is extensive and features many vegetarian and vegan options. Of the vegetarian starters, the *kurkuri bhindi* (crispy okra and red onions flavored by a lime and *chaat masala*) is not to be missed, while the non-vegetarian cochin lamb chops, rubbed with southern spices and served with onions and garlic, is so good that it might tempt a vegetarian to cross over to the dark side. Long, crispy *dosas* (thin crepes stuffed with spiced potatoes and peas), are also available at Chola and, according to the menu, a favorite of Martha Stewart's. After a few bites, I concurred with Martha. Of the "Southern Specialties" on the menu *savitri amma's avail,* vegetables in a yogurt sauce, was unlike anything I had ever tasted in an Indian restaurant, but very much want to again. Chicken korma, seemingly a conventional Indian dish, was anything but at Chola, with the tender roasted chicken coated in a rich cashew sauce. Probably the best way to experience Chola and to sample a wide variety of its dishes is to visit the restaurant for its popular weekend "maharaja" buffet.

225 E. 58th St. (btwn Second and Third aves.). **℗ 212/688-4619.** wwwfineindian dining.com. Main courses: $14–$23; lunch buffet $14. AE, DC, DISC, MC, V. Mon–Fri noon–3pm; Sat–Sun 11am–3pm; nightly 5–11pm. Subway: 4, 5, 6, N, R, W to 59th St.

Mia Dona ☆☆ ITALIAN/GREEK   This newest (2008) venture by the team of Chef Michael Psilakis and partner Donatella Arpaia (**Anthos,** p. 89) is a celebration of mostly rustic Italian dishes with a few nods to Greece. The combination is a natural and best of all, at Mia Dona, easy on the wallet. The appetizer of grilled calamari and caponata salad (a combination of sweet [from currants] and sour from the pickled eggplant) works terrifically, the calamari grilled to tender perfection; while the crispy rabbit with salt and fingerling chips is a starter you most likely won't find anywhere else. Another original is the *gnudi*, gnocchilike pasta served with sheep's milk ricotta in a truffle butter sauce; it's the standout in a selection of very good pastas. Of the entrees, the olive oil poached cod with broccoli rabe in a sun-dried tomato pesto tasted as good as its description, while the hearty braised veal breast with escarole and cannellini beans is Italian comfort food at its best. The current trend in New York dining is high decibel and here it's no exception, making the noise-level the only negative to the Mia Dona experience.

206 E. 58th St. (btwn Second and Third aves.). **℗ 212/750-8170.** www.miadona. com. Reservations recommended. Pastas $15–$16; entrees $17–$24. AE, DC, DISC, MC, V. Mon–Fri noon–2:30pm; Sat–Sun 11am–2pm; Mon–Thurs 5–10:30pm; Fri–Sun 5–11pm. Subway: 4, 5, 6, N, R, W to 59th St.-Lexington Ave.

INEXPENSIVE

For a glorious meal, dining under an impressive curved and tiled ceiling, try the New York landmark **Oyster Bar & Restaurant** ☆ (**℗ 212/490-6650;** www.oysterbarny.com). For a complete list of vendors, check out www.grandcentralterminal.com.

In addition to the listings below, there's also **Ess-A-Bagel** (see "The Hole Truth: N.Y.'s Best Bagels," p. 88) at 831 Third Ave., at 51st Street (**℗ 212/980-1010**).

11 Upper West Side
VERY EXPENSIVE

Porter House New York ☆☆ STEAKHOUSE   The space, in the Time Warner Center on Columbus Circles is sleek with large leather banquettes for groups along with smaller, white table-clothed tables by the floor-to-ceiling windows overlooking Central Park. Along with the view, this steakhouse satisfies the essentials of the best red

Where to Dine Uptown

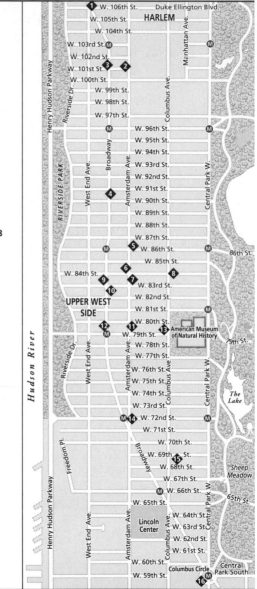

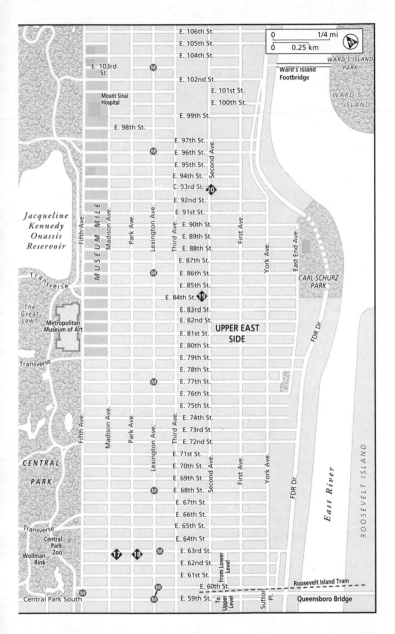

meat emporiums, with a few inventive twists. I gambled by ordering the chili-rubbed ribeye—would chili obscure the natural flavor of the meat? It paid off; the chili was subtle and brought out the cut's essence. If you want your steak straight ahead, the dry-aged prime strip steak, cooked to perfection, won't let you down. Sides are somewhat steakhouse unconventional: they add pieces of thick, smoky bacon to the creamed spinach and offer porcini mushrooms on a bed of polenta as an alternative to mashed potatoes. But it's the meat—and that you are eating it overlooking Central Park—that makes Porter House New York so special.

10 Columbus Circle (4th Floor) in the Time Warner Center (at 60th St.). ℭ **212/823-9500**. www.porterhousenewyork.com. Main courses: $24–$39. AE, DC, DISC, MC, V. Mon–Sat noon–4pm; Sun noon–3pm; Mon–Thurs 5–10:30pm; Fri–Sat 5–11pm. Subway: A,B,C,D,1 trains to 59th St-Columbus Circle.

EXPENSIVE

Ouest 𝒦𝒦𝒦 CONTEMPORARY AMERICAN   With plush red banquettes and an intimate balcony area, Ouest is both cozy and clubby. Service is personable but also professional—so good you'll need to keep reminding yourself that you are on the Upper West Side. But what really draws the crowds is chef Tom Valenti's mastery in the kitchen, especially with meats such as his signature braised lamb shank or his melt-in-your-mouth braised beef short ribs. The sautéed skate is perfectly prepared with a simple sauce of parsley and olive oil, while the baby calamari in a spicy tomato sopressata sauce appetizer was so good I actually smiled as I ate it.

2315 Broadway (at 84th St.). ℭ **212/580-8700**. www.ouestny.com. Reservations required well in advance. Main courses $23–$36. AE, DC, DISC, MC, V. Mon–Thurs 5:30–11pm; Fri–Sat 5:30–11:30pm; Sun 11am–10pm. Subway: 1, 2 to 86th St.

Telepan 𝒦𝒦 AMERICAN   Telepan is in an Upper West Side townhouse with a dining room painted in soothing lime green. The cool design complements the menu which changes seasonally but always features farm fresh products. In the spring I was greeted with fresh ramps, fiddleheads, and young peas in many of the dishes. There was no fresh produce, however, in the foie gras donuts listed as a "share." The "donuts" are dusted with cocoa and cinnamon and might work as well with a cup of java as with a cocktail. Of the appetizers, the standout was the wild green frittata which came with in-season ramps. Telepan offers Mid Courses and of them, the pea pancakes with pea agnolotti looked and, more importantly, tasted greenmarket fresh. Save room for an entrée, specifically the haddock with a sweet lobster sauce. Whatever you choose to eat, you'll have no problem finding a complementary wine from the restaurant's long and impressive list. Telepan is a pre-Lincoln Center favorite so if you want to avoid the crush, make a reservation for after curtain.

72 W. 69th St. (at Columbus Ave.). ℂ **212/580-4300.** www.telepan-ny.com. Reservations recommended. Main courses: $29–$36; four-course tasting menu $59; five-course tasting menu $69. AE, DC, MC, V. Lunch Wed–Fri 11:30am–2:30pm; dinner Mon–Thurs 5–11pm, Fri–Sat 5–11:30pm, Sun 5–10:30pm; brunch Sat–Sun 11am–2:30pm. Subway: B, C to 72nd St.

MODERATE

Carmine's ★ *Kids* FAMILY-STYLE SOUTHERN ITALIAN
Everything is B-I-G at this rollicking family-style mainstay with two locations, on the Upper West Side (the original) and in Times Square. In many cases big means bad, but not here. Carmine's, with a dining room vast enough to deserve its own zip code, and massive portions, turns out better pasta and entrees than most 20-table Italian restaurants. I've never had pasta here that wasn't *al dente*, and the marinara sauce is as good as any I've had in Manhattan. The salads are always fresh and the fried calamari perfectly tender. Rigatoni marinara, linguine with white-clam sauce, and ziti with broccoli are pasta standouts, while the best meat entrees include veal parmigiana, broiled porterhouse steak, shrimp scampi, and the remarkable chicken *scarpariello* (chicken pan-broiled with a lemon-rosemary sauce). The tiramisu is pie-size, thick, creamy, and bathed in Kahlúa and Marsala. Order half of what you think you'll need. Don't expect intimate conversation; in fact, it's downright loud.

2450 Broadway (btwn 90th and 91st sts.). ℂ **212/362-2200.** www.carminesnyc. com. Reservations recommended before 6pm; accepted only for 6 or more after 6pm. Family-style main courses $19–$65 (most $23 or less). AE, DC, DISC, MC, V. Sun–Thurs 11:30am–11pm; Fri–Sat 11:30am–midnight. Subway: 1, 2, 3 to 96th St. Also at 200 W. 44th St. (btwn Broadway and Eighth Ave.). ℂ **212/221-3800.** Subway: A, C, E, N, R, S, 1, 2, 3, 7 to 42nd St./Times Sq.

Kefi ★★★ *Finds* GREEK Chef/owner Michael Psilakis has transformed what was formerly nouveau-Greek Onera back to something much closer to your father's Greek. More accurately, Kefi is like your Greek mother's (if you had a Greek mother) kitchen and in fact, the restaurant was inspired by Psilakis's mother and her traditional recipes. So gone is the Offal Tasting menu of Onera and in are Greek standards like moussaka, spinach pie, Greek salad, and grilled fish. But oh, what Psilakis does with the standards! The *mezes* (Greek appetizers) are good enough to make up a meal; it's hard to resist the selection of spreads accompanied by pita, the warm feta, tomatoes, capers and anchovies, and the grilled octopus salad, as good as I've had anywhere. But something's gotta give if you want to save room for entrées like the flat noodles with braised rabbit, the grilled whole branzino with potatoes, olives, tomatoes and feta, or the slow cooked lamb shank on a bed of orzo. If it is humanly possible after indulging in all of the above, don't miss out on the desserts, most notably the walnut cake with maple walnut ice cream.

505 Columbus Ave (at 84th St.) ℂ 212/873-0200. Reservations recommended. Main courses $10–$20. AE, DC, DISC, MC, V. Tue–Thurs 5–10:30pm; Fri–Sat 5–11pm; Sun 5–10pm. Subway: 1 to 79th St.

Ocean Grill ⓡⓡ SEAFOOD   The Stephen Hanson/BRGuest Restaurant empire (Primehouse, Blue Water Grill, Dos Caminos, and Fiamma to name a few) is vast, and sometimes the brawny restaurants in the group can be a wee bit impersonal. But Ocean Grill, despite its size, defies that generalization. Maybe it's because the restaurant is across from the Museum of Natural History and feeds off that building's wondrous vibe? Or maybe because it is in the heart of the family-friendly Upper West Side that Ocean Grill feels more like an intimate neighborhood joint. And what makes Ocean Grill even more special is that the always-fresh seafood, usually prepared without too many frills, complements that relaxed good feeling. Like other Hanson-run restaurants, there are numerous menu options, including a touch of Asian in the preparation of the seafood, specifically Japanese, with a generous selection of house made maki rolls— the creamy wasabi tuna is so good you will immediately forget any mercury warnings you've read about. But if raw tuna terrifies you, try one of the fish entrees such as the Chilean sea bass in a violet mustard emulsion served with polenta fries, or any of the fish grilled with a choice of sauces, such as black olive tapenade or a soy-ginger vinaigrette, and sides such as bok choy or broccoli rabe.

384 Columbus Ave (btwn 79th and 80th sts.). ℂ 212/579-2300. www.brguest restaurants.com. Reservations recommended. Main courses: $20–$33. AE, DC, DISC, MC, V. Mon–Fri 11:30am–5pm; Sat 11:30am–4:30pm; Sun 10:30am–4:30pm; Mon–Tues 5–11pm; Wed–Thurs 5–11:30pm; Fri 5pm–midnight; Sat 4:30pm–midnight; Sun 4:30–11pm. Subway: B, C to 81st St.

Savann ⓡ MEDITERRANEAN   The restaurant scene on Amsterdam Avenue in the low 80s is particularly volatile, but for over 9 years, Savann has survived on that difficult stretch of real estate thanks to consistently top-notch food, personable service, and a casual, low-key atmosphere. This is a neighborhood place with regulars who swear by the food. Some favorites include the home-cured gravlax, here served over a chickpea-scallion pancake in a flying-fish caviar and dill sauce; the grilled calamari; the Seafood Savann, a medley of seafood in a light tomato sauce served over linguine; the mixed seafood phyllo purse; and the perfectly cooked filet mignon. For dessert don't miss the *tarte tatine*, a homemade apple tart served with cinnamon ice cream and warm honey. In warm weather, the sidewalk cafe is a great place for people-watching.

414 Amsterdam Ave. (btwn 79th and 80th sts.) ⓒ 212/580-0202. www.savann. com. Reservations recommended. Main courses $12–$27 (most under $20). AE, MC, V. Mon–Fri noon–3:30pm; Sat–Sun 11am–3:30pm; daily 4–11pm. Subway: 1 to 79th St.

INEXPENSIVE

For breakfast or lunch, also consider **Artie's Delicatessen,** 2290 Broadway, between 82nd and 83rd streets (ⓒ **212/579-5959;** www. arties.com), and **Barney Greengrass, the Sturgeon King,** 541 Amsterdam Ave., between 86th and 87th streets (ⓒ **212/724-4707**), two of the best Jewish delis in town. See "The New York Deli News" sidebar on p. 96 for further details.

You'll find some of the best bagels in New York on the Upper West Side, including **H&H Bagels,** 2239 Broadway, at 80th Street (ⓒ **212/595-8003**), and **Absolute Bagels,** 2788 Broadway, between 106th and 107th streets (ⓒ **212/932-2052**). For more information, see "The Hole Truth: N.Y.'s Best Bagels," on p. 88.

For non-vegetarians and the non-health-minded, consider the cheapest, yet in some ways most comforting, indulgence: **Gray's Papaya,** 2090 Broadway, at 72nd Street (ⓒ **212/799-0243**). This 24-hour hot-dog stand is a New York institution.

Celeste 🅰🅰 *Finds* ITALIAN   Tiny, charming Celeste features its own wood-burning pizza oven, which churns out thin-crusted, delicious pizzas. Pizza is not the only attraction; the *"fritti"* (fried) course is unique; the *fritto misto de pesce* (fried mixed seafood) is delectable, but the fried zucchini blossoms, usually available in the summer and fall, are amazing. The fresh pastas are better than the dried pasta; I never thought the fresh egg noodles with cabbage, shrimp, and sheep's cheese would work, but it was delicious. Not on the menu, but usually available, are plates of artisanal Italian cheeses served with homemade jams. Though the main courses are good, stick with the pizzas, antipasto, *frittis,* and pastas. For dessert, try the gelato; the pistachio was the best I've had in New York. The restaurant has been "discovered," so go early or late or expect a wait.

502 Amsterdam Ave. (btwn 84th & 85th sts.). ⓒ **212/874-4559.** Reservations not accepted. Pizza $10–$12; antipasto $7–$10; pasta $10; main courses $14–$16. No credit cards. Mon–Sat 5–11pm; Sun noon–3pm. Subway: 1 to 86th St.

Flor de Mayo *Finds* CUBAN/CHINESE   Cuban/Chinese cuisine is a New York phenomenon that started in the late 1950s when Cubans of Chinese heritage immigrated to New York after the revolution. Most of the immigrants took up residence on the Upper West Side, and Cuban/Chinese restaurants flourished. Many have disappeared, but the best one, Flor de Mayo, still remains and is so popular that a new branch opened further south on Amsterdam Avenue. The kitchen excels at both sides of the massive menu, but the best dish is the *la brasa* half-chicken lunch special—beautifully spiced and slow-roasted until it's fork tender and falling off the bone, served with a pile of fried rice, bounteous with roast pork, shrimp, and veggies. Offered Monday through Saturday until 4:30pm, the whole meal is $6.95, and it's enough to fortify you for the day. Service and atmosphere are reminiscent of Chinatown: efficient and lightning-quick. My favorite combo: the noodles-, greens-, shrimp-, and pork-laden Chinese soup with yellow rice and black beans.

2651 Broadway (btwn 100th & 101st sts.). ℂ **212/663-5520** or 212/595-2525. Reservations not accepted. Main courses $4.50–$19 (most under $10); lunch specials $5–$7 (Mon–Sat to 4:30pm). AE, MC, V ($15 minimum). Daily noon–midnight. Subway: 1 to 103rd St. Also at 484 Amsterdam Ave. (btwn 83rd & 84th sts.). ℂ **212/ 787-3388.** Subway: 1 to 86th St.

Good Enough to Eat *Kids* *Finds* AMERICAN HOME COOKING   For 25 years the crowds have been lining up on weekends outside Good Enough to Eat to experience chef/owner Carrie Levin's incredible breakfasts. As a result, lunch and dinner have been somewhat overlooked. That's too bad, because these meals can be as great as the breakfasts. The restaurant's cow motif and farmhouse knick-knacks imply hearty, home-cooked food, and that's what's done best here. Stick with the classics: meatloaf with gravy and mashed potatoes; turkey dinner with cranberry relish, gravy, and cornbread stuffing; macaroni and cheese; griddled corn bread; Vermont spinach salad; and the BBQ sandwich, roast chicken with barbecue sauce and homemade potato chips. And save room for the desserts; though the selection is often overwhelming, I can never resist the coconut cake. This is food you loved as a kid, which is one reason why the kids will love it today. There are only 20 tables here, so expect a wait on weekends during the day or for dinner after six.

483 Amsterdam Ave. (btwn 83rd and 84th sts.). ℂ **212/496-0163.** www.good enoughtoeat.com. Breakfast $5.25–$12; lunch $8.50–$15; dinner $8.50–$23 (most under $18). AE, MC, V. Breakfast Mon–Fri 8:30am–4pm, Sat–Sun 9am–4pm; lunch Mon noon–4pm, Tues–Fri 11:30am–4pm; dinner Mon–Thurs & Sun 5:30–10:30pm, Fri–Sat 5:30–11pm. Subway: 1 to 86th St.

Noche Mexicana ★ *Finds* MEXICAN   This tiny restaurant serves some of the best tamales in New York. Wrapped in cornhusks, as a good tamale should be, they come in two varieties: in a red mole sauce with shredded chicken or in a green tomatillo sauce with shredded pork. There are three tamales in each order, which costs only $6, making it a cheap and almost perfect lunch. The burritos are authentic and meals unto themselves. The *tinga* burrito, shredded chicken in a tomato-and-onion chipotle sauce, is my favorite. Each is stuffed with rice, beans, and guacamole. Don't get fancy here; stick with the tamales, burritos, and soft tacos, the best being the taco *al pastor,* a taco stuffed with pork marinated with pineapple and onions.

852 Amsterdam Ave. (btwn 101st and 102nd sts.). ℂ **212/662-6900** or 212/662-7400. Burritos $6.50–$8.50; tacos $2; tamales $6; Mexican dishes $9.50–$11. AE, DISC, MC, V. Sun–Thurs 10am–11pm; Fri–Sat 10am–midnight. Subway: 1 to 103rd St.

12 Upper East Side

To locate the restaurants in this section, see the map on p. 102.

EXPENSIVE

Paola's ★ ITALIAN   There is no shortage of Italian restaurants on the Upper East Side, but many are mediocre. There is nothing mediocre about Paola's, and having survived and thrived in the neighborhood for over 10 years is testament to the restaurant's quality and charms. The charm begins with Paola herself, almost always present and always the gracious hostess. The two dining rooms are inviting; the larger centered on a wood-burning oven used to cook many of the restaurant's meat dishes, the other the smaller, but cozy, wine room. Most appealing of all is the menu. Hope that Paola has found baby artichokes the day you visit, because you will want to begin with the *carciofi alla Giudea,* artichokes prepared in the style of the Roman Jews—cooked twice and addictively crispy. The pastas are usually homemade; the pappardelle with a duck-meat ragout is a standout, while the hand-rolled *trofie* served with pesto is a specialty. The *stinco d'agnello,* slow-roasted lamb shank with sage and parmesan polenta, is a hearty main course, roasted in the wood-burning oven, as are the naturally raised, corn-fed poussins, served with potato gratin and sautéed greens. Fig ice cream topped with port-soaked figs is the decadent way to finish your meal.

245 E. 84th St. (btwn Second & Third aves.). ℂ **212/794-1890.** www.paolas restaurant.com. Reservations recommended. Pasta $14–$17; main courses $22–$30. AE, MC, V. Sun–Fri 1–4pm; Sun–Wed 5–10pm; Thurs–Sat 5–11pm. Subway: 4, 5, 6 to 86th St.

Dining Uptown: The Soul of Harlem

There is much soul in Manhattan, but Harlem seems to possess the mother lode when it comes to food. Here is one man's primer to Harlem's soul food (see map on p. 112):

Amy Ruth's, 113 W. 116th St., between Lenox and Seventh avenues (© **212/280-8779**). Amy Ruth's has become a mecca for Harlem celebs, with the gimmick of naming platters after them, like the Rev. Al Sharpton (chicken and waffles) and the Rev. Calvin O. Butts III (chicken wings and waffles). Most of the celebrities gained their fame in Harlem, as did the chicken and waffles, or fried whiting and waffles, or steak and waffles. You can't go wrong with anything here as long as waffles are included.

Charles' Southern Style Kitchen ⭐, 2837 Eighth Ave., between 151st and 152nd streets (© **877/813-2920** or 212/926-4313). Nothing fancy about this place, just a brightly lit, 25-seater on a not-very-attractive block in upper Harlem. But you don't come here for fancy, you come for soul food at its simplest and freshest. And come hungry. The $13 all-you-can-eat buffet features crunchy, moist, pan-fried chicken; ribs in a tangy sauce, with meat falling off the bone; stewed oxtails in a thick brown onion gravy; macaroni and cheese; collard greens with bits of smoked turkey; black-eyed peas; and corn bread, warm and not overly sweet. Hours can be erratic, so call before you head there.

M&G Diner, 383 W. 125th St., at St. Nicholas Avenue (© **212/864-7326**). All the soul-food joints I've listed serve

Park Avenue Winter ⭐⭐ AMERICAN/MEDITERRANEAN
Not only might the name of this restaurant be different when you visit, but the look (created by award-winning design firm AvroKO) and the menu will be changed as well. The gimmick here is that the restaurant transforms itself each season. And though a restaurant with a gimmick is sometimes frowned upon, in this case, it's more than a gimmick: Park Avenue Winter (the season I happened to visit it) is first rate. For the winter look, the large, high-ceilinged dining room was a snowy, glacial white and the menu reflected the season. Starters included the hearty porcini ravioli with Swiss chard in a flavorful

top-notch fried chicken, but the best I've had is the perfectly pan-fried, supermoist bird at the M&G. This small, no-frills diner, open 8am–11:30pm, is a treat any time. Start your day with a breakfast of eggs with salmon croquettes or eggs with grits or finish it with the chicken, chitterlings, or meat-loaf. All the sides are freshly made, and the desserts, espe-cially the sweet-potato pie, are phenomenal. There's a great jukebox loaded with soul to complement the food.

Miss Mamie's Spoonbread Too, 366 W. 110th St., between Columbus and Manhattan avenues (© 212/865-6744). Entering this strawberry-curtained charmer is like stepping into South Carolina. But you are in Harlem, or at least the southern fringe of Harlem, and you won't be paying South Carolina soul prices, or Harlem soul prices, either. Still, despite the prices, Miss Mamie's is the real deal, especially their barbecued ribs, falling off the bone in a sweet peppery sauce, and the smothered chicken, fried and then covered with thick pan gravy.

Sylvia's, 328 Lenox Ave., between 126th and 127th streets (© 212/996-0660; www.sylviassoulfood.com). Sylvia is the self-proclaimed queen of not only Harlem soul food but *all* soul food. In reality, Sylvia's is a "brand," offering canned food, beauty products, and fragrances, and the food at her original restaurant has suffered and it's more of a tourist trap. If you plan to go, make it on Sunday for the gospel brunch, which is an absolute joy.

gorgonzola cream sauce, while you might not find a more comforting cold weather dish than the entree of filet mignon on a bed of shred-ded short ribs accompanied by root vegetables. But surprisingly, the winter fare here has a welcome light touch as evidenced in the deli-cate cornbread-crusted red snapper on a citrus salad. Even the side of potato latkes, notoriously leaden, here were actually light and airy. Like most restaurants these days, the decibel level is thunderous.

100 E. 63rd St. (at Park Ave.). © 212/644-1900. www.parkavenuenyc.com. Reservations recommended. Main courses: $26–$48. AE, DC, DISC, MC, V. Mon–Fri 11:30am–3pm; Sat–Sun 11am–3pm; Mon–Thurs 5:30–11pm; Fri–Sat 5:30–11:30pm; Sun 5:30–10pm. Subway: F at Lexington Ave-63rd St.

Where to Dine in Harlem

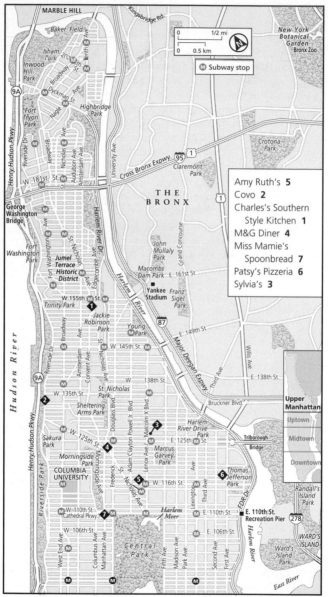

0   1/2 mi
0   0.5 km

Ⓜ Subway stop

Amy Ruth's **5**
Covo **2**
Charles's Southern
 Style Kitchen **1**
M&G Diner **4**
Miss Mamie's
 Spoonbread **7**
Patsy's Pizzeria **6**
Sylvia's **3**

The Post House ★★ STEAKHOUSE The Post House is not your traditional meat and potatoes steakhouse. There are as many non–red meat items on the menu as there are steak and chops. Most of the appetizers come from the sea and the cornmeal fried oysters layered on a potato chip with cole slaw is something I've never had in a steakhouse before. Dover Sole, lobster, and grilled chicken, are just a few of the non–red meat entree options you'll find at the Post House, but I've categorized the restaurant as a steakhouse because you need to forget those other options and order the Cajun rib eye steak, broiled in a subtle cayenne rub that perfectly melds with the richness of the meat. The starchy side dishes are traditional and served family-style (meaning large) so make sure you are eating with a family before ordering a platter of hash browns or onion rings. For dessert it will be worth your while to wait the extra ten minutes it takes to prepare the restaurant's classic chocolate soufflé.

28 E. 63rd St. (btwn Park and Madison aves.). © **212/935-2888**. www.theposthouse. com. Reservations recommended. Main courses: $26–$70. AE, DC, DISC, MC, V. Mon–Fri noon–5pm; Mon–Thurs 5–11pm; Fri–Sun 5pm–midnight. Subway: 4, 5, 6, N, R, W at Lexington Ave-59th St

INEXPENSIVE

Nick's Family-Style Restaurant and Pizzeria ★ *Kids* ITALIAN Since 1994, Nick Angelis has wowed them in Forest Hills, Queens, with his pizza. In 2003 he took his act to Manhattan, where the pizza is garnering equally high praise. The pizza is thin-crusted, with the proper proportions of creamy, homemade mozzarella and fresh tomato sauce. But this is much more than a pizzeria: Try the light, lemony baked clams or "Josephine's" perfectly breaded eggplant parmigiana. If you dare combine pizza with a calzone, this is the place; Nick's calzone, stuffed with ricotta and mozzarella cheese, is spectacular. The orecchiette with broccoli rabe and sausage is the pasta winner, while the filet of sole oreganato Livornese with mussels is the standout main course. Save room for an extra-large cannoli for dessert; the shell is flaky and the filling ultra-creamy. Full orders are enough to feed two or three and are a great bargain for a group, but half-orders are also available. The room is comfortable and far from fancy. Go early or be prepared to wait.

1814 Second Ave. (at 94th St.). © **212/987-5700**. Pizza $12–$14; macaroni half-orders $6–$12, full orders $12–$24; entree half-orders $8.50–$12, full orders $17–$24. AE, DC, DISC, MC, V. Sun–Thurs 11:30am–11pm; Fri–Sat 11:30am–11:30pm. Subway: 6 to 96th St.

Covo Trattoria & Pizzeria *(R) (Finds)* ITALIAN   "*Covo*" means cave in Italian and the location of Covo, under the West Side Highway and down steep steps from Riverside Park, could be called cavelike. But this *covo* has a wood-burning pizza and bread oven manned by a Neapolitan pizza maker, along with an affordable menu of rustic Italian dishes. Try the *paesana* pizza, made with tomato sauces, pecorino cheese, and black olives or an antipasti of bruschetta slathered with tomato and chick peas. Of the pastas, the homemade pappardelle with a honey-braised short rib ragu is addictive, while the *rigatoni alla norma* (pasta with tomato sauce, eggplant, basil and fresh ricotta cheese) is the restaurant's signature dish. Save room for a "secondi" especially the *coniglio*, braised, tender rabbit served with olive oil, rosemary, and black olives. The list of Italian wines is decent and easy on the wallet, but because you are in a *covo*, the sound level when it's busy can be deafening. Be prepared.

701 W. 135th St. (at 12th Ave.). *(C)* **212/234-9573**. www.covony.com. Pizza $8–$13; main courses $10–$19. AE, DC, DISC, MC, V. Daily noon–midnight. Subway: 1 to 137th St.

4

Exploring New York City

Don't try to tame New York—you can't. Decide on a few must-see attractions, and then let the city take you on its own ride. Inevitably, as you make your way around town, you'll be blown off course by unplanned diversions that are as much fun as what you meant to see. After all, the true New York is in the details. As you dash from sight to sight, take time to admire a cornice on a prewar building, linger over coffee at a sidewalk cafe, or just idle away a few minutes on a bench watching New Yorkers parade through their daily lives.

1 The Top Attractions

American Museum of Natural History *Kids* This is one of the hottest museum tickets in town, thanks to the **Rose Center for Earth and Space**, whose four-story-tall planetarium sphere hosts the show, *Cosmic Collisions,* narrated by Robert Redford, about the violent beginnings of the universe. Prepare to be blown away by this astounding, literally earth-shaking short film.

Buy your tickets in advance for the Space Show in order to guarantee admission (they're available online); I also recommend buying tickets in advance for a specific IMAX film or special exhibition, such as the Butterfly Conservatory (see below), especially during peak seasons (summer, autumn, holiday time) and for weekend visits; otherwise, you might miss out.

Other must-sees include the Big Bang Theater, which re-creates the theoretical birth of the universe; the Hall of the Universe, with its 16-ton meteorite; and the terrific Hall of Planet Earth, which focuses on the geologic processes of our home planet (great volcano display!). All in all, you'll need at least 2 hours to fully explore the Rose Center. *Tip:* Friday night is a great time to plan your visit, as the center isn't overcrowded, live jazz and food fill the Hall of the Universe, and, bathed in blue light, the sphere looks magical.

Downtown Attractions

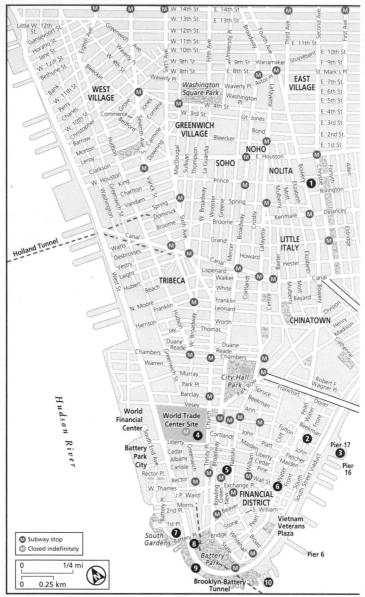

Little W. 12th St.
Gansevoort St.
Horatio St.
Jane St.
W. 12th St.
Bethune St.
Bank
W. 11th St.
Perry
Charles
W. 10th St.
Christopher
Barrow
Morton
Leroy
Clarkson
W. Houston
King
Charlton
Vandam
Spring
Dominick
Broome

Eighth Ave.
Greenwich Ave.
Waverly Pl.
W. 4th St.
Bleecker
Grove
Commerce
Bedford
Seventh Ave. S.
Hudson
Washington
Greenwich St.
West St.

Sixth Ave.
Jones
Cornelia
Downing
Varick St.
Carmine

WEST VILLAGE

GREENWICH VILLAGE

W. 14th St.
W. 13th St.
W. 12th St.
W. 11th St.
W. 10th St.
W. 9th St.
W. 8th St.
Waverly Pl.

Washington Square Park
Washington Pl.
W. 4th St.
W. 3rd St.

Fifth Ave.
University Pl.
Broadway

E. 14th St
E. 13th St.
E. 11th St.
E. 10th St.
E. 9th St.
St. Mark's Pl.
E. 7th St.
E. 6th St.
E. 5th St.
E. 4th St.
E. 3rd St.
E. 2nd St.
E. 1st St.

Third Ave.
Fourth Ave.
Astor Pl.
Lafayette
Stuyvesant
Wanamaker

Second Ave.
First Ave.

EAST VILLAGE

Gt. Jones
Bond
Bleecker

NOHO

E. Houston

SOHO

MacDougal
Sullivan
Thompson
W. Broadway
Wooster
Greene
Mercer
La Guardia

Prince
Spring
Broome
Grand
Canal

Crosby
Broadway
Lafayette
Howard
Lispenard
Walker
White
Franklin
Leonard
Worth

NOLITA

Bowery
Mott
Mulberry
Elizabeth
Kenmare
Chrystie
Forsyth
Allen
Rivington
Delancey
Eldridge

LITTLE ITALY

Baxter
Hester
Mott
Mulberry
Elizabeth

Canal

CHINATOWN

Bayard
Centre
Division
Henry
Madison
Catherine

Holland Tunnel

Watts
Desbrosses
Vestry
Laight
Hubert
Beach
N. Moore
Franklin
Harrison
Jay
Duane
Reade
Chambers
Warren
Murray
Park Pl.
Barclay
Vesey

Sixth Ave.
W. Broadway
Hudson

TRIBECA

Thomas
Duane
Reade
Chambers

Hudson River

World Financial Center

Battery Park City

South End Ave.

Rector Pl.
Rector
W. Thames
J.P. Ward
Morris
2nd Pl.
1st Pl.

South Gardens

World Trade Center Site

Liberty
Cedar
Albany
Carlisle

Greenwich St.
Church
Trinity Pl.
Broadway
Nassau
Cortlandt
John

City Hall Park

Park Row
Spruce
Beekman
Ann

Frankfort

Robert F. Wagner Pl.

Dover
Water
Pearl
Front
Beekman

Fulton
John
Maiden
Liberty
Cedar
Pine
Wall St.
Exchange Pl.
New
Beaver

Platt
Maiden
William
Cliff
Gold

South Street Viaduct

Pier 17

Pier 16

FINANCIAL DISTRICT

Bowling Green
Whitehall
State
Broad
Pearl
Stone
S. William
Bridge
Battery Pl.

Vietnam Veterans Plaza

Pier 6

Battery Park

Brooklyn-Battery Tunnel

❶
❷
❸
❹
❺
❻
❼
❽
❾
❿

Ⓜ Subway stop
Ⓜ Closed indefinitely

0   1/4 mi
0   0.25 km

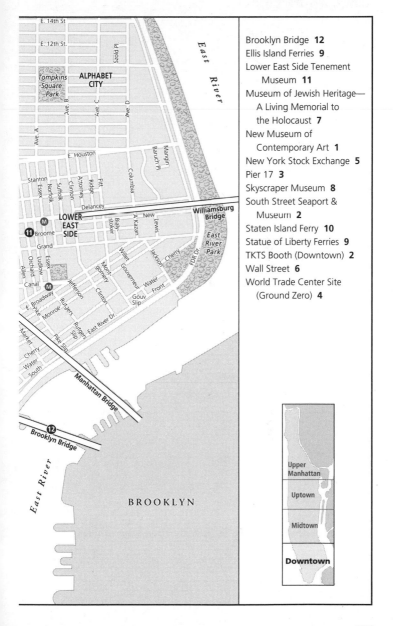

Brooklyn Bridge **12**
Ellis Island Ferries **9**
Lower East Side Tenement
  Museum **11**
Museum of Jewish Heritage—
  A Living Memorial to
  the Holocaust **7**
New Museum of
  Contemporary Art **1**
New York Stock Exchange **5**
Pier 17 **3**
Skyscraper Museum **8**
South Street Seaport &
  Museum **2**
Staten Island Ferry **10**
Statue of Liberty Ferries **9**
TKTS Booth (Downtown) **2**
Wall Street **6**
World Trade Center Site
  (Ground Zero) **4**

Midtown Attractions

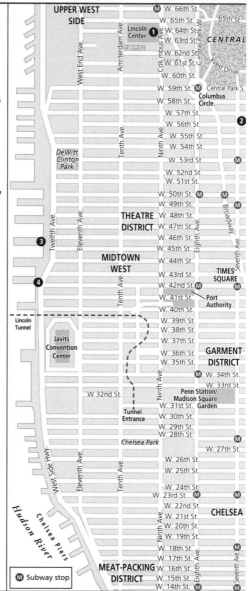

Uptown Attractions

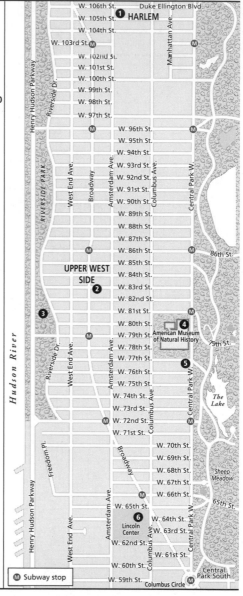

120

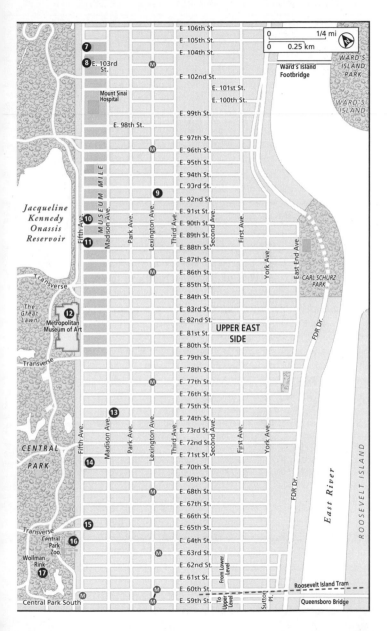

7

8 E. 103rd St.

E. 106th St.
E. 105th St.
E. 104th St.

E. 102nd St.

E. 101st St.
E. 100th St.

E. 99th St.

Mount Sinai
Hospital

E. 98th St.

E. 97th St.

E. 96th St.
E. 95th St.
E. 94th St.
E. 93rd St.

9 E. 92nd St.
E. 91st St.

10 E. 90th St.
E. 89th St.

11 E. 88th St.
E. 87th St.
E. 86th St.
E. 85th St.
E. 84th St.
E. 83rd St.
E. 82nd St.

12
Metropolitan
Museum of Art
E. 81st St.
E. 80th St.
E. 79th St.
E. 78th St.
E. 77th St.
E. 76th St.
E. 75th St.

13 E. 74th St.
E. 73rd St.
E. 72nd St.
E. 71st St.

14 E. 70th St.
E. 69th St.
E. 68th St.
E. 67th St.
E. 66th St.
E. 65th St.

15 E. 64th St.

Central
Park
Zoo **16** E. 63rd St.
E. 62nd St.
Wollman
Rink E. 61st St.
17 E. 60th St.

Central Park South E. 59th St.

*Jacqueline
Kennedy
Onassis
Reservoir*

MUSEUM MILE

Fifth Ave.
Madison Ave.
Park Ave.
Lexington Ave.
Third Ave.
Second Ave.
First Ave.
York Ave.
East End Ave.

UPPER EAST
SIDE

CENTRAL
PARK

The
Great
Lawn

Transverse
Transverse
Transverse

Ward's Island
Footbridge

*WARD'S
ISLAND
PARK*

*WARD'S
ISLAND*

CARL SCHURZ
PARK

FDR Dr.

East River

ROOSEVELT ISLAND

From Lower
Level

To
Upper
Level

Sutton
Pl.

Roosevelt Island Tram

Queensboro Bridge

0		1/4 mi
0	0.25 km	

The rest of the 4-square-block museum is nothing to sneeze at. Founded in 1869, it houses the world's greatest natural-science collection in a group of buildings made of towers and turrets, pink granite, and red brick. The diversity of the holdings is astounding: some 36 million specimens, ranging from microscopic organisms to the world's largest cut gem, the Brazilian Princess Topaz (21,005 carats). Rose Center aside, it would take you all day to see the entire museum, and then you *still* wouldn't get to everything. You can see the best of the best on free **highlights tours** offered daily every hour at 15 minutes after the hour from 10:15am to 3:15pm. Free daily **spotlight tours,** thematic tours that change monthly, are also offered; stop by an information desk for the schedule. **Audio Expeditions,** high-tech audio tours that allow you to access narration in the order you choose, are also available to help you make sense of it all.

If you only see one exhibit, see the **dinosaurs** ⟨★⟩, which take up the fourth floor.

Kids 5 and up should head to the **Discovery Room,** with lots of hands-on exhibits. The **Hall of Human Origins** in the Anne and Bernard Spitzer Hall traces the evolution of man and offers children's workshops where kids can compare skull casts of early humans.

The museum excels at **special exhibitions,** so check to see what will be on while you're in town in case any advance planning is required. The magical **Butterfly Conservatory** ⟨★⟩, a walk-in enclosure housing nearly 500 free-flying tropical butterflies, has developed into a can't-miss fixture from October through May; check to see if it's in the house while you're in town.

Central Park West (btwn 77th and 81st sts.). ⟨℃⟩ **212/769-5100** for information, or 212/769-5200 for tickets (tickets can also be ordered online for an additional $4 charge). www.amnh.org. Suggested admission $14 adults, $11 seniors and students, $8 children 2–12; Space Show and museum admission $22 adults, $17 seniors and students, $13 children under 12. Additional charges for IMAX movies and some special exhibitions. Daily 10am–5:45pm; Rose Center open 1st Fri of every month until 8:45pm. Subway: B, C to 81st St.; 1 to 79th St.

Brooklyn Bridge ⟨★★⟩ (Moments)   Its Gothic-inspired stone pylons and intricate steel-cable webs have moved poets like Walt Whitman and Hart Crane to sing the praises of this great span, the first to cross the East River and connect Manhattan to Brooklyn. Begun in 1867 and completed in 1883, the Brooklyn Bridge is the city's best-known symbol of the age of growth that seized the city during the late 19th century. Walk across the bridge and imagine the awe that New Yorkers of that age felt at seeing two boroughs joined by this span. It's still astounding.

(Value) **A Money & Time-Saving Tip**

CityPass may be New York's best sightseeing deal. Pay one price ($65, or $49 for kids 12–17) for admission to six major attractions: The American Museum of Natural History (admission only; does not include Space Show), the Guggenheim Museum, the Empire State Building, the Museum of Modern Art, the Metropolitan Museum of Art and the Cloisters, and a 2-hour Circle Line harbor cruise. Individual tickets would cost more than twice as much (though I should point out that the Met is a "suggested" admission fee).

More important, CityPass is not a coupon book. It contains actual tickets, so you can bypass lengthy lines. This can save you hours, as sights such as the Empire State Building often have ticket lines of an hour or more.

CityPass is good for 9 days from the first time you use it. It's sold at all participating attractions and online at **http://city pass.com**. To avoid online service and shipping fees, you may wish to buy the pass at your first attraction (start at an attraction that's likely to have the shortest admission line, such as the Guggenheim). However, if you begin your sightseeing on a weekend or during holidays, when lines are longest, online purchase may be worthwhile.

For more information, call CityPass at © **888/330-5008** (note, however, that CityPass is not sold over the phone).

Walking the bridge: Walking the Brooklyn Bridge is one of my all-time favorite New York activities, although there's no doubt that the Lower Manhattan views from the bridge now have a painful resonance as well as a joyous spirit. A wide wood-plank pedestrian walkway is elevated above the traffic, making it a relatively peaceful, and popular, walk. There's a sidewalk entrance on Park Row, just across from City Hall Park (take the 4, 5, or 6 train to Brooklyn Bridge/City Hall). But why do this walk *away* from Manhattan, toward the less impressive Brooklyn skyline? For Manhattan skyline views, take an A or C train to High Street, one stop into Brooklyn. Come out above ground, and then walk through the little park to Cadman Plaza East and head downslope (left) to the stairwell that will take you up to the footpath. (Following Prospect Place under the bridge, turning right onto Cadman Plaza East, will also take you directly to the stairwell.) It's a 20- to 40-minute stroll over the bridge to Manhattan, depending on your pace, the amount of foot traffic, and the number of stops you make to behold the spectacular views (there are benches along the way). The footpath will deposit you right at City Hall Park.

Tasty tips: The perfect complement to your stroll over the bridge is a stop for pizza at **Grimaldi's** (see "Pizza, New York–Style," on p. 94), followed by homemade ice cream at the **Brooklyn Ice Cream Factory** (© **718/246-3963**), located at the Fulton Ferry Fire Boat House on the river and in the shadow of the bridge. The pizza and ice cream will fortify you for your stroll into Manhattan.

Subway: A, C to High St.; 4, 5, 6 to Brooklyn Bridge–City Hall.

Ellis Island 🗹🗹 One of New York's most moving sights, the restored Ellis Island opened in 1990, slightly north of Liberty Island. Roughly 40% of Americans (myself included) can trace their heritage back to an ancestor who came through here. For the 62 years when it was America's main entry point for immigrants (1892–1954), Ellis Island processed some 12 million people. The greeting was often brusque—especially in the early years of the century (until 1924), when as many as 12,000 came through in a single day. The statistics can be overwhelming, but the **Immigration Museum** skillfully relates the story of Ellis Island and immigration in America by placing the emphasis on personal experience.

It's difficult to leave the museum unmoved. Today you enter the Main Building's baggage room, just as the immigrants did, and then climb the stairs to the **Registry Room,** with its dramatic vaulted tiled ceiling, where millions waited anxiously for medical and legal processing. A step-by-step account of the immigrants' voyage is detailed in the exhibit, with haunting photos and touching oral histories. What might be the most poignant exhibit is **Treasures from Home,** 1,000 objects and photos donated by descendants of immigrants, including family heirlooms, religious articles, and rare clothing and jewelry. Outside, the **American Immigrant Wall of Honor** commemorates the names of more than 500,000 immigrants and their families. You can even research your own family's history at the interactive **American Family Immigration History Center.** You might also make time to see the award-winning short film *Island of Hope, Island of Tears,* which plays on a continuous loop in two theaters. Short live theatrical performances depicting the immigrant experience are also often part of the day's events.

Touring tip: Ferries run daily to Ellis Island and Liberty Island from Battery Park and Liberty State Park at frequent intervals; see the Statue of Liberty listing (p. 131) for details.

In New York Harbor. © **212/363-3200** (general info), or 212/269-5755 (ticket/ferry info). www.nps.gov/elis, www.ellisisland.org, or www.statuecruises.com. Free admission (ferry ticket charge). Daily 9:30am–5:15pm (last ferry departs around 3:30pm). For subway and ferry details, see the Statue of Liberty listing on p. 131 (ferry trip includes stops at both sights).

Empire State Building ★★★   It took 60,000 tons of steel, 10 million bricks, 2.5 million feet of electrical wire, 120 miles of pipe, and seven million man-hours to build. King Kong climbed it in 1933—and again in 2005. A plane slammed into it in 1945. The World Trade Center superseded it in 1970 as the island's tallest building. And in 1997, a gunman ascended it to stage a deadly shooting. On that horrific day of September 11, 2001, it once again regained its status as New York City's tallest building, after 31 years of taking second place. And through it all, the Empire State Building has remained one of the city's favorite landmarks and its signature high-rise. Completed in 1931, the limestone-and-stainless-steel Streamline Deco dazzler climbs 102 stories (1,454 ft.) and now harbors the offices of fashion firms, and, in its upper reaches, a jumble of high-tech broadcast equipment.

Always a conversation piece, the Empire State Building glows every night, bathed in colored floodlights to commemorate events of significance—red, white, and blue for Independence Day; green for St. Patrick's Day; red, black, and green for Martin Luther King Day; blue and white for Hanukkah; even blue for the New York Giants' Super Bowl appearance in 2008 (you can find a lighting schedule online). The familiar silver spire can be seen from all over the city.

The best views, and what keeps the nearly three million visitors coming every year, are the ones from the 86th- and 102nd-floor observatories. The lower one is best—you can walk out on a windy deck and look through coin-operated viewers (bring quarters!) over what, on a clear day, can be as much as an 80-mile radius. The panorama is magnificent. One surprise is the flurry of rooftop activity, an aspect of city life that thrives unnoticed from our everyday sidewalk vantage point. The higher observation deck is glass-enclosed and cramped.

Light fog can create an admirably moody effect, but it goes without saying that a clear day is best. Dusk brings the most remarkable views and the biggest crowds. Consider going in the morning, when the light is still low on the horizon, keeping glare to a minimum. Starry nights are pure magic.

In your haste to go up, don't rush through the three-story-high marble lobby without pausing to admire its features, which include a wonderful Streamline mural.

350 Fifth Ave. (at 34th St.). © **212/736-3100.** www.esbnyc.com. Observatory admission $19 adults, $17 seniors and children 12–17, $13 children 6–11, free for children under 6. Daily open 8am–2am, last elevator at 1:15am. Subway: B, D, F, N, R, Q, V, W to 34th St.; 6 to 33rd St.

Grand Central Terminal ✶✶✶   Even if you're not catching one of the subway lines or Metro-North commuter trains that rumble through Grand Central Terminal, come for a visit; it's one of the most magnificent public places in the country. And even if you arrive and leave by subway, be sure to exit the station, walking a couple of blocks south, to about 40th Street, before you turn around to admire Jules-Alexis Coutan's neoclassical sculpture *Transportation* hovering over the south entrance, with a majestic Mercury, the Roman god of commerce and travel, as its central figure.

The greatest visual impact comes when you enter the vast majestic **main concourse.** The high windows allow sunlight to penetrate the space, glinting off the half-acre Tennessee-marble floor. The brass clock over the central kiosk gleams, as do the gold- and nickel-plated chandeliers piercing the side archways. The masterful **sky ceiling,** a brilliant greenish blue, depicts the constellations of the winter sky above New York. They're lit with 59 stars, surrounded by dazzling 24-carat gold and emitting light fed through fiber-optic cables, their intensities roughly replicating the magnitude of the actual stars as seen from Earth. Look carefully and you'll see a patch near one corner left unrestored as a reminder of the neglect once visited on this splendid overhead masterpiece. On the east end of the main concourse is a grand **marble staircase.**

This Beaux Arts splendor serves as a hub of social activity as well. Excellent-quality shops and restaurants have taken over the mezzanine and lower levels. Off the main concourse at street level, there's a mix of specialty shops and national retailers, as well as the **Grand Central Market** for gourmet foods. The **New York Transit Museum Store,** in the shuttle passage, houses transit-related exhibits and a gift shop that's worth a look. The **lower dining concourse** ✶ houses a food court and the famous **Oyster Bar & Restaurant.**

42nd St. at Park Ave. © **212/340-2210** (events hot line). www.grandcentral terminal.com. Subway: S, 4, 5, 6, or 7 to 42nd St./Grand Central.

Metropolitan Museum of Art ✶✶✶   Home of blockbuster after blockbuster exhibition, the Metropolitan Museum of Art attracts some five million people a year, more than any other spot in New York City. At 1.6 million square feet, this is the largest museum in the Western Hemisphere. Nearly all the world's cultures are on display—from Egyptian mummies to Greek statuary to Islamic carvings to Renaissance paintings to Native American masks to 20th-century decorative arts—and masterpieces are the rule. You could go once a week for a lifetime and still find something new on each visit.

So unless you plan on spending your entire vacation in the museum (some do), you cannot see the entire collection. My recommendation is to give it a good day—or better yet, 2 half-days so you don't burn out. One good way to get an overview is to take the **Museum Highlights Tour,** offered every day at various times (usually between 10:15am and 3:15pm; tours also offered in Spanish, Italian, German, and Korean). Visit the museum's website for a schedule of this and subject-specific tours (Old Masters Paintings, American Period Rooms, Arts of China, Islamic Art, and so on); you can get a schedule of the day's tours at the Visitor Services desk when you arrive. A daily schedule of **Gallery Talks** is also available.

The least overwhelming way to see the Met on your own is to pick up a map at the round desk in the entry hall and concentrate on what you like, whether it's 17th-century paintings, American furniture, or the art of the South Pacific. Highlights include the American Wing's **Garden Court,** with its 19th-century sculpture; the **Costume Hall;** and the **Frank Lloyd Wright room.** The beautifully renovated **Roman and Greek galleries** are overwhelming, but in a marvelous way, as are the collections of **Byzantine Art** and **Chinese art.** The highlight of the **Egyptian collection** is the **Temple of Dendur,** in a dramatic, purpose-built glass-walled gallery with Central Park views.

In response to the huge crowds, the Met now opens on "holiday Mondays." On those Mondays, such as Memorial Day or Labor Day, the museum is open from 9:30am to 5:30pm.

To purchase tickets for concerts and lectures, call ✆ **212/570-3949** (Mon–Sat 9:30am–5pm). The museum contains several dining facilities, including a **full-service restaurant** serving Continental cuisine (✆ **212/570-3964** for reservations). The roof garden is worth visiting if you're here from spring to autumn, offering peaceful views over Central Park and the city.

The Met's medieval collections are housed in upper Manhattan at **The Cloisters** ✮✮; see the full listing on p. 135.

Fifth Ave. at 82nd St. ✆ 212/535-7710. www.metmuseum.org. Suggested admission (includes same-day entrance to the Cloisters) $20 adults, $15 seniors and $10 students, free for children under 12 when accompanied by an adult. Sun, holiday Mon (Memorial Day, Labor Day, and so forth), and Tues–Thurs 9:30am–5:30pm; Fri–Sat 9:30am–9pm. Strollers are permitted in most areas—inquire at Information

Desks for gallery limitations. Oversized and jogging strollers are prohibited. Subway: 4, 5, 6 to 86th St.

Museum of Modern Art ☆☆   The newer, larger MoMA, after a 2-year renovation, is almost twice the space of the original. The renovation, designed by Yoshio Taniguchi, highlights space and light, with open rooms, high ceilings, and gardens—a beautiful work of architecture and a complement to the art within. This is where you'll find van Gogh's *Starry Night,* Cezanne's *Bather,* Picasso's *Les Demoiselles d'Avignon,* and the great sculpture by Rodin, *Monument to Balzac.* Whenever I visit, I like to browse the fun "Architecture and Design" department, with examples of design for appliances, furniture, and even sports cars. MoMA also features edgy new exhibits and a celebrated film series. The heart of the museum remains the Abby Aldrich Rockefeller Sculpture Garden, which has been enlarged; the museum's new design affords additional views of this lovely space from other parts of the museum. And, as of Spring 2008, MoMA has installed a museum-wide Wi-Fi network so that visitors can access a mobile Web site on handheld devices (which basically iPhones and iPod Touch). They can then load up audio tours and commentary; content is available in eight languages as well as in specialized versions for children, teenagers, and the visually impaired. MoMA is one of the most expensive museums in New York, but does have a "free" day: on Fridays from 4 to 8pm.

11 W. 53rd St. (btwn Fifth and Sixth aves.). © 212/708-9400. www.moma.org. Admission $20 adults, $16 seniors, $12 students, children under 16 free if accompanied by an adult. Sat–Mon and Wed–Thurs 10:30am–5:30pm; Fri 10:30am–8pm. Subway: E, V to Fifth Ave.; B, D, F to 47th–50th/Rockefeller Center.

Rockefeller Center ☆☆   A streamline moderne masterpiece, Rockefeller Center is one of New York's central gathering spots for visitors and New Yorkers alike. A prime example of the city's skyscraper spirit and historic sense of optimism, it was erected mainly in the 1930s, when the city was deep in the Depression as well as its most passionate Art Deco phase. Designated a National Historic Landmark in 1988, it's the world's largest privately owned business-and-entertainment center, with 18 buildings on 21 acres.

For a dramatic approach to the complex, start at Fifth Avenue between 49th and 50th streets. The builders purposely created the gentle slope of the Promenade, known as the **Channel Gardens** because it's flanked to the south by La Maison Française and to the north by the British Building. (The Channel, get it?)

The **Rink at Rockefeller Center** ☆ (© **212/332-7654;** www.rockefellercenter.com) is tiny but romantic, especially during the

Heading for the Top of the Rock

Giving the Empire State Building some friendly competition when it comes to spectacular views, is the observation deck of 30 Rockefeller Plaza known as the **Top of the Rock** 👁👁. The stately deck, which comprises floors 67 to 70, was constructed in 1933 to resemble the grandeur of a luxury ocean liner. It's more spacious than the Empire State Building's lookout, and the views, though not quite as high, are as stunning. You might have just as much fun getting up there as you will on the deck; the sky-shuttle elevators with glass ceilings project images from the 1930s through the present day as they zoom upward. Reserved-time tickets help minimize the lines and are available online at **www.topoftherocknyc.com**. The observation deck is open daily from 8:30am to midnight; admission rates are $18.50 for adults, $16 for seniors, $11.25 for ages 6 to 11, and free for children under 6. For more information, call ℭ **877/ NYC-ROCK (877/692-7625)** or **212/698-2000** or visit www. topoftherocknyc.com.

holidays, when the Christmas tree's multicolored lights twinkle from above. The rink is open from mid-October to mid-March, and you'll skate under the magnificent tree for the month of December.

The focal point of this "city within a city" is the building at **30 Rockefeller Plaza** 👁, a 70-story showpiece towering over the plaza. It's still one of the city's most impressive buildings; walk through for a look at the granite-and-marble lobby, lined with monumental sepia-toned murals by José Maria Sert. You can pick up a walking-tour brochure highlighting the center's art and architecture at the information desk. On the 65th floor, the legendary Rainbow Room is open to the public on a limited basis.

NBC television maintains studios throughout the complex. *Saturday Night Live* and *Late Night with Conan O'Brien* originate at 30 Rock. NBC's ***Today*** show is broadcast live on weekdays from 7 to 10am from the glass-enclosed studio on the southwest corner of 49th Street and Rockefeller Plaza; come early if you want a visible spot, and bring your HI MOM! sign.

The 70-minute **NBC Studio Tour** (ℭ **212/664-3700**; www.nbc universalstore.com) will take you behind the scenes at the Peacock network. The tour changes daily but might include the *Today* show, *NBC Nightly News, Dateline NBC,* and/or *Saturday Night Live* sets. Who knows? You may even run into Brian Williams or Meredith Viera. Tours run every 15 to 30 minutes Monday through Saturday from 8:30am to 5:30pm, Sunday from 9:30am to 4:30pm (later on certain summer days); of course, you'll have a better chance of encountering some real live action on a weekday. Tickets are $19 for adults, $16 for seniors and children 6 to 12. You can reserve your tickets in advance (reservations are recommended) or buy them right up to tour time at the NBC Experience store, on Rockefeller Plaza at 49th Street. They also offer a 60-minute Rockefeller Center Tour Monday to Saturday on the hour from 11am to 5pm, and Sunday 11am to 3pm. Tickets are $12 for adults, $10 for seniors and children 6 to 12; two-tour combination packages are available for $23. Call ✆ **212/664-7174.**

Radio City Music Hall ✇, 1260 Sixth Ave., at 50th Street (✆ **212/247-4777;** www.radiocity.com), is perhaps the most impressive architectural feat of the complex. Designed by Donald Deskey and opened in 1932, it's one of the largest indoor theaters, with 6,200 seats. But its true grandeur derives from its magnificent Art Deco appointments. The crowning touch is the stage's great proscenium arch, which from the distant seats evokes a faraway sun setting on the horizon of the sea. The men's and women's lounges are also splendid. The theater hosts the annual **Christmas Spectacular,** starring the Rockettes. The illuminating 1-hour **Stage Door Tour** is offered Monday through Saturday from 10am to 5pm, Sunday from 11am to 5pm; tickets are $17 for adults, $10 for children under 12. Btwn 48th & 50th sts., from Fifth to Sixth aves. ✆ 212/332-6868. www.rockefeller center.com. Subway: B, D, F, V to 47th–50th sts./Rockefeller Center.

Solomon R. Guggenheim Museum ✇ It's been called a bun, a snail, a concrete tornado, and even a giant wedding cake; bring your kids, and they'll probably see it as New York's coolest opportunity for skateboarding. Whatever description you choose to apply, Frank Lloyd Wright's only New York building, completed in 1959, is best summed up as a brilliant work of architecture—so consistently brilliant that it competes with the art for your attention. If you're looking for the city's best modern art, head to MoMA or the Whitney first; come to the Guggenheim to see the house.

But the restoration has no effect on what's inside, and it's easy to see the bulk of what's on display in 2 to 4 hours. The museum's spiraling rotunda circles over a slowly inclined ramp that leads you past changing exhibits. Usually the progression is counterintuitive: from the first floor up, rather than from the sixth floor down. If you're not sure, ask a guard before you begin. Permanent exhibits of 19th- and 20th-century art, including strong holdings of Kandinsky, Klee, Picasso, and French Impressionists, occupy a stark annex called the Tower Galleries, an addition (accessible at every level) that some critics have claimed made the entire structure look like a toilet bowl backed by a water tank (see what you think).

The Guggenheim runs some special programs, including free docent tours daily, a limited schedule of lectures, free family films, avant-garde screenings for grown-ups, and curator-led guided gallery tours on select Friday afternoons.

1071 Fifth Ave. (at 89th St.). ✆ 212/423-3500. www.guggenheim.org. Admission $18 adults, $15 seniors and students, free for children under 12, pay what you wish Fri 5:45–7:15pm. Sat–Wed 10am–5:45pm; Fri 10am–7:45pm. Subway: 4, 5, 6 to 86th St.

Staten Island Ferry ✪ (Value)   In 2006, the Staten Island Ferry celebrated its 100th anniversary. Over the years it has been one of New York's best bargains—sometimes costing a nickel and most of the time, like now, costing nothing at all. It's New York's best freebie—especially if you just want to glimpse the Statue of Liberty and not climb her steps. You get an hour-long excursion (round-trip) into the world's biggest harbor. This is not strictly a sightseeing ride but commuter transportation. As a result, during business hours, you'll share the boat with working stiffs reading and drinking coffee.

You should go on deck and enjoy the busy harbor traffic. The old orange-and-green boats usually have open decks along the sides or at the bow and stern; try to catch one of these if you can, since the newer white boats don't have decks. Grab a seat on the right side of the boat for the best view. On the way out of Manhattan, you'll pass the Statue of Liberty (the boat comes closest to Lady Liberty on the way to Staten Island), Ellis Island, and from the left side of the boat, Governor's Island; you'll see the Verrazano Narrows Bridge spanning from Brooklyn to Staten Island in the distance. Once you've docked, there's usually another boat waiting to depart for Manhattan. The skylight views are awesome on the return trip.

Departs from the Whitehall Ferry Terminal at the southern tip of Manhattan. ✆ 718/727-2508. www.ci.nyc.ny.us/html/dot. Free admission. 24 hr.; every 20–30 min. weekdays, less frequently during off-peak and weekend hours. Subway: R, W to Whitehall St.; 4, 5 to Bowling Green; 1 to South Ferry (ride in one of the 1st 5 cars).

Statue of Liberty ✪✪✪ (Kids)   For the millions who came by ship to America in the last century—either as privileged tourists or needy, hopeful immigrants—Lady Liberty, standing in the Upper Bay, was their first glimpse of America. No monument so embodies the nation's, and the world's, notion of political freedom and economic potential. Even if you don't make it to Liberty Island, you can get a spine-tingling glimpse from Battery Park, from the New Jersey side of the bay, or during a ride on the Staten Island Ferry (see above). It's always reassuring to see her torch lighting the way.

Proposed by French statesman Edouard de Laboulaye as a gift from France to the United States, commemorating the two nations' friendship and joint notions of liberty, the statue was designed by sculptor Frédéric-Auguste Bartholdi with the engineering help of Alexandre-Gustave Eiffel (who was responsible for the famed Paris tower) and unveiled on October 28, 1886. *Touring tips:* Ferries leave daily every half-hour to 45 minutes from 9am to about 3:30pm, with more frequent ferries in the morning and extended hours in summer. Try to go early on a weekday to avoid the crowds that swarm in the afternoon, on weekends, and on holidays. A stop at **Ellis Island** ☆☆ (p. 124) is included in the fare, but if you catch the last ferry, you can visit the statue or Ellis Island, not both.

You can order ferry tickets in advance via **www.statuereservations. com**, which will allow you to board without standing in the some-times-long ticket line; however, there is an additional service charge of $1.75 per ticket. Even if you've already purchased tickets, arrive as much as 30 minutes before your desired ferry time to allow for increased security procedures prior to boarding. The ferry ride takes about 20 minutes. Once on Liberty Island, you'll start to get an idea of the statue's immensity: She weighs 225 tons and measures 152 feet from foot to flame. Her nose alone is 4½ feet long, and her index finger is 8 feet long.

On Liberty Island in New York Harbor. ⓒ 212/363-3200 (general info), or 212/269-5755 (ticket/ferry info). www.nps.gov/stli or www.statuecruises.com. Free admission; ferry ticket to Statue of Liberty and Ellis Island $12 adults, $10 seniors, $5 children 3–17. Daily 9am–3:30pm (last ferry departs around 3:30pm); extended hours in summer. Subway: 4, 5 to Bowling Green; 1 to South Ferry. Walk south through Battery Park to Castle Clinton, the fort housing the ferry ticket booth.

Times Square *Overrated*   There's no doubt that Times Square has evolved into something much different than it was over a decade ago when it had a deservedly sleazy reputation. Yet there is much debate among New Yorkers about which incarnation was better. For New Yorkers, Times Square is a place we go out of our way to avoid. The crowds, even by New York standards, are stifling; the restaurants, mostly national chains, aren't very good; the shops, also mostly

World Trade Center Site (Ground Zero)

Do you call a place where over 3,000 people lost their lives an "attraction"? Or is it a shrine? This is the quandary of the World Trade Center site. What had been a big hole for 5 years is a little more than that; construction began in early 2006 on the proposed "Freedom Tower" to be built at the site. But even though work is ongoing, there is still much bickering as to what will rise from that hole. The new design retains essential elements of the original—it soars 1,776 feet, its illuminated mast evoking the Statue of Liberty's torch. From the square base, the Tower will taper into eight tall isosceles triangles, forming an octagon at its center. An observation deck will be 1,362 feet above ground.

For now, you can see the site through a viewing wall on the Church Street side of the site; on that "Wall of Heroes" are the names of those who lost their lives that day along with the history of the site, including photos of the construction of the World Trade Center in the late 1960s and how, after it opened in 1972, it changed the New York skyline and downtown. A walk along the Wall of Heroes remains a painfully moving experience.

The site is bounded by Church, Barclay, Liberty, and West streets. Call ℂ **212/484-1222,** or go to **www.nycvisit. com** or **www.southstseaport.org** for viewing information; go to **www.downtownny.com** for lower-Manhattan area information and rebuilding updates. The Tribute Center gives guided tours of the site. Call ℂ **212/422-3520,** or visit **www.tributewtc.org** for more information. Tours are given Monday to Friday at 11am and 1 and 3pm; Saturday and Sunday at noon, 1, 2, and 3pm. The fee is $10 for adults; under 12 free.

national chains, are unimaginative; and the attractions, like **Madame Tussauds New York** wax museum, are kitschy. I suppose it's a little too Vegas for us. Still, you've come all this way; you've got to at least take a peek, if only for the amazing neon spectacle of it.

Most Broadway theaters are around Times Square, so plan your visit around your show tickets. For your pre-dinner meal, walk 2 blocks west to Ninth Avenue where you'll find many relatively inexpensive, good restaurants. If you are with kids, the Ferris wheel in the **Toys "R" Us** store makes a visit to Times Square worthwhile. Subway: 1, 2, 3, 7, N, Q, R, S, W to Times Sq.; A, C, E to 42nd St.–Port Authority.

Wall Street & the New York Stock Exchange Wall Street—it's an iconic name, and the world's prime hub for bulls and bears everywhere. This narrow 18th-century lane (you'll be surprised at how little it is) is appropriately monumental, lined with neoclassical towers that reach as far skyward as the dreams and greed of investors who built it into the world's most famous financial market.

At the heart of the action is the **New York Stock Exchange (NYSE),** the world's largest securities trader, where billions change hands. The NYSE came into being in 1792, when merchants met daily under a nearby buttonwood tree to try to pass off to each other the U.S. bonds that had been sold to fund the Revolutionary War. By 1903, they were trading stocks of publicly held companies in this Corinthian-columned Beaux Arts "temple" designed by George Post. About 3,000 companies are now listed on the exchange, trading nearly 314 billion shares valued at about $16 trillion. Unfortunately, the NYSE is no longer open to the public for tours.

20 Broad St. (between Wall St. and Exchange Place). 𝄞 **212/656-3000.** www.nyse. com. Subway: J, M, Z to Broad St.; 2, 3, 4, 5 to Wall St.

Whitney Museum of American Art 𝕬𝕬 What is arguably the finest collection of 20th-century American art in the world belongs to the Whitney thanks to the efforts of Gertrude Vanderbilt Whitney. A sculptor, Whitney organized exhibitions by American artists shunned by traditional academies, assembled a sizable collection, and founded the museum in 1930 in Greenwich Village.

Today's museum is an imposing presence on Madison Avenue—an inverted three-tiered pyramid of concrete and gray granite with seven seemingly random windows designed by Marcel Breuer, a leader of the Bauhaus movement. The rotating permanent collection consists of an intelligent selection of major works by Edward Hopper, George Bellows, Georgia O'Keeffe, Roy Lichtenstein, Jasper Johns, and other artists. A second-floor exhibit space is devoted exclusively to works from its permanent collection from 1900 to 1950, while the rest is dedicated to rotating exhibits.

Shows are usually all well curated and more edgy than what you'd see at MoMA or the Guggenheim. Topics range from topical surveys, such as "American Art in the Age of Technology" and "The Warhol Look: Glamour Style Fashion" to in-depth retrospectives of famous or lesser-known movements (such as Fluxus, the movement that spawned Yoko Ono, among others) and artists (Mark Rothko, Keith Haring, Duane Hanson, Bob Thompson). Free **gallery tours** are offered daily, and music, screenings, and lectures fill the calendar.

945 Madison Ave. (at 75th St.). (C) **800/WHITNEY** or 212/570-3676. www.whitney. org. Admission $15 adults, $10 seniors students free with valid IDs, free for children under 12, pay what you wish Fri 6–9pm. Wed–Thurs and Sat–Sun 11am–6pm; Fri 1–9pm. Subway: 6 to 77th St.

2 More Manhattan Museums & Galleries

ART GALLERIES   SoHo remains colorful, if less edgy than it used to be, with the action centered on West Broadway and encroaching onto the edge of Chinatown. Start with the **Peter Blum Gallery,** 99 Wooster St. ((C) **212/343-0441**), who showcased Kim Sooja, a Korean artist who uses traditional Korean bedcovers to comment on the promise of wedded bliss; **O. K. Harris,** 383 W. Broadway ((C) **212/ 431-3600;** www.okharris.com), which shows a fascinating variety of contemporary painting, sculpture, and photography; and **Louis K. Meisel,** 141 Prince St. ((C) **212/677-1340;** www.meiselgallery.com), specializing in photorealism and American pinup art (yep, Petty and Vargas girls). In TriBeCa, try **Cheryl Hazan Arts Gallery,** 35 N. Moore St. ((C) **212/343-8964;** www.cherylhazanarts.com), or DFN Gallery, 210 11th Ave. 6th Fl. ((C) 212/334-3400; www.dfngallery. com), which focus on fresh, distinctive contemporary art.

Children's Museum of Manhattan (*) (Kids)   Here's a great place to take the kids when they're tired of being told not to touch. Designed for ages 2 to 12, this museum is strictly hands-on. Interactive exhibits and activity centers encourage self-discovery. The Time Warner Media Center takes children through the world of animation and helps them produce their own videos. The Body Odyssey is a zany, scientific journey through the human body. This isn't just a museum for the 5-and-up set—there are exhibits designed for babies and toddlers, too. The schedule also includes art classes and storytellers, and a full slate of entertainment on weekends.

212 W. 83rd St. (btwn Broadway and Amsterdam Ave.). (C) **212/721-1234.** www. cmom.org. Admission $9 children and adults, $6 seniors. School season Wed–Sun and school holidays 10am–5pm; summer Tues–Sun 10am–5pm. Subway: 1 to 86th St.

The Cloisters (*)(*)   If it weren't for this branch of the Metropolitan Museum of Art, many New Yorkers would never get to this northernmost point in Manhattan. This remote yet lovely spot is devoted to the art and architecture of medieval Europe. Atop a cliff overlooking the Hudson River, you'll find a 12th-century chapter

Finds **Cutting-Edge Art in Chelsea**

The area in the West 20s between Tenth and Eleventh avenues is home to the avant-garde of today's New York art scene, with West 26th serving as the unofficial "gallery row"—and nearly all the art is free to the public. Do yourself a favor and take a stroll through the neighborhood. Take the C, E to 23rd Street, Tuesday through Saturday, 10am until 6pm. See *Time Out New York* or the *New York Times* for listings, and note that many of the galleries are closed during the summer.

house, parts of five cloisters from medieval monasteries, a Romanesque chapel, and a 12th-century Spanish apse brought intact from Europe. Surrounded by peaceful gardens, this is the one place on the island that can even approximate the kind of solitude suitable to such a collection. Inside you'll find extraordinary works that include the famed Unicorn tapestries, sculpture, illuminated manuscripts, stained glass, ivory, and precious metal work.

Despite its remoteness, the Cloisters are popular, especially in fine weather, so try to schedule your visit during the week rather than on a crowded weekend afternoon. A free guided **Highlights Tour** is offered Tuesday through Friday at 3pm and Sunday at noon; gallery talks are also a regular feature. Additionally, **Garden Tours** are offered Tuesday through Sunday at 1pm in May, June, September, and October; lectures and other special programming are always on Sunday from noon to 2pm; and medieval music concerts are regularly held in the stunning 12th-century Spanish chapel. For an extra-special experience, you may want to plan your visit around one.

At the north end of Fort Tryon Park. ☏ **212/923-3700.** www.metmuseum.org. Suggested admission (includes same-day entrance to the Metropolitan Museum of Art) $20 adults, $15 seniors, $10 students, free for children under 12. Nov–Feb Tues–Sun 9:30am–4:45pm; Mar–Oct Tues–Sun 9:30am–5:15pm. Subway: A to 190th St., then a 10-min. walk north along Margaret Corbin Dr., or pick up the M4 bus at the station (1 stop to Cloisters). Bus: M4 Madison Ave. (Fort Tryon Park–The Cloisters).

Cooper-Hewitt National Design Museum ☆   Part of the Smithsonian Institution, the Cooper-Hewitt is housed in the Carnegie Mansion, built by steel magnate Andrew Carnegie in 1901, and undergoing a renovation of the Fox and Miller town houses and the Museum Mansion, which will create a third floor and expand gallery space by 80%. The renovation is scheduled to be completed in 2010. During the renovations, the museum remains open and galleries will continue to be devoted to changing exhibits that are invariably well conceived, engaging, and educational. Shows are both historic and contemporary in nature, and topics range from "The Work of Charles and Ray Eames: A Legacy of Invention" to "Russell Wright: Creating American Lifestyle" to "The Architecture of Reassurance: Designing the Disney Theme Parks." Many installations are drawn from the museum's own vast collection of industrial design, drawings, textiles, wall coverings, books, and prints. And be sure to visit the garden, ringed with Central Park benches from various eras.

2 E. 91st St. (at Fifth Ave.). ℂ 212/849-8400. www.cooperhewitt.org. Admission $15 adults, $10 seniors and students, free for children under 12, free to all Fri 5–9pm. Mon–Thurs 10am–5pm; Fri 10am–9pm; Sat 10am–6pm; Sun noon–6pm. Subway: 4, 5, 6 to 86th St.

El Museo del Barrio   What started in 1969 with a small display in a local school classroom in East Harlem is today the only museum in America dedicated to Puerto Rican, Caribbean, and Latin American art. The northernmost Museum Mile institution has a permanent exhibit ranging from pre-Columbian artifacts to photographic art and video. The display of *santos de palo* (wood-carved religious figurines) is especially noteworthy, as is "Taíno, Ancient Voyagers of the Caribbean," dedicated to the active, highly developed cultures that Columbus encountered when he landed in the "New World." The well-curated changing exhibitions tend to focus on 20th-century artists and contemporary subjects.

1230 Fifth Ave. (at 104th St.). ℂ 212/831-7272. www.elmuseo.org. Suggested admission $6 adults, $4 seniors (free on Thurs) and students, free for children under 12. Wed–Sun 11am–5pm. Subway: 6 to 103rd St.

The Frick Collection 𝕬𝕬   Henry Clay Frick could afford to be an avid collector of European art after amassing a fortune as a pioneer in the coke and steel industries at the turn of the 20th century. To house his treasures and himself, he hired architects Carrère & Hastings to build this 18th-century French-style mansion (1914), one of the most beautiful remaining on Fifth Avenue.

Most appealing about the Frick is its intimate size and setting. This is a living testament to New York's vanished Gilded Age—the interior still feels like a private home (albeit a really, really rich guy's home) graced with beautiful paintings, rather than a museum. Come here to see the classics by some of the world's most famous painters: Titian, Bellini, Rembrandt, Turner, Vermeer, El Greco, and Goya, to name only a few. A highlight of the collection is the **Fragonard Room,** graced with the sensual rococo series "The Progress of Love." The portrait of Montesquieu by Whistler is also stunning. Included in the price of admission, the AcousticGuide audio tour is particularly useful because it allows you to follow your own path rather than a proscribed route. A free 22-minute video presentation is screened in the Music Room every half-hour from 10am to 4:30pm (from 1:30 on Sun); starting with this helps to set the tone for what you'll see.

1 E. 70th St. (at Fifth Ave.). ℂ 212/288-0700. www.frick.org. Admission $15 adults, $10 seniors, $5 students. Children under 10 not admitted; children under 16 must be accompanied by an adult. Tues–Sat 10am–6pm; Sun 11am–5pm. Closed all major holidays. Subway: 6 to 68th St./Hunter College.

International Center of Photography ⟨𝒦 ⟨Finds   The ICP is one of the world's premier educators, collectors, and exhibitors of photographic art. The state-of-the-art gallery space is ideal for viewing rotating exhibitions of the museum's 50,000-plus prints as well as visiting shows. The emphasis is on contemporary photographic works, but historically important photographers aren't ignored. This is a must on any photography buff's list.

1133 Sixth Ave. (at 43rd St.). ℂ 212/857-0000. www.icp.org. Admission $12 adults, $8 seniors and students, under 12 free. Tues–Thurs and Sat–Sun 10am–6pm; Fri 10am–8pm. Subway: B, D, F, V to 42nd St.

USS *Intrepid* Sea-Air-Space Museum ⟨𝒦𝒦 ⟨Kids   After almost 2 years in drydock, the USS *Intrepid* is scheduled to return to its refurbished home on Pier 86 in October, 2008; and the museum will reopen on Veteran's Day, November 11, 2008. The most astonishing thing about the aircraft carrier USS *Intrepid* is how it can be simultaneously so big and so small. It's a few football fields long, weighs 40,000 tons, holds 40 aircraft, and sometimes doubles as a ballroom for society functions. But stand there and think about landing an A-12 jet on the deck and suddenly it's minuscule. And in the narrow passageways below, you'll find it isn't the roomiest of vessels. Now a National Historic Landmark, the exhibit also includes the naval destroyer USS *Edson* and the submarine USS *Growler,* the only intact strategic missile submarine open to the public anywhere, as well as a collection of vintage and modern aircraft, including the A-12 Blackbird, and a retired British Airways Concorde jet.

Kids love this place. They, and you, can climb inside a replica Revolutionary War submarine, sit in an A-6 Intruder cockpit, and follow the progress of America's astronauts as they work in space. There are even flight simulators—including a "Fly with the Blue Angels" program—for educational thrill rides. Look for family-oriented activities and events at least 1 Saturday a month.

Dress warmly for a winter visit—it's almost impossible to heat an aircraft carrier.

Pier 86 (W. 46th St. at Twelfth Ave.). ℂ 212/245-0072. www.intrepidmuseum.org. At press time, rate and hours were not announced. Call or check the website for the most up-to-date information, and to see if the museum reopening is still on schedule. Subway: A, C, E to 42nd St./Port Authority. Bus: M42 Crosstown.

Lower East Side Tenement Museum 𝕽 *Kids*   This museum is the first-ever National Trust for Historic Preservation site that was not the home of someone rich or famous. It's something quite different: a five-story tenement that 10,000 people from 25 countries called home between 1863 and 1935—people who had come to the United States looking for the American dream and made 97 Orchard St. their first stop. The tenement museum tells the story of the great immigration boom of the late 19th and early 20th centuries, when the Lower East Side was considered the "Gateway to America." A visit here makes a good follow-up to an Ellis Island trip.

The only way to see the museum is by guided tour. Two primary tenement tours, held on all open days and lasting an hour, offer a satisfying exploration of the museum: **Piecing It Together: Immigrants in the Garment Industry,** which focuses on the restored apartment and the lives of its turn-of-the-20th-century tenants, an immigrant Jewish family named Levine from Poland; and **Getting By: Weathering the Great Depressions of 1873 and 1929,** featuring the homes of the German-Jewish Gumpertz family and the Sicilian-Catholic Baldizzi family, respectively. A knowledgeable guide leads you into each urban time capsule, where several apartments have been restored to their lived-in condition, and recounts the real stories of the families who occupied them. You can pair the tours for an in-depth look at the museum, since the apartments and stories are so different; however, one tour serves as an excellent introduction.

These tours are not really for kids, who won't enjoy the serious tone and "don't touch" policy. Much better for them is the 45-minute, weekends-only **Confino Family Apartment** tour, a living-history program geared to families, which allows kids to converse with an interpreter who plays teenage immigrant Victoria Confino (ca. 1916); kids can also handle whatever they like and try on period clothes.

The hour-long **Streets Where We Lived** neighborhood heritage walking tour is also offered on weekends from April through December. Small permanent and rotating exhibits, including photos, videos, and a model tenement, are housed in the visitor center and exhibition space in the tenement building at 97 Orchard St. Special tours and programs are sometimes on the schedule.

Tours are limited in number and sell out quickly, so it pays to buy tickets in advance, which you can do online or over the phone by calling Ticketweb at ℂ **800/965-4827.**

108 Orchard St. (btwn Delancey and Broome sts.). ℂ 212/431-0233. www.tenement. org. Tenement and walking tours $15 adults, $11 seniors and students; Confino Apt. $17 adults, $13 seniors and students. Tenement tours depart Tues–Fri every 40 min. 1–4pm; Sat–Sun every half-hour 11am–4:45pm. Confino Apt. tour Sat–Sun hourly noon–3pm. Walking tour Apr–Dec Sat–Sun 1 and 3pm. Subway: F to Delancey St.; J, M, Z to Essex St.

Morgan Library ⭐⭐ *(Finds)*   This New York treasure, boasting one of the world's most important collections of original manuscripts, rare books and bindings, master drawings, and personal writings has reopened after 2 years of extensive renovations. Those renovations include a welcoming entrance on Madison Avenue; new and renovated galleries, so that more of the library's holdings can be exhibited; a modern auditorium; and a Reading Room with greater capacity and electronic resources and expanded space for collections storage. Some of the Library's recent exhibitions include one on the life of Bob Dylan through music, letters, and memorabilia and an exhibit on illustrator Saul Steinberg. You can lunch in the intimate **Morgan Dining Room** as if you were dining in JP's own quarters.

225 Madison Ave. (between 36th and 37th sts). ℂ 212/685-0008. www.the morgan.org. $12 adults, $8 seniors and students, under 12 free. Tues–Thurs 10:30am–5pm, Fri 10:30am–9pm, Sat 10am–6pm, Sun 11am–6pm. Subway: 6 to 33rd St.

Museum of the City of New York   A wide variety of objects— costumes, photographs, prints, maps, dioramas, and memorabilia— trace the history of New York City from its beginnings as a humble Dutch colony in the 16th century to its present-day prominence. Two outstanding permanent exhibits are the re-creation of John D. Rockefeller's master bedroom and dressing room, and the space devoted to "Broadway!," a history of New York theater. Kids will love "New York Toy Stories," a permanent exhibit showcasing toys and dolls owned and adored by centuries of New York children. The permanent "Painting the Town: Cityscapes of New York" explores the changing cityscape from 1809 to 1997, and carries new profundity in the wake of the September 11, 2001 terrorist attacks. In 2008, the exhibits, "Manhattan Noon: The photographs of Gus Powell" and "Catholics in New York" were featured.

1220 Fifth Ave. (at 103rd St.). © **212/534-1672.** www.mcny.org. Suggested admission $9 adults, $5 seniors, students, and children, $20 families. Tues–Sun 10am–5pm. Admission free Sun 10am–noon. Subway: 6 to 103rd St.

Museum of Jewish Heritage—A Living Memorial to the Holocaust ⟨⟩

In the south end of Battery Park City, the Museum of Jewish Heritage occupies a strikingly spare six-sided building designed by award-winning architect Kevin Roche, with a six-tier roof alluding to the Star of David and the six million murdered in the Holocaust. The permanent exhibits—"Jewish Life a Century Ago, The War Against the Jews," and "Jewish Renewal"—recount their prewar lives, the unforgettable horror that destroyed them, and the tenacious renewal experienced by European and immigrant Jews in the years from the late 19th century to the present. The museum's power derives from the way it tells that story: through the objects, photographs, documents, and, most poignantly, the videotaped testimonies of Holocaust victims, survivors, and their families, chronicled by Steven Spielberg's Survivors of the Shoah Visual History Foundation. Thursday evening is dedicated to panel discussions, performances, and music, while Sunday is for family programs and workshops; a film series is also a part of the calendar.

While advance tickets are not usually necessary, you may want to purchase them to guarantee admission; call © **212/945-0039.** Audio tours narrated by Meryl Streep and Itzhak Perlman are available at the museum for an additional $5.

36 Battery Place (at 1st Place), Battery Park City. © **646/437-4200.** www.mjhnyc. org. Admission $10 adults, $7 seniors, $5 students, free for children under 12 and for everyone Wed 4–8pm. Check website for $2-off admission coupon (available at press time). Sun–Tues and Thurs 10am–5:45pm; Wed 10am–8pm; Fri and eves of Jewish holidays 10am–3pm. Subway: 4, 5 to Bowling Green.

New Museum of Contemporary Art ⟨⟩

Like boxes haphazardly piled upon one another, the seven-story New Museum of Contemporary Art, rising above the tenements of the Lower East Side, is New York's newest (2007) museum icon. But it's not only the exterior that catches the eye; the exhibits reflect the slightly offbeat, slanted look of the museum. The museum's debut exhibition, "Unmonumental," a four-part series displaying 21st-century sculptures, objects, video, and collages by 30 international artists, was a fitting beginning to what promises to be a bright future. On the first Saturday of each month, the museum offers programs for families with thematic tours, conversations with artists, and creative activities, all free of charge. Advance registration is required.

235 Bowery (at Prince St.) ℭ **212/219-1222**. www.newmuseum.org. Admission: $12 adult, $8 Senior, $6 student, 18 and under free; free for all Thurs 7–10pm. Wed noon–6pm; Thurs–Fri noon–1pm; Sat–Sun noon–6pm. Subway: 6 to Spring St; N, R to Prince St.

New-York Historical Society ☆   Launched in 1804, the New-York Historical Society is a major repository of American history, culture, and art, with a special focus on New York and its broader cultural significance. The grand neoclassical edifice near the Museum of Natural History has finally emerged from the renovation tent. Now open on the fourth floor is the **Henry Luce III Center for the Study of American Culture,** a state-of-the-art study facility and gallery of fine and decorative arts, which displays more than 40,000 objects amassed over 200 years—including paintings, sculpture, Tiffany lamps, textiles, furniture, even carriages—that had previously been in storage for decades. Of particular interest to scholars and ephemera buffs are the extensive Library Collections, which include books, manuscripts, maps, newspapers, photographs, and more documents chronicling the American experience. (An appointment may be necessary to view some or all of the Library Collections, so call ahead.) The 2006 exhibit "Slavery in New York" was so popular it has now become permanent and the companion exhibit, "New York Divided: Slavery and the Civil War" was featured in 2007.

An extensive, top-quality calendar of programs runs the gamut from story hours to Irving Berlin music nights to lectures by such luminaries as Ric Burns to expert-led walks through Manhattan neighborhoods; call or check the website for the schedule.

170 Central Park West (at 77th St.). ℭ **212/873-3400**. www.nyhistory.org. Admission $10 adults, $7 seniors and educators, $6 students, free for children 12 and under; free Fri 6–8pm. Tues–Sun 10am–6pm (Fri until 8pm). Subway: B, C to 81st St.; 1 to 79th St.

The Paley Center for Media   Formerly known as the Museum of Television and Radio, if you can resist the allure of this museum, I'd wager you've spent the last 70 years in a bubble. You can watch and hear all the great personalities of TV and radio—from Uncle Miltie to Johnny Carson to Jerry Seinfeld—at a private console (available for 2 hrs.). You can also conduct computer searches to pick out the great moments of history, viewing almost anything that made its way onto the airwaves, from the Beatles' first appearance on *The Ed Sullivan Show* to the crumbling of the Berlin Wall (the collection consists of 75,000 programs and commercials). Selected programs are also presented in two theaters and two screening rooms,

Moments **Sacred Ground**

In 1991, during the construction of a federal building on the corner of Duane Street and Broadway, workers unearthed human remains. Those remains, it turned out, were of enslaved and free African slaves, and the site where they were discovered was part of the largest Colonial Era cemetery for blacks in the United States. Building on the site was halted and in 1993 it was declared a National Historic Landmark. In 2006, it became a national monument and put under the jurisdiction of the National Parks Services. In 2007, after almost 16 years, the **African Burial Ground Memorial** (between Duane and Elk sts.; (C) **212/637-2019;** www.nps. gov/afbg) was constructed to honor the final resting place of an estimated 15,000 Africans.

The granite memorial sandwiched between glass-and-steel federal buildings has seven design elements, including a triangular structure that symbolizes the ship passage to the new world from Africa, and religious symbols from 20 countries of the African Diaspora on a spiral wall that leads to a map of the world centered in West Africa. It's a moving memorial and well worth visiting while exploring downtown.

There is a small **visitor's center** in the IRS building at 290 Broadway, adjacent to the memorial, but you have to go through a security check to enter. The Memorial is open to the public, free of charge, from 9am until 5pm daily except Thanksgiving, Christmas, and New Year's Day.

which can range from "Barbra Streisand: The Television Performances" to little-seen Monty Python episodes.

25 W. 52nd St. (btwn Fifth and Sixth aves.). (C) **212/621-6600.** www.mtr.org. Admission $10 adults, $8 seniors and students, $5 children under 14. Tues–Sun noon–6pm (Thurs until 8pm) Subway: B, D, F, V to 47th–50th sts./Rockefeller Center; E, V to 53rd St.

Skyscraper Museum   Wowed by the sheer verticality in this town? Awed by the architectural marvel that is the high-rise? You're not alone. If you'd like to learn more about the technology, culture, and muscle behind it all, seek out this formerly itinerant museum, which moved into its first permanent home in 2004 in the 38-story

Skidmore, Owings & Merrill tower that also houses the Ritz-Carlton New York, Battery Park. The space comprises two galleries, one housing a permanent exhibition dedicated to the evolution of Manhattan's commercial skyline, the other for changing shows. In 2008 the museum featured "Vertical Cities: Hong Kong/New York," an exhibition of the world's two major skyscraper cities.

39 Battery Place (Little West St. and 1st Place). (✆ 212/968-1961. www.skyscraper. org. Admission: $5 adults, $2.50 seniors and students. Wed–Sun noon–6pm. Subway: 4, 5 to Bowling Green.

South Street Seaport & Museum (Kids   Dating back to the 17th century, this historic district on the East River encompasses 11 square blocks of historic buildings, a maritime museum, several piers, shops, and restaurants. You can explore most of the Seaport on your own. It's a beautiful but somewhat odd place. The 18th- and 19th-century buildings lining the cobbled streets and alleyways are impeccably restored but nevertheless have a theme-park air about them, no doubt due to the mall-familiar shops housed within. The Seaport's biggest tourist attraction is Pier 17, a historic barge converted into a mall, complete with food court and cheap-jewelry kiosks.

Despite its rampant commercialism, the Seaport is well worth a look. There's a good amount of history to be discovered here, most of it around the **South Street Seaport Museum,** a fitting tribute to the sea commerce that once thrived here. On weekends the museum dedicates Saturday and Sunday afternoons to family fun with music, art, and other activities for children 4 and older.

In addition to the galleries—which house paintings and prints, ship models, scrimshaw, and nautical designs, as well as frequently changing exhibitions—there are a number of historic ships berthed at the pier to explore, including the 1911 four-masted *Peking* and the 1893 Gloucester fishing schooner *Lettie G. Howard.* A few of the boats are living museums and restoration works in progress; the 1885 cargo schooner *Pioneer* ((✆ 212/748-8786) offers 2-hour public sails daily from early May through September. Even **Pier 17** has its merits. Head up to the third-level deck overlooking the East River, where the long wooden chairs will have you thinking about what it was like to cross the Atlantic on the *Normandie.* From this level you can see south to the Statue of Liberty, north to the Gothic majesty of the Brooklyn Bridge, and Brooklyn Heights on the opposite shore.

At the gateway to the Seaport, at Fulton and Water streets, is the *Titanic* **Memorial Lighthouse,** a monument to those who lost their lives when the ocean liner sank on April 15, 1912. It was erected overlooking the East River in 1913 and moved to this spot in 1968, just after the historic district was so designated.

At Water and South sts.; museum visitor center is at 12 Fulton St. ℭ **212/748-8600** or 212/SEA-PORT. www.southstseaport.org. Museum admission $8 adults, $6 students and seniors, $4 children 5–12, free for children under 5 Museum Apr–Oct Tues–Sun 10am–6pm, Thurs 10am–8pm; Nov–Mar Fri–Mon 10am–5pm. Subway: 2, 3, 4, 5 to Fulton St. (walk east, or downslope, on Fulton St. to Water St.).

3 Skyscrapers & Other Architectural Highlights

For details on the **Empire State Building** ✺✺✺, see p. 125; for **Grand Central Terminal** ✺✺, p. 126; for **Rockefeller Center** ✺✺, p. 128; and for the **Brooklyn Bridge** ✺✺, p. 122. You might also wish to check out "Places of Worship," below, for treasures like **St. Patrick's Cathedral, Temple Emanu-El,** and the **Cathedral of St. John the Divine** ✺.

The Upper West Side is home to two of the city's prime examples of residential architecture. On Broadway, taking up the block between 73rd and 74th streets, is the **Ansonia,** looking for all the world like a flamboyant architectural wedding cake. This splendid Beaux Arts building has been home to the likes of Stravinsky, Toscanini, and Caruso, thanks to its virtually soundproof apartments. (It was also where members of the Chicago White Sox plotted to throw the 1919 World Series, a year before Babe Ruth moved in after donning the New York Yankees' pinstripes.) Even more notable is the **Dakota,** at 72nd Street and Central Park West. Legend has it that the angular 1884 apartment house—accented with gables, dormers, and oriel windows that give it a brooding appeal—earned its name when its forward-thinking developer, Edward S. Clark, was teased by friends that he was building so far north of the city that he might as well be building in the Dakotas. The building's most famous resident, John Lennon, was gunned down outside the 72nd Street entrance on December 8, 1980; Yoko Ono still lives inside.

Chrysler Building ✺✺ Built as Chrysler Corporation headquarters in 1930, this is perhaps the 20th century's most romantic architectural achievement, especially at night when the lights in its triangular openings play off its steely crown. As you admire its facade, be sure to note the gargoyles reaching out from the upper floors, looking, for all the world, like streamline-Gothic hood ornaments. The observation deck closed long ago, but you can visit its lavish ground-floor interior, which is Art Deco to the max.

405 Lexington Ave. (at 42nd St.). Subway: S, 4, 5, 6, 7 to 42nd St./Grand Central.

Flatiron Building   This triangular masterpiece was one of the first skyscrapers. Its wedge shape is the only way the building could fill the triangular property created by the intersection of Fifth Avenue and Broadway, and that happy coincidence created one of the city's most distinctive buildings. Built in 1902 and fronted with limestone and terra cotta (not iron), the Flatiron measures only 6 feet across at its narrow end. So called for its resemblance to the laundry appliance, it was originally named the Fuller Building, then later "Burnham's Folly" because folks were certain that architect Daniel Burnham's 21-story structure would fall down. It didn't.

175 Fifth Ave. (at 23rd St.). Subway: R to 23rd St.

New York Public Library 🌟🌟   The New York Public Library, adjacent to **Bryant Park** 🌟 and designed by Carrère & Hastings (1911), is one of the country's finest examples of Beaux Arts architecture, a majestic structure of white Vermont marble with Corinthian columns and allegorical statues. Before climbing the broad flight of steps to the Fifth Avenue entrance, note the famous lion sculptures—*Fortitude* on the right, and *Patience* on the left—so dubbed by whip-smart former mayor Fiorello La Guardia. At Christmastime, they don natty wreaths to keep warm.

This library is actually the **Humanities and Social Sciences Library,** only one of the research libraries in the New York Public Library system. The interior is one of the finest in the city and features **Astor Hall,** with high arched marble ceilings and grand staircases. Thanks to restoration and modernization, the stupendous **Main Reading Rooms** have been returned to their stately glory and moved into the computer age (goodbye, card catalogs!). After a $5-million restoration, what was once known only as Room 117, a Beaux Arts masterpiece with incredible views of Fifth Avenue and 42nd Street, reopened and is now known as the Lionel Pincus and Princess Firyal Map Division. Here you will find possibly the finest and most extensive collection of maps in the world.

Even if you don't stop in to peruse the periodicals, you may want to check out one of the excellent rotating **exhibitions.** And in 2008, the Library's facade will begin a 3-year restoration, to be completed for the building's centennial in 2011.

Fifth Ave. at 42nd St. ✆ **212/930-0830** (exhibits and events) or 212/661-7220 (library hours). www.nypl.org. Free admission to all exhibitions. Tues–Wed 11am–7:30pm. Thurs–Sat 10am–6pm; Sun 1 to 5pm. Subway: B, D, F, V to 42nd St.; S, 4, 5, 6, 7 to Grand Central/42nd St.

United Nations   In the midst of New York City is this working monument to world peace. The U.N. headquarters occupies 18 acres of international territory—neither the city nor the United States has jurisdiction here—along the East River from 42nd to 48th streets. Designed by an international team of architects (led by American Wallace K. Harrison and including Le Corbusier) and finished in 1952, the complex along the East River weds the 39-story glass slab Secretariat with the free-form General Assembly on beautifully landscaped grounds donated by John D. Rockefeller, Jr. One hundred eighty nations use the facilities to arbitrate worldwide disputes. **Guided tours** leave every half-hour and last 45 minutes to an hour.

At First Ave. and 46th St. ✆ **212/963-8687.** www.un.org/tours. Guided tours $14 adults, $9 seniors, high school, and college students, $7.50 children 5–14. Children under 5 not permitted. Daily tours every half-hour 9:30am–4:45pm; Jan–Feb Sat–Sun 10am–4:30pm; limited schedule may be in effect during the general debate (late Sept to mid-Oct). Subway: S, 4, 5, 6, 7 to 42nd St./Grand Central.

4 Places of Worship

Abyssinian Baptist Church ✵   The most famous of Harlem's more than 400 houses of worship is this Baptist church, founded downtown in 1808 by African-American and Ethiopian merchants. It was moved uptown to Harlem back in the 1920s by Adam Clayton Powell, Sr., who built it into the largest Protestant congregation—white or black—in America. His son, Adam Clayton Powell, Jr. (for whom the adjoining boulevard was named), carried on his tradition, and also became a U.S. congressman. Abyssinian is now the domain of the fiery, activist-minded Rev. Calvin O. Butts, whom the chamber of commerce has declared a "living treasure." The Sunday morning services—at 9 and 11am—offer a wonderful opportunity to experience the Harlem gospel tradition.

132 Odell Clark Place (W. 138th St., btwn Adam Clayton Powell Blvd. & Lenox Ave.). ✆ **212/862-7474.** www.abyssinian.org. Subway: 2, 3, B, C to 135th St.

Cathedral of St. John the Divine ✵   The world's largest Gothic cathedral, St. John the Divine has been a work-in-progress since 1892. Its sheer size is amazing enough—a nave that stretches two football fields and a seating capacity of 5,000—but keep in mind that there is no steel structural support. The church is being built

using traditional Gothic engineering—blocks of granite and limestone are carved out by master masons and their apprentices—which
may explain why construction is still ongoing, more than 100 years
after it began, with no end in sight. In fact, a December 2001 fire
destroyed the north transept, which housed the gift shop. But this
phoenix rose from the ashes quickly; the cathedral was reopened to
visitors within a month. That's precisely what makes this place so
wonderful: Finishing isn't necessarily the point. Though maybe it is;
in late 2007 scaffolding was finally removed from the church's southwest tower exposing that magnificent structure for the first time in
over 15 years. And in late 2008, after a $16.5 million cleaning and
repair from the 2001 fire, the great nave is expected to open.

Though it's the seat of the Episcopal Diocese of New York, St.
John's embraces an interfaith tradition. Internationalism is a theme
found throughout the cathedral's iconography. Each chapel is dedicated to a different national, ethnic, or social group. The genocide
memorial in the Missionary chapel—dedicated to the victims of the
Ottoman Empire in Armenia (1915–23), of the Holocaust
(1939–45), and in Bosnia-Herzegovina since 1992—moved me to
tears, as did the FDNY memorial in the Labor chapel. Although it
was conceived to honor 12 firefighters killed in 1966, hundreds of
personal notes and trinkets of remembrance have made it into a tribute to the 343 firefighters killed on September 11, 2001.

1047 Amsterdam Ave. (at 112th St.). © **212/316-7490** or 212/932-7347 for tour
information and reservations, 212/662-2133 for event information and tickets.
www.stjohndivine.org. Suggested admission $2; tour $5. Mon–Sat 7am–6pm; Sun
7am–7pm. Tours offered Tues–Sat 11am; Sun 1pm. Worship services Mon–Sat 8 and
8:30am (morning prayer and holy Eucharist), 12:15 and 5:30pm (1st Thurs service
7:15am); Sun 8, 9, and 11am and 6pm; AIDS memorial service 4th Sat of the month
at 12:15pm. Subway: B, C, 1 to Cathedral Pkwy.

St. Patrick's Cathedral This Gothic white-marble-and-stone
structure is the largest Roman Catholic cathedral in the United States,
as well as the seat of the Archdiocese of New York. Designed by James
Renwick, begun in 1859, and consecrated in 1879, St. Patrick's wasn't
completed until 1906. Strangely, Irish Catholics picked one of the
city's WASPiest neighborhoods for St. Patrick's. After the death of the
beloved John Cardinal O'Connor in 2000, Pope John Paul II
installed Bishop Edward Egan, whom he elevated to cardinal in 2001.
The cathedral seats a congregation of 2,200; if you don't want to
come for Mass, you can pop in between services to get a look at the
impressive interior. The St. Michael and St. Louis altar came from

Tiffany & Co. (also located here on Fifth Ave.), while the St. Elizabeth altar—honoring Mother Elizabeth Ann Seton, the first American-born saint—was designed by Paolo Medici of Rome.

Fifth Ave. (btwn 50th & 51st sts.). © 212/753-2261. www.ny-archdiocese.org. Free admission. Sun–Fri 7am–8:30pm; Sat 8am–8:30pm. Mass Mon–Fri 7, 7:30, and 8am, noon, and 12:30, 1, and 5:30pm; Sat 8am, noon, and 12:30 and 5:30pm; Sun 7, 8, 9, and 10:15am (Cardinal's mass), noon, and 1 and 5:30pm; holy days 7, 7:30, 8, 8:30, and 11:30am, noon, and 12:30, 1, and 5:30pm. Subway: B, D, F, V to 47th–50th sts./Rockefeller Center.

Temple Emanu-El   Many of New York's most prominent and wealthy families are members of this Reform congregation—the first in New York City—housed in the city's most famous synagogue. The largest house of Jewish worship in the world is a majestic blend of Moorish and Romanesque styles, symbolizing the mingling of Eastern and Western cultures. The temple houses a small but remarkable collection of Judaica in the Herbert & Eileen Bernard Museum, including a collection of Hanukkah lamps with examples ranging from the 14th to the 20th centuries. Three galleries also tell the story of the congregation Emanu-El from 1845 to the present. Tours are given after morning services Saturday at noon. Inquire for a schedule of lectures, films, music, symposiums, and other events.

1 E. 65th St. (at Fifth Ave.). © 212/744-1400. www.emanuelnyc.org. Free admission. Daily 10am–5pm. Services Sun–Thurs 5:30pm; Fri 5:15pm; Sat 10:30am. Subway: N, R to Fifth Ave.; 6 to 68th St.

Trinity Church   Serving God and Mammon, this Wall Street house of worship—with neo-Gothic flying buttresses, beautiful stained-glass windows, and vaulted ceilings—was designed by Richard Upjohn and consecrated in 1846. At that time, its 280-foot spire dominated the skyline. Its main doors, embellished with biblical scenes, were inspired in part by Ghiberti's famed doors on Florence's Baptistery. The historic Episcopal church stood strong while office towers crumbled around it on September 11, 2001; however, an electronic organ has temporarily replaced the historic pipe organ, which was damaged by dust and debris. The gates to the church currently serve as a memorial to the victims of 9/11, with countless tokens of remembrance left by locals and visitors.

The church runs a tour daily at 2pm (a second Sun tour follows the 11:15am Eucharist); groups of five or more should call © 212/602-0872 to reserve. Also part of Trinity Church is **St. Paul's Chapel,** at Broadway and Fulton Street, New York's only surviving pre-Revolutionary church, and a transition shelter for homeless men until it was transformed into a relief center after September 11, 2001; it returned to its former duties in mid-2002. Built by Thomas McBean, with a temple-like portico and Ionic columns supporting a massive pediment, the chapel resembles London's St. Martin-in-the-Fields. In the graveyard, 18th- and 19th-century notables rest in peace and modern businesspeople sit for lunch.

At Broadway & Wall St. ☎ **212/602-0800** or 212/602-0872 for concert information. www.trinitywallstreet.org. Free admission and free tours; $2 suggested donation for noonday concerts. Museum Mon–Fri 9–11:45am; Sun–Fri 1–3:45pm; Sat 10am–3:45pm. Services Mon–Fri 8:15am, 12:05, and 5:15pm (additional Healing Service Thurs at 12:30pm); Sat 8:45am; Sun 9 and 11:15am (also 8am Eucharist service at St. Paul's Chapel, between Vesey and Fulton sts.). Subway: 4, 5 to Wall St.

5 Central Park & Other Places to Play

CENTRAL PARK

Without the miracle of civic planning that is **Central Park** ⊛⊛⊛, Manhattan might be an unbroken block of buildings. Instead, smack in the middle of Gotham, an 843-acre natural retreat provides a daily escape valve and tranquilizer for millions.

While you're in the city, be sure to take advantage of the park's many charms—not the least of which is its sublime layout. Frederick Law Olmsted and Calvert Vaux won a competition with a plan that marries flowing paths with sinewy bridges, integrating them into the rolling landscape with its rocky outcroppings, man-made lakes, and wooded pockets. Designers hid traffic from the eyes and ears of park-goers by building roads that are largely hidden from the bucolic view.

GETTING THERE　To reach the southernmost entrance on the west side, take the A, B, C, D, 1 to 59th Street/Columbus Circle. To reach the southeast corner entrance, take the N, R, W to Fifth Avenue; from here, it's an easy walk into the park to the Information Center in the **Dairy** (☎ **212/794-6564;** daily 11am–5pm, to 4pm in winter), midpark at about 65th Street. Here you can ask questions, pick up park information, and purchase a good park map.

If your time for exploring is limited, I suggest entering the park at 72nd or 79th street for maximum exposure (subway: B, C to 72nd St. or 81st St./Museum of Natural History). From here, you can pick up park information at the visitor center at **Belvedere Castle** (☎ **212/772-0210;** Tues–Sun 10am–5pm, to 4pm in winter), midpark at 79th Street. There's also a third visitor center at the **Charles A. Dana Discovery Center** (☎ **212/860-1370;** daily 11am–5pm, to 4pm in winter), at the northeast corner of the park at Harlem

Central Park

Meer, at 110th Street between Fifth and Lenox avenues (subway: 2, 3 to Central Park N./110th St.). The Dana Center is also an environmental education center hosting workshops, exhibits, music programs, and park tours, and lends fishing poles for fishing in Harlem Meer. (Park policy is catch-and-release.)

Food carts and vendors are set up at all of the park's main gathering points. You'll also find a fixed food counter at the **Conservatory,** on the east side of the park north of the 72nd Street entrance, and both casual snacks and more sophisticated New American dining at **The Boat House,** on the lake near 72nd Street and Park Drive North (℅ **212/517-2233**).

GUIDED WALKS The **Central Park Conservancy** offers a slate of free walking tours of the park; call ℅ **212/360-2726** or check **www.centralparknyc.org** for the current schedule (click on the "Walking Tours" button on the left). The Dana Center hosts ranger-guided tours on occasion (call ℅ **212/860-1370** or 800/201-PARK for a schedule). Also consider a private walking tour; many of the companies listed in "Organized Sightseeing Tours," below, offer guided tours of the park.

FOR FURTHER INFORMATION Call the main number at ℅ **212/360-3444** for recorded information, or 212/310-6600 or 212/628-1036 to speak to a live person. Call ℅ **888/NY-PARKS** for special events information. The park also has two comprehensive websites that are worth checking out before you go: The city parks department's site at **www.centralpark.org**, and the Central Park Conservancy's site at **www.centralparknyc.org**, both of which feature excellent maps and a far more complete rundown of park attractions and activities than I have room to include here. If you have an **emergency** in the park, dial ℅ **800/201-PARK,** which will link you directly to the park rangers.

SAFETY TIP Even though the park has the lowest crime rate of any of the city's precincts, keep your wits about you, especially in the more remote northern end. It's a good idea to avoid the park entirely after dark, unless you're heading to one of the restaurants for dinner or to a **Shakespeare in the Park** event.

EXPLORING THE PARK

The best way to see Central Park is to wander along its 58 miles of winding pedestrian paths, keeping in mind the following highlights.

Before starting, stop by the **Information Center** in the Dairy (℅ **212/794-6464;** daily 11am–5pm, to 4pm in winter), midpark in a 19th-century-style building overlooking Wollman Rink at about 65th Street, to get a map and other information on sights and events, and to peruse the kid-friendly exhibit on the park's history and design.

GOING TO THE ZOO

Central Park Zoo/Tisch Children's Zoo ★ (Kids)   Here is a pleasant refuge within a refuge where sea lions frolic in the central pool area with beguiling style, gigantic but graceful polar bears glide back and forth across a watery pool that has glass walls through which you can observe very large paws doing smooth strokes, monkeys seem to regard those on the other side of the fence with disdain, and in the hot and humid Tropic Zone, colorful birds swoop around in freedom, sometimes landing next to nonplused visitors.

Because of its small size, the zoo is at its best with its displays of smaller animals. The indoor multilevel Tropic Zone is a highlight, its steamy rainforest home to everything from black-and-white colobus monkeys to Emerald tree boa constrictors to a leaf-cutter ant farm; look for the new dart-poison-frog exhibit, which is very cool. So is the large penguin enclosure in the Polar Circle, which is better than the one at San Diego's SeaWorld. In the Temperate Territory, look for the Asian red pandas (cousins to the big black-and-white ones), which look like the world's most beautiful raccoons. Despite their pool and piles of ice, however, the polar bears still look sad.

The entire zoo is good for short attention spans; you can cover the whole thing in 1½ to 3 hours, depending on the size of the crowds and how long you like to linger. It's also very kid-friendly, with lots of well-written and -illustrated placards that older kids can understand. For the littlest ones, there's the $6-million **Tisch Children's Zoo** ★. With goats, llamas, potbellied pigs, and more, this petting zoo and playground is a real blast for the 5-and-under set.

830 Fifth Ave. (at 64th St., just inside Central Park). © 212/439-6500. www.wcs. org/zoos. Admission $8 adults, $4 seniors, $3 children 3–12, free for children under 3. Apr–Oct Mon–Fri 10am–5pm, Sat–Sun 10am–5:30pm; Nov–Mar daily 10am–4:30pm. Last entrance 30 min. before closing. Subway: N, R to Fifth Ave; 6 to 68th St.

ACTIVITIES

The 6-mile rolling road circling the park, **Central Park Drive,** has a lane set aside for bikers, joggers, and in-line skaters. The best time to use it is when the park is closed to traffic: Monday to Friday 10am to 3pm (except Thanksgiving to New Year's) and 7 to 10pm. It's also closed from 7pm Friday to 6am Monday, but when the weather is nice, the crowds can be hellish.

BIKING Off-road biking isn't permitted; stay on Central Park Drive or your bike may be confiscated by park police.

You can rent 3- and 10-speed bikes as well as tandems in Central Park at the **Loeb Boathouse,** midpark near 72nd Street and Park Drive North, just in from Fifth Avenue (✆ **212/517-2233** or 212/517-3623), for $9 to $15 an hour, with a complete selection of kids' bikes, cruisers, tandems, and the like ($200 deposit required); at **Metro Bicycles,** 1311 Lexington Ave., at 88th Street (✆ **212/427-4450**), for about $7 an hour, or $35 a day; and at **Toga Bike Shop,** 110 West End Ave., at 64th Street (✆ **212/799-9625;** www.toga bikes.com), for $30 a day. No matter where you rent, be prepared to leave a credit card deposit.

BOATING From March through November, gondola rides and rowboat rentals are available at the **Loeb Boathouse,** midpark near 74th Street and Park Drive North, just in from Fifth Avenue (✆ **212/517-2233** or 212/517-3623). Rowboats cost $10 for the first hour, $2.50 for every 15 minutes thereafter, and a $30 deposit is required; reservations are accepted. (Note that rates were not set for the summer season at press time, so these may change.)

HORSE-DRAWN CARRIAGE RIDES At the entrance to the park at 59th Street and Central Park South, you'll see a line of **horse-drawn carriages** waiting to take passengers through the park or along certain city streets. Horses belong on city streets as much as chamber pots belong in our homes. You won't need me to tell you how forlorn most of these horses look; if you insist, a ride is about $50 for two for a half-hour, but I suggest skipping it.

ICE-SKATING Central Park's **Wollman Rink** ✪, on the east side of the park between 62nd and 63rd streets (✆ **212/439-6900;** www.wollmanskatingrink.com), is the city's best outdoor skating spot, more spacious than the rink at Rockefeller Center. It's open for skating from mid-October to mid-April, depending on the weather. Rates are $9.50 for adults ($12 on weekends), $4.75 for seniors and kids under 12 ($8.25 on weekends), and skate rental is $5; lockers are available (locks are $3.75). **Lasker Rink** ✆ **212/534-7639,** on the east side around 106th Street, is a less expensive alternative to the more crowded Wollman Rink. Open November through March, rates are $4.50 for adults, $2.25 for kids under 12, and skate rental is $4.75.

IN-LINE SKATING Central Park is the city's most popular place for blading. See the beginning of this section for details on Central Park Drive, the main drag for skaters. On weekends, head to West

Drive at 67th Street, behind Tavern on the Green, where you'll find trick skaters weaving through a New York Roller Skating Association (NYRSA) slalom course, or to the Mall in front of the band shell (above Bethesda Fountain) for twirling to tunes. In summer, **Wollman Rink** ✟ converts to a hotshot roller rink, with half-pipes and lessons available. (See "Ice-Skating," above.)

You can rent skates for $20 a day from **Blades Board and Skate,** 120 W. 72nd St., between Broadway and Columbus Avenue (✆ 212/ 787-3911; www.blades.com). Wollman Rink (see above) also rents in-line skates for park use at similar rates.

PLAYGROUNDS   Nineteen Adventure Playgrounds are scattered throughout the park, perfect for jumping, sliding, tottering, swinging, and digging. At Central Park West and 81st Street is the **Diana Ross Playground** ✟, voted the city's best by *New York* magazine. Also on the west side is the **Spector Playground,** at 85th Street and Central Park West, and, a little farther north, the **Wild West Playground,** at 93rd Street. On the east side is the **Rustic Playground,** at 67th Street and Fifth Avenue, a delightfully landscaped space rife with islands, bridges, and big slides; and the **Pat Hoffman Friedman Playground,** right behind the Metropolitan Museum of Art at East 79th Street, is geared toward older toddlers.

RUNNING   Marathoners and wannabes regularly run in Central Park along the 6-mile **Central Park Drive,** which circles the park (please run toward oncoming traffic to avoid being mowed down by wayward cyclists and in-line skaters, who go with the flow of traffic). The **New York Road Runners** (✆ 212/860-4455; www.nyrrc.org), organizers of the New York City Marathon, schedules group runs 7 days a week at 6am and 6pm, leaving from the entrance to the park at 90th Street and Fifth Avenue.

SWIMMING   **Lasker Pool** (on the east side at around 106th Street; ✆ 212/534-7639), is open July 1 through Labor Day weekend. Rates are $4 for adults, $2 for kids under 12. Bring a towel.

6 Organized Sightseeing Tours

Reservations are required for some of the tours below, but even if they're not, call ahead to confirm prices, times, and meeting places.

DOUBLE-DECKER BUS TOURS
Gray Line New York Tours   Gray Line offers just about every sightseeing tour option and combination you could want. There are bus tours by day and night that run uptown, downtown, and all

around the town, as well as bus combos with Circle Line cruises, helicopter flights, museum admittance, and guided visits of sights. There's no real point to purchasing some combination tours—you don't need a guide to take you to the Statue of Liberty, and you don't save any money on admission by buying the combo ticket.

777 Eighth Ave. (btwn 47th & 48th sts.). Tours depart from various locations. ℂ **800/669-0051** or 212/445-0848; www.graylinenewyork.com. Hop-on, hop off bus tours start at $49 adults, $39 children 3 to 11.

HARBOR CRUISES

Circle Line Sightseeing Cruises *☆☆*   A New York institution, the Circle Line is famous for its 3-hour tour around the entire 35 miles of Manhattan. This **Full Island** cruise passes by the Statue of Liberty, Ellis Island, the Brooklyn Bridge, the United Nations, Yankee Stadium, the George Washington Bridge, and more, including Manhattan's wild northern tip. The panorama is riveting, and the commentary isn't bad. The big boats are basic but fine, with lots of deck room for everybody to enjoy the view. Snacks, soft drinks, coffee, and beer are available onboard for purchase.

If 3 hours is more than you or the kids can handle, go for either the 2-hour **Semi-Circle** or the **Sunset/Harbor Lights** cruise, both of which show you the highlights of the skyline. There's also a 1-hour **Seaport Liberty** version that sticks close to the south end of the island. But of all the tours, the kids might like **The Beast** best, a thrill-a-minute speedboat ride offered in summer only.

In addition, a number of adults-only **Live Music and DJ Cruises** sail regularly from the seaport from May through September ($20–$40 per person). Depending on the night of the week, you can groove to the sounds of jazz, Latin, gospel, dance tunes, or blues as you sail along viewing the skyline.

Departing from Pier 83, at W. 42nd St. and Twelfth Ave. Also departing from Pier 16 at South St. Seaport, 207 Front St. ℂ **212/563-3200.** www.circleline42.com and www.seaportmusiccruises.com. Check the website or call for the most up to date schedule. Sightseeing cruises $12–$29 adults, $16–$24 seniors, $13–$16 children 12 and under. Subway to Pier 83: A, C, E to 42nd St. Subway to Pier 16: J, M, Z, 2, 3, 4, 5 to Fulton St.

SPECIALTY TOURS

The **Municipal Art Society** *☆* (ℂ **212/439-1049** or 212/935-3960; www.mas.org) offers historical and architectural walking tours aimed at intelligent, individualistic travelers. Each is led by a highly qualified guide who offers insights into the significance of buildings, neighborhoods, and history. Topics range from the urban history of Greenwich Village to "Williamsburg: Beyond the Bridge," to an examination of the "new" Times Square. Weekday walking tours are $12; weekend tours are $15. Reservations may be required depending on the tour, so it's best to call ahead. The full schedule is available online or by calling © 212/439-1049.

The **92nd Street Y** ℱ (© 212/415-5500; www.92ndsty.org) offers a wonderful variety of walking and bus tours, many featuring funky themes or behind-the-scenes visits. Subjects can range from "Diplomat for a Day at the U.N." to "Secrets of the Chelsea Hotel," or from "Artists of the Meatpacking District" to "Jewish Harlem." Prices range from $25 to $60 (sometimes more for bus tours), but many include ferry rides, afternoon tea, dinner, or whatever suits the program. Guides are well-chosen experts on their subjects, ranging from respected historians to an East Village poet, mystic, and art critic (for "Allen Ginsberg's New York" and "East Village Night Spots"), and many routes travel into the outer boroughs; some day trips even reach beyond the city. Advance registration is required for all walking and bus tours. Schedules are planned a few months in advance, so check the website for tours that might interest you.

Myra Alperson, founder and lead tour guide for **NoshWalks** (© 212/222-2243; www.noshwalks.com), knows food in New York City and where to find it. For the past 6 years, Alperson has been leading hungry walkers to some of the city's most delicious neighborhoods. From the Uzbek, Tadjik, and Russian markets of Rego Park, Queens; to the Dominican coffee shops of Washington Heights in upper Manhattan, Alperson has left no ethnic neighborhood unexplored. Tours are held on Saturday and Sunday, leaving around 11:30am and 2:30pm. The preferred means of transport is subway; tours last around 3 hours and cost about $33 not including the food you will undoubtedly buy on the tour. Space is limited, so book well in advance.

Harlem Spirituals (© 800/660-2166 or 212/391-0900; www.harlemspirituals.com) specializes in gospel and jazz tours of Harlem that can be combined with a traditional soul-food meal. A variety of options are available, including a tour of Harlem sights with gospel service and a soul-food lunch or brunch as an optional add-on. The Harlem jazz tour includes a neighborhood tour, dinner at a family-style soul-food restaurant, and a visit to a local jazz club; there's also an Apollo Theater variation on this tour. Bronx and Brooklyn tours are also an option for those who want a taste of the outer boroughs. Prices start at $49, $39 for children, for a Harlem Heritage tour, and go up from there based on length and inclusions (tours that include food and entertainment are pay-one-price). All tours leave from

Harlem Spirituals' Midtown office (690 Eighth Ave., between 43rd and 44th sts.), and transportation is included.

Active visitors can hook up with **Bike the Big Apple** (© 201/837-1133; www.bikethebigapple.com). Tours by Bike offers guided half-day, full-day, and customized tours through a variety of city neighborhoods, including the fascinating but little-explored upper Manhattan and Harlem; an ethnic tour that takes you over the legendary Brooklyn Bridge, through Chinatown and Little Italy, and to Ground Zero; and around Flushing, Queens, where you'll feel like you're biking around Hong Kong. You don't have to be an Ironman candidate to participate; tours are designed for the average rider, with an emphasis on safety and fun; shorter rides are available, but the rides generally last around 5 hours. Tours are offered year-round; prices run $80 and include all gear and a bike.

For a bit more whimsy on your tour, **Levy's Unique New York** (© 877/692-5869; www.levysuniqueny.com) offers a lighter look at the city's history and landmarks. The tours are all custom-planned, depending on the size and needs of the group; most are walking but some are conducted by bus. A few of their tours include the "Bohemians and Beats of Greenwich Village Literary Tours," and "Hey Ho! Let's Go! Punk Rock on the Bowery" tour. The group is Brooklyn-based, and they are extremely knowledgeable about their home borough; tours of Coney Island and another called "Edible Ethnic Brooklyn Eats" are just a few that feature Brooklyn. Tours range from $25 to $65 per person.

7 Highlights of the Outer Boroughs

THE BRONX

Bronx Zoo Wildlife Conservation Park ★★★ (Kids)   Founded in 1899, the Bronx Zoo is the largest metropolitan animal park in the United States, with more than 4,000 animals living on 265 acres, and one of the city's best attractions.

One of the most impressive exhibits is the **Wild Asia Complex.** This zoo-within-a-zoo comprises the **Wild Asia Plaza** education center; **Jungle World,** an indoor re-creation of Asian forests, with birds, lizards, gibbons, and leopards; and the **Bengali Express Monorail** (open May–Oct), which takes you on a narrated ride high above free-roaming Siberian tigers, Asian elephants, Indian rhinoceroses, and other nonnative New Yorkers (keep your eyes peeled— the animals aren't as interested in seeing you). The **Himalayan Highlands** is home to 17 extremely rare snow leopards, as well as red pandas and white-naped cranes. The 6½-acre **Congo Gorilla Forest** is home to Western lowland gorillas, okapi, red river hogs, and other African rainforest animals.

The **Children's Zoo** (open Apr–Oct) allows young humans to learn about their wildlife counterparts. If the natural settings and breeding programs aren't enough to keep zoo residents entertained, they can always choose to ogle the two million annual visitors. But there are ways to beat the crowds. Try to visit on a weekday or on a nice winter's day. In summer, come early in the day, before the heat of the day sends the animals back into their enclosures. Expect to spend an entire day here—you'll need it.

Getting there: Liberty Lines' BxM11 express bus, which makes various stops on Madison Avenue, will take you directly to the zoo; call ☎ **718/652-8400.** By subway, take the no. 2 train to Pelham Parkway and then walk west to the Bronxdale entrance.

Fordham Rd. and Bronx River Pkwy., the Bronx. ☎ **718/367-1010.** www.bronxzoo. com. Admission $14 adults, $12 seniors, and $10 for children 2–12; discounted admission Nov–Mar; free Wed year-round. There may be nominal additional charges for some exhibits. Nov–Mar daily 10am–4:30pm (extended hours for Holiday Lights late Nov–early Jan); Apr–Oct Mon–Fri 10am–5pm, Sat–Sun 10am–5:30pm. Transportation: See "Getting there," in the paragraph above.

New York Botanical Garden ✦   A National Historic Landmark, the 250-acre New York Botanical Garden was founded in 1891 and today, is one of America's foremost public gardens. The setting is spectacular—a natural terrain of rocky outcroppings, a river with cascading waterfalls, hills, ponds, and wetlands.

Highlights of the Botanical Garden include the 27 **specialty gardens,** an exceptional **orchid collection,** and 40 acres of **uncut forest,** as close as New York gets to its virgin state before the arrival of Europeans. The **Enid A. Haupt Conservatory,** a stunning series of Victorian glass pavilions that recall London's former Crystal Palace, shelters a rich collection of tropical, subtropical, and desert plants as well as seasonal flower shows. There's also a **Children's Adventure Garden.** *Getting there:* Take Metro-North (☎ **800/METRO-INFO** or 212/532-4900; www.mta.nyc.ny.us/mnr) from Grand Central Terminal to the New York Botanical Garden station; the easy ride takes about 20 minutes. By subway, take the D or 4 train to Bedford Park, then take bus Bx26 or walk southeast on Bedford Park Boulevard for 8 long blocks.

200th St. and Kazimiroff Blvd., the Bronx. ☎ **718/817-8700.** www.nybg.org. Admission $6 adults, $3 seniors, $2 students, $1 children 2–12. Extra charges for Everett Children's Adventure Garden, Enid A. Haupt Conservatory, T. H. Everett Rock

Garden, Native Plant Garden, and narrated tram tour; entire Garden Passport package $13 adults, $11 seniors and students, $5 children 2–12. Apr–Oct Tues–Sun and Mon holidays 10am–6pm; Nov–Mar Tues–Sun and Mon holidays 10am–5pm. Transportation: See "Getting there," in the paragraph above.

BROOKLYN

It's easy to link visits to the Brooklyn Botanic Garden, the Brooklyn Museum of Art, and Prospect Park, since they're all an easy walk from one another, just off **Grand Army Plaza.** Designed by Frederick Law Olmsted and Calvert Vaux as a grand entrance to their Prospect Park, it boasts a Civil War memorial arch designed by John H. Duncan (1892–1901) and the main **Brooklyn Public Library,** an Art Deco masterpiece completed in 1941 (the garden and museum are just on the other side of the library, down Eastern Pkwy.). The entire area is a half-hour subway ride from midtown Manhattan.

Brooklyn Botanic Garden 🐾   Just down the street from the Brooklyn Museum of Art (see below) is the most popular botanic garden in the city. This peaceful 52-acre sanctuary is at its most spectacular in May when the thousands of deep pink blossoms of cherry trees are abloom. Well worth seeing is the spectacular **Cranford Rose Garden,** one of the largest and finest in the country; the **Shakespeare Garden,** an English garden featuring plants mentioned in his writings; a **Children's Garden;** the **Osborne Garden,** a 3-acre formal garden; the **Fragrance Garden,** designed for the blind but appreciated by all noses; and the extraordinary **Japanese Hill-and-Pond Garden.** The renowned **C. V. Starr Bonsai Museum** is home to the world's oldest and largest collection of bonsai, while the impressive $2.5-million Steinhardt Conservatory holds the garden's extensive indoor plant collection.

900 Washington Ave. (at Eastern Pkwy.), Brooklyn. ✆ **718/623-7200.** www.bbg. org. Admission $8 adults, $4 seniors and students, free for children under 16, free to all Tues and Sat 10am–noon year-round, plus Wed–Fri from mid-Nov through Feb. Apr–Sept Tues–Fri 8am–6pm, Sat–Sun 10am–6pm; Oct–Mar Tues–Fri 8am–4:30pm, Sat–Sun 10am–4:30pm. Subway: Q to Prospect Park; 2, 3 to Eastern Pkwy./Brooklyn Museum.

Brooklyn Museum of Art 🐾🐾   One of the nation's premier art institutions, the Brooklyn Museum of Art rocketed back into public consciousness in 1999 with the hugely controversial "Sensation: Young British Artists from the Saatchi Collection," which drew international media attention and record crowds who came to see just what an artist—and a few conservative politicians—could make out of a little elephant dung.

Indeed, the museum is best known for its remarkable temporary exhibitions as well as its excellent permanent collection. The museum's grand Beaux Arts building, designed by McKim, Mead & White (1897), befits its outstanding holdings, most notably the Egyptian, Classical, and Ancient Middle Eastern collection of sculpture, wall reliefs, and mummies. The decorative-arts collection includes 28 American period rooms from 1675 to 1928 (the extravagant Moorish-style smoking room from John D. Rockefeller's 54th St. mansion is my favorite). Other highlights are the African and Asian arts galleries, dozens of works by Rodin, a good costumes and textiles collection, and a diverse collection of American and European painting and sculpture that includes works by Homer, O'Keeffe, Monet, Cézanne, and Degas.

200 Eastern Pkwy. (at Washington Ave.), Brooklyn. (C) **718/638-5000.** www.brooklyn museum.org. Suggested admission $8 adults, $4 seniors and students, free for children under 12, free to all 1st Sat of the month 11am–11pm. Wed–Fri 10am–5pm; 1st Sat of the month 11am–11pm, each Sat thereafter 11am–6pm; Sun 11am–6pm. Subway: 2, 3 to Eastern Pkwy./Brooklyn Museum.

Coney Island ᖊᖊ *Moments*   Sure, Coney Island is just a shell of what it was in its heyday in the early 20th century. But it's that shell and what remains that make it such an intriguing attraction. The almost-mythical Parachute Jump, recently refurbished, though long inoperable, stands as a monument to Coney Island. But this is not a dead amusement park: Astroland, home of the famed Cyclone roller coaster, has some great rides for children and adults, though 2008 will be its last season. The new owners will keep the National Historic Landmark Cyclone, however; and the Wonder Wheel, next door at Deno's, will still be turning. The best amusement of all, however, is the people-watching. Maybe because it is at the extreme edge of New York City, but Coney Island attracts more than its share of the odd, freaky, and funky. It's here where Nathan's Famous Hot Dogs holds its annual hot-dog-eating contest on July 4 at noon; where the wholly entertaining **Mermaid Parade** ᖊ spoofs the old bathing-beauty parades (late June); and where members of the Polar Bear Swim Club show their masochistic gusto by taking a plunge into the icy ocean on January 1. The best time to visit is between Memorial Day and mid-September, when the rides and amusement park are open. Bring your bathing suit and test the waters.

If you are here in the summer, or even if you are not, I recommend a visit to Coney Island just to see it; and you can always visit the nearby **Coney Island Museum,** 1208 Surf Ave. ((C) **718/372-5159;** www.coneyisland.com). Open Saturdays and Sundays year round, here you will find relics from Coney Island's heyday as the premier amusement park in the world. Check out an original "steeple chase horse," vintage bumper cars, or fun-house distortion mirrors. And for a mere 99¢, even if all you want to do is use the clean bathroom, the museum is a bargain.

Brooklyn. Subway: D, F, N, Q to Coney Island–Stillwell Ave.

New York Aquarium *(Kids)*   Because of the long subway ride (about an hour from midtown Manhattan) and its proximity to Coney Island, it's best to combine the two attractions, preferably in the summer. This small but good aquarium is home to hundreds of sea creatures. Taking center stage are Atlantic bottle-nosed dolphins and California sea lions that perform daily during summer at the **Aquatheater.** Also in the spotlight are Pacific octopuses, sharks, and a brand-new seahorse exhibit. Black-footed penguins, California sea otters, and a variety of seals live at the **Sea Cliffs exhibit,** a re-creation of a Pacific coastal habitat. But my favorites are the beautiful Beluga whales, which exude buckets of aquatic charm. Children love the hands-on exhibits at **Discovery Cove.** There's an indoor ocean-view cafeteria and an outdoor snack bar, plus picnic tables.

502 Surf Ave. (at W. 8th St.), Coney Island, Brooklyn. ✆ 718/265-FISH. www.ny aquarium.com. Admission $12 adults, $8 seniors and children 2–12. Daily 10am–4:30pm. Subway: F, Q to West 8th St.

8 Shopping Highlights

CHINATOWN

Don't expect to find the purchase of a lifetime on Chinatown's crowded streets, but there's some quality browsing to be done. The fish and herbal markets along Canal, Mott, Mulberry, and Elizabeth streets are fun for their bustle and exotica. Dispersed among them (especially along **Canal St.**), you'll find a mind-boggling collection of knockoff sunglasses and watches, cheap backpacks, discount leather goods, and exotic souvenirs. It's a fun daytime browse, but don't expect quality—and be sure to bargain.

Mott Street, between Pell Street and Chatham Square, boasts the most interesting of Chinatown's off-Canal shopping, with an antiques shop or two dispersed among the tiny storefronts selling blue-and-white Chinese dinnerware. Just around the corner, peek into **Ting's Gift Shop** (18 Doyer St.; ✆ 212/962-1081), one of the oldest operating businesses in Chinatown. Under a vintage pressed-tin ceiling, it sells good-quality Chinese toys, kits, and lanterns.

THE LOWER EAST SIDE

The bargains aren't what they used to be in the **Historic Orchard Street Shopping District**—which runs from Houston to Canal along Allen, Orchard, and Ludlow streets, spreading outward along both sides of Delancey Street—but prices on leather bags, luggage, linens, and fabrics on the bolt are still good. Be aware, though, that the hard sell on Orchard Street can be hard to take. Still, the district is a nice place to discover a part of New York that's disappearing. Come during the week; many stores are Jewish-owned and close Friday afternoon and all day Saturday. Sunday tends to be a madhouse.

The artists and other trendsetters who have been turning this neighborhood into a bastion of hip have also added a cutting edge. You'll find a growing—and increasingly upscale—crop of alterna-shops south of Houston and north of Grand Street, between Allen and Clinton streets to the east and west, specializing in up-to-the-minute fashions and club clothes for 20-somethings, plus funky retro furnishings, Japanese toys, and other offbeat items. Stop in at the **Lower East Side Visitor Center,** 261 Broome St., between Orchard and Allen streets (© **866/224-0206** or 212/226-9010; Subway: F to Delancey St.), for a shopping guide that includes vendors both old-world and new. Or visit **www.lowereastsideny.com**.

SOHO

People love to complain about super-fashionable SoHo—it's become too trendy, too tony, too Mall of America. True, **J. Crew** is only one of the big names that have supplanted the artists' lofts that used to inhabit its historic buildings. But SoHo is still one of the best shopping 'hoods in the city—and few are more fun to browse. The cast-iron architecture, the cobblestone streets, and the rich-artist vibe: SoHo has a look and feel unlike any other Manhattan neighborhood.

SoHo's shopping grid runs from Broadway west to Sixth Avenue, and Houston Street south to Canal Street. **Broadway** is the most commercial strip, with such recognizable names as **Pottery Barn, Banana Republic, Sephora,** and **A/X Armani Exchange. H&M,** the popular Swedish department store with cutting-edge fashions sold at unbelievably low prices, has two stores that face one another on Broadway. **Bloomingdale's** has opened up a downtown branch in the old Canal Jean space. **Prada**'s flagship store, also on Broadway, is worth visiting for its spacious, almost soothing design alone (by Dutch architect Rem Koolhaus). A definite highlight is the two-story **Pearl River** Chinese emporium, which offers everything from silk cheongsam (traditional Chinese high-necked dresses) to teaware.

The big names in avant-garde fashion have landed in SoHo, but you'll also find one-of-a-kind boutiques, such as the **Hat Shop,** 120 Thompson St., between Prince and Spring streets (© **212/219-1445**), a full service milliner for women.

NOLITA

Not so long ago, **Elizabeth Street** was a quiet adjunct to Little Italy. Today it's one of the hottest shopping strips in the neighborhood known as Nolita. Elizabeth and neighboring **Mott and Mulberry streets** are dotted with an increasing number of shops between Houston Street and the Bowery. It's an easy walk from the Broadway/ Lafayette stop on the F, V line to the neighborhood, since it starts just east of Lafayette Street; you can take the no. 6 train to Spring Street, or the N, R to Prince Street, and walk east from there.

Its wall-to-wall boutiques are largely the province of shopkeepers specializing in high-quality fashion-forward products. More and more, it's become a beacon of ethnic designs from around the world. **Indomix** (232 Mulberry St.; © **212/334-6356;** www.indomix.com) offers beaded tunics and other colorful south-Asian styles by five top designers in India. Texan-born designer and skateboarder **Tracy Feith** (209 Mulberry St.; © **212/334-3097**) creates irresistibly pretty slip dresses, skirts, and tops in eye-popping colors and light-as-air Indian silk in his eponymous store on Mulberry Street.

Nolita is also an accessories bonanza; stop in at **Sigerson Morrison** (20 Prince St.; © **212/219-3893** for great shoes or **Push** (240 Mulberry St.; © **212/965-9699**) for eye-catching jewelry.

THE EAST VILLAGE

The East Village personifies bohemian hip, though many New Yorkers would argue that SoHo's gentrification has engulfed it as well. The easiest subway access is the no. 6 train to Astor Place.

East 9th Street between Second Avenue and Avenue A is lined with an increasingly smart collection of boutiques, proof that the East Village isn't just for kids anymore. Designers, including **Jill Anderson** (331 E. 9th St.; © **212/253-1747**) and **Huminska** (315 E. 9th St.; © **212/677-3458**) sell excellent-quality and original fashions for women along here.

If it's strange, illegal, or funky, it's probably available on **St. Marks Place,** which takes over for 8th Street, running east from Third Avenue to Avenue A. This strip is a permanent street market, with countless T-shirt, tattoo and boho jewelry stands. The height of the action is between Second and Third. If you're in search of the harder-edge East Village and feeling a little brave, explore the side streets closer to Avenue A and southward toward the Bowery.

GREENWICH VILLAGE

The West Village is great for browsing and gift shopping. Specialty bookstores and record stores, antiques and craft shops, and gourmet food markets dominate. On 8th Street—NYU territory between Broadway and Sixth Avenue—you can find trendy footwear and affordable fashions.

But the biggest shopping boom of late has happened on **Bleecker Street** west of Sixth Avenue. Between Carmine Street and Seventh Avenue, foodies will delight in the strip of boutique food shops, including **Amy's Bread, Wild Edibles,** and **Murray's Cheese.** In between are record stores, guitar shops, and a sprinkling of artsy boutiques. On **Christopher Street,** you'll find such wonders as **Aedes De Venutas,** a gorgeous little boutique selling fabulous perfumes and scented candles that are difficult to find in the States, and **The Porcelain Room,** 13 Christopher St. (✆ **212/367-8206**),

---

Tips Additional Sources for Serious Shoppers

If you're looking for specific items, check the shopping listings at **www.newyork.citysearch.com, www.timeoutny.com,** and **www.nymag.com** before you leave home.

For an online guide to sample sales/designer bargains, visit **www.nysale.com,** which will let you in on unadvertised sales taking place throughout the city.

Information about current sales, new shops, sample and close-out sales, and arts, crafts, and antiques shows is found in the "Check Out" section of *Time Out New York* or the "Sales & Bargains," "Best Bets," and "Smart City" sections of *New York* magazine. *New York* also runs daily updates of sales at **www.nymag.com,** and *Time Out* publishes a twice-yearly shopping guide available on newsstands for about $6.

Other Web sources include **www.dailycandy.com,** a daily online newsletter highlighting store openings and where to find the day's sales, and **www.girlshop.com,** a website dedicated to New York insider fashion news. In 2005, the flagship **Girlshop Boutique** opened at 819 Washington St., between Little W. 12th and Gansevoort sts.; (✆ **212/255-4985**).

Tips **Sales Tax**

New York City sales tax is 8.375%, but it is not added to clothing and footwear items under $110. If you're visiting from out of state, consider having your purchases shipped directly home to avoid paying sales tax. As with any shipped purchase, be sure to get documentation of the sale and keep those receipts handy until the merchandise arrives at your door.

---

which is located below street level and offers amazing antique and contemporary porcelains that have to be seen to be believed.

The Oscar Wilde Bookshop, the world's first gay bookstore, has been on the eastern end of Christopher Street since 1967. Follow the street westward, where Bleecker becomes boutique alley, and one jewel box of a shop follows another. Among them: **Intermix, Olive & Bette, Ralph Lauren, Lulu Guinness,** and **Marc Jacobs.**

Those who love to browse should also wander **west of Seventh Avenue** and along **Hudson Street,** where charming shops such as **House of Cards and Curiosities,** 23 Eighth Ave., between Jane and 12th streets (℗ 212/675-6178), the Village's own funky take on an old-fashioned 5-and-10, are tucked among the brownstones.

CHELSEA/MEATPACKING DISTRICT

Far west Chelsea has been transformed into the **Chelsea Art District,** where more than 200 galleries have sprouted up in a once-moribund enclave of repair shops and warehouses. The district unofficially stretches between 14th to 29th streets and the West Side Highway and Seventh Avenue, but the high-density area lies between 20th and 26th streets, between Tenth and Eleventh avenues.

The Meatpacking District has also zoomed from quaint to hot (and some say over) in no time, with such big-name designers as **Stella McCartney** (429 W. 14th St.; ℗ 212/255-1556), **Christian Louboutin** (59 Horatio St.; ℗ 212/255-1910), and **Alexander McQueen** (417 W. 14th St.; ℗ 212/645-1797) in residence. **Jeffrey New York,** an offshoot of the Atlanta department store, has pricey designer clothes, an amazing shoe collection, and the friendliest staff in New York.

UNION SQUARE/THE FLATIRON DISTRICT

The hottest shopping/eating/hanging-out neighborhood in the city may be Union Square. The south side of the square is a mega–shopping area with **Whole Foods, Filene's Basement,** and **DSW (Designer Shoe Warehouse).** On the north side, **Barnes & Noble** is situated in a beautifully restored 1880 cast iron building. Of course, the beating heart of Union Square is the 4-days-a-week **Greenmarket,** the biggest farmers' market in the city.

On Broadway, a few blocks north of Union Square, is the amazing emporium **ABC Carpet & Home,** where the loft-size floors hold brilliantly decadent displays of furniture, housewares, linens (thread counts off the charts), and tchotchkes of all sizes and shapes.

Upscale retailers who have rediscovered the architectural majesty of **lower Fifth Avenue** include **Banana Republic, Victoria's Secret,** and **Kenneth Cole.** You won't find much that's new along here, but it's a pleasing stretch nonetheless.

When 23rd Street was the epitome of New York uptown fashion more than 100 years ago, the major department stores stretched along **Sixth Avenue** for about a mile from 14th Street up. These elegant stores stood in huge cast iron buildings that were long ago abandoned and left to rust. In the last several years, however, the area has become the city's discount shopping center, with superstores and off-pricers filling up the renovated spaces: **Filene's Basement, TJ Maxx,** and **Bed Bath & Beyond** are all at 620 Sixth Ave., while **Old Navy** is next door, and **Barnes & Noble** is just a couple of blocks away, at Sixth Avenue near 22nd Street.

HERALD SQUARE & THE GARMENT DISTRICT

Herald Square—where 34th Street, Sixth Avenue, and Broadway converge—is dominated by **Macy's** (© 212/695-4400) the "world's biggest department store." At Sixth Avenue and 33rd Street is the **Manhattan Mall** (© 212/465-0500; www.manhattanmallny.com), which is just that (a mall), with mostly chain stores (apparel, housewares, electronics) and a food court.

TIMES SQUARE & THE THEATER DISTRICT

You won't find much in the heart of Times Square to entice the serious shopper, since you can find most of the goods sold here back home. Among the exceptions is the fabulous **Toys "R" Us** flagship on Broadway and 44th Street, which even has its own full-scale Ferris wheel.

West 47th Street between Fifth and Sixth avenues is the city's famous **Diamond District.** The street is lined shoulder-to-shoulder with showrooms; and you'll be wheeling and dealing with the largely Hasidic dealers, who offer quite a juxtaposition to the crowds.

FIFTH AVENUE & 57TH STREET

The heart of Manhattan retail ranges up Fifth Avenue to 57th Street and across. **Tiffany & Co.,** which has long reigned supreme, sits a stone's throw from **NIKETOWN, the NBA Store,** and the huge **Louis Vuitton** flagship at the corner of 57th Street and Fifth Avenue. In addition, a good number of mainstream retailers, such as **Banana Republic,** have flagships along Fifth, shifting the breadth of higher-end shopping to Madison Avenue north of 59th Street. You will find a number of big-name, big-ticket designers radiating from the crossroads, including **Versace, Chanel, Dior,** and **Cartier.** You'll also find big-name jewelers here, as well as grand old department stores such as **Bergdorf Goodman, Henri Bendel,** and **Saks Fifth Avenue**—all Fifth Avenue mainstays that must at least be browsed, even if your budget won't allow for more than longing glances.

A few blocks east on Lexington is the world's flagship **Bloomingdale's,** 1000 Third Ave. (Lexington Ave. at 59th St.; ✆ 212/705-2000; www.bloomingdales.com) and a great place to shop.

MADISON AVENUE

Madison Avenue from 57th to 79th streets boasts the most expensive retail real estate in the world. Bring lots of plastic. This ultra-deluxe strip—particularly in the high 60s—is home to *the* most luxurious designer boutiques, with **Barneys New York** as the anchor. Don't be intimidated by the glamour or any of the celebrities you're likely to bump into. There are affordable treasures to be had, such as the Ginger Flower room spray at **Shanghai Tang** (714 Madison Ave.; ✆ 212/888-0111) or a pair of crystal cufflinks at the **Lalique** boutique next door at 712 Madison Ave. (✆ 212/355-6550).

UPPER WEST SIDE

The Upper West Side's best shopping street is **Columbus Avenue.** Small shops catering to the neighborhood's white-collar mix of young hipsters and families line both sides of the pleasant avenue from 66th Street (where you'll find an excellent branch of **Barnes & Noble**) to about 86th Street. Highlights include **Maxilla & Mandible** for museum-quality natural-science-based gifts and **Harry's Shoes,** but you won't lack for browsing along here. **The Shops at Columbus Circle,** which is also a mall, albeit one of the most upscale around, with some of the city's top restaurants, and retailers ranging from Armani to Coach to a Whole Foods Market.

5

New York City After Dark

For the latest, most comprehensive nightlife listings, from theater and performing-arts to live rock, jazz, and dance-club coverage, *Time Out New York* (www.timeoutny.com) is my favorite weekly source; a new issue comes out every Thursday. The free weekly *Village Voice* (www.villagevoice.com), is available late Tuesday downtown and early Wednesday in the rest of the city. Just about every live-music venue advertises here. The **New York Times** *(www. nytoday.com) features terrific entertainment coverage, particu*-larly in the two-part Friday "Weekend" section. Other great sources are the **New Yorker** (www.newyorker.com), in its "Goings on About Town" section; **New York** magazine (www.nymag.com) features the latest happenings in its "The Week" section.

Bar-hoppers shouldn't pass up *Shecky's New York Bar, Club & Lounge Guide,* printed annually. The website (**www.sheckys.com**) is offers updated nightlife news at the click of a button.

1 The Theater Scene

Nobody does theater better than New York. No other city—not even London—has a theater scene with so much breadth and depth, with so many wide-open alternatives. Broadway, of course, gets the most ink and the most airplay, and deservedly so. It's where you'll find the big stage productions, from crowd-pleasing warhorses like *The Lion King* to more recent hits like *Jersey Boys*. But today's scene is thriving beyond the bounds of just Broadway—smaller, "alternative" theater has taken hold of the popular imagination, too. With bankable stars onstage, crowds lining up for hot tickets, and hits popular enough to generate major-label cast albums, Off-Broadway isn't just for culture vultures anymore. (And Off-Off-Broadway is the cheapest theater in town, usually under $20 a ticket.)

I can't tell you precisely what will be on while you're in town, so check the publications listed at the start of this chapter or the websites listed in "Online Sources for Theatergoers & Performing-Arts Fans," to get an idea of what you might like to see. Another source is the **Broadway Line** (© **888/BROADWAY;** www.live broadway.com), where you can get details on current Broadway shows, hear about special offers and discounts, and choose to be transferred to Telecharge or Ticketmaster to buy tickets. The recorded service **NYC/Onstage** (© **212/768-1818;** www.tdf.org) provides the same kind of info for Broadway and Off-Broadway.

WHEN YOU ARRIVE

Once you arrive in the city, getting your hands on tickets can take some street smarts—and failing those; cold, hard cash. Even if it seems unlikely that seats are available, always **call or visit the box office** first. Single seats are often easiest to obtain, so people willing to sit apart from each other may find themselves in luck.

You can also try the **Broadway Ticket Center,** run by the League of American Theatres and Producers (the same people behind Live-Broadway.com) at the Times Square Visitors Center, 1560 Broadway, between 46th and 47th streets (Mon–Sat 10am–6pm; Sun 10am–3pm; hours subject to seasonal changes). They often have tickets available for otherwise sold-out shows, both for advance and same-day purchase, and only charge about $5 extra per ticket.

Even if saving money isn't an issue for you, check the boards at the **TKTS Booth** in Times Square; more on that can be found under "Reduced-Price Ticket Deals," below.

In addition, your **hotel concierge** may be able to arrange tickets. These are usually purchased through a broker and a premium will be attached, but they're usually good seats and you can count on them being legitimate. (A $20 tip to the concierge for this service is reasonable—perhaps more if the tickets are for a very hot show. By the time you've paid this tip, you might come out better by contacting a broker or ticket agency yourself.) If you want to deal with a licensed broker, **Keith Prowse & Co.** has an office at 234 W. 44th St., between Seventh and Eighth avenues, Suite 1000 (© **800/669-8687;** Mon–Sat 9am–8pm; Sun noon–7pm).

If you buy from one of the **scalpers** in front of the theater, you're taking a risk. They may be legitimate—a couple from the 'burbs whose companions couldn't make it for the evening, say—but they could also be swindlers passing off fakes. It's a risk not worth taking.

One preferred **insiders' trick** is to make the rounds of Broadway theaters at about 6pm, when unclaimed house seats are made available. These tickets—reserved for VIPs, friends of the cast, the press, and so forth—offer great locations and are sold at face value.

Also, **Monday** is often a good day to cop big-name show tickets. Though most theaters are dark on that day, some sought-after choices aren't. Locals are at home on the first night of the work week, so all the odds are in your favor. Your chances will always be better on weeknights, or for Wednesday matinees, rather than weekends.

REDUCED-PRICE TICKET DEALS

You may be able to purchase **reduced-price theater tickets** in advance over the phone (or in person at the box office) by joining one or more of the online theater clubs. Membership is free and can garner you discounts of up to 50% on select Broadway and Off-Broadway shows. For further details, see "Online Resources for Theatergoers & Performing-Arts Fans," below.

Broadway shows—even blockbusters—sometimes have a limited number of cheaper tickets set aside for students and seniors, or drawn by lottery before each show; call the box office to inquire.

The best deal in town on same-day tickets for Broadway and Off-Broadway shows is at the **Times Square Theatre Centre,** better known as the **TKTS** booth run by the non-profit Theatre Development Fund. A fancy new TKTS booth was scheduled to (finally!) reopen in Duffy Square, October 2008. The new booth is set to open by the end of 2008. It's open 3–8pm for evening performances, 10am–2pm for Wed and Sat matinees, from 11am–8pm on Sun for all performances.

Tickets for that day's performances are usually offered at half price, with a few reduced 25%, plus a $2.50-per-ticket service charge. Boards outside the ticket windows list available shows; you're unlikely to find the newest hit, but most other shows turn up. Only cash and traveler's checks are accepted (no credit cards). There's often a huge line, so show up early for best availability and be prepared to wait. Visit **www.tdf.org** or call **NYC/Onstage** at ℂ **212/768-1818** and press "8" for the latest TKTS information.

ONLINE RESOURCES FOR THEATERGOERS & PERFORMING ARTS FANS

Some of your best, most comprehensive, and up-to-date information sources for what's going on about town are in cyberspace.

Broadway.com (**www.broadway.com**), **Playbill Online** (**www. playbill.com** or www.playbillclub.com), and **TheaterMania** (**www. theatermania.com**)—offer lots of information on Broadway and

Off-Broadway shows, with links to buy tickets. Each offers an **online theater club** that's free to join and can yield substantial discounts—as much as 50%—on advance-purchase theater tickets for some shows. You can also sign up for their regular email blasts.

For information on Broadway shows, visit **LiveBroadway.com** (**www.livebroadway.com**), the official website of Broadway, sponsored by the League of American Theatres and Producers.

2 Performing Arts: Major Concert Halls & Companies

Apollo Theater *(★ (Moments)* Built in 1914, this legendary Harlem theater launched or abetted the careers of countless musical icons—including Bessie Smith, Billie Holiday, Dinah Washington, Duke Ellington, Ella Fitzgerald, Sarah Vaughan, Count Basie, and Aretha Franklin. Thousands lined the streets in December of 2006 to pay their last respects to the Godfather of Soul on the Apollo stage, the place where he performed some of the greatest shows of all time. Currently, there's a $65-million restoration project going on, which should be completed by 2009. The first phase—refurbishing the terra-cotta facade, a new box office, and a high-tech marquee retaining the original 1940s style and features—was unveiled in 2005. The theater remains open during the renovations and is still internationally renowned for its African-American acts of all musical genres, from hip-hop to Wynton Marsalis's "Jazz for Young People" events. Wednesday's "Amateur Night at the Apollo" is a loud, fun-filled night that draws in young talent from all over the country with high hopes of making it big. 253 W. 125th St. (btwn Adam Clayton Powell and Frederick Douglass boulevards). *©* **212/531-5300** or 212/531-5301. www.apollo theater.com. Subway: 1 to 125th St.

Brooklyn Academy of Music *(Finds)* BAM is the city's most renowned contemporary-arts institution, presenting cutting-edge theater, opera, dance, and music. Offerings have included historically informed presentations of baroque opera by William Christie and Les Arts Florissants; pop opera from Lou Reed; Marianne Faithfull singing the music of Kurt Weill; dance by Mark Morris and Mikhail Baryshnikov; the Royal Dramatic Theater of Sweden directed by Ingmar Bergman; and many more experimental works by renowned and lesser-known artists as well as companies from all over.

Of particular note is the **Next Wave Festival,** September through December, this country's foremost showcase for new experimental works. The **BAM Rose Cinemas** show first-run independent films, and there's free live music every Thursday, Friday, and Saturday night at **BAMcafé,** which can range from electronica by cornetist Graham Haynes to radical jazz from the Harold Rubin Trio to the tango band Tanguardia! 30 Lafayette Ave. (off Flatbush Ave.), Brooklyn. ✆ 718/636-4100. www.bam.org. Subway: 2, 3, 4, 5, M, N, Q, R, W to Pacific St./Atlantic Ave.

Carnegie Hall ✸✸   Perhaps the world's most famous performance space (How *do* you get there?), Carnegie Hall offers everything from grand classics to the music of Ravi Shankar. The **Isaac Stern Auditorium,** the 2,804-seat main hall, welcomes orchestras from across the country and the world. Many of the world's premier soloists and ensembles give recitals. The legendary hall is both visually and acoustically brilliant; don't miss an opportunity to experience it if there's something on that interests you.

There's also the intimate 268-seat **Weill Recital Hall,** usually used to showcase chamber music and vocal and instrumental recitals. Carnegie Hall has also, after being occupied by a movie theater for 38 years, reclaimed the ornate underground 650-seat **Zankel Concert Hall.** 881 Seventh Ave. (at 57th St.). ✆ 212/247-7800. www.carnegiehall. org. Subway: N, Q, R, W to 57th St.

Lincoln Center for the Performing Arts   New York is the world's premier performing-arts city, and Lincoln Center is its premier

---

Lincoln Center Renovates for its 50th

The massive performing arts complex is turning 50 in 2009, and marking the anniversary with renovations that will add new performing spaces, a restaurant, visitor center, and redesign its open spaces. **Alice Tully Hall** is closed for an 18-month renovation (it will reopen in 2009). Construction has also blocked off some of the entrances and public spaces, and may displace some of the companies for all or part of their 2008–09 seasons. For a description of the entire project, complete with videos, timelines and illustrations of what it will all look like, visit **www.lincolncenter.org/load_screen.asp? screen=transforming**. You can also call ✆ **212/LINCOLN** for current prerecorded information and speak to a live person by calling Customer Service at ✆ **212/875-5456,** Monday through Friday from 9am to 8pm.

Jazz at Lincoln Center: Not Actually at Lincoln Center

Jazz at Lincoln Center can be found a few blocks south at the Time Warner Center at Broadway and 60th Street on Columbus Circle (℗ 212/258-9800; www.jalc.org). Though the move was downtown, it was definitely a move up. The complex on the fourth floor of Time Warner's northern tower features two performance spaces, a jazz club, a mini jazz Hall of Fame, and a 7,000-square-foot atrium with views of Central Park. The largest venue is the **Rose Theater,** where you might see the Lincoln Center Jazz Orchestra, led by Wynton Marsalis, performing the swing music of Thad Jones. Acoustics are perfect and seating is spacious. The glittering jewel of the Center is the **Allen Room** with its 4,500-square-foot glass backdrop behind the main stage offering views of Central Park and the Manhattan night sky. It's hard to believe that what was once played in smoky basements is now presented in venues as spectacular and opulent as these.

Also at Jazz at Lincoln Center is **Dizzy's Club Coca-Cola** (℗ 212/258-9595; p. 179), a stylish, intimate jazz club that's open every day.

institution. Whenever you're planning an evening's entertainment, check the offerings here—which can include opera, dance, symphonies, jazz, theater, film, and more, from the classics to the contemporary. Lincoln Center's many buildings serve as permanent homes to their own companies as well as major stops for world-class performance troupes from around the globe.

Resident companies include the **Metropolitan Opera** (℗ 212/362-6000; www.metopera.org), with its full production of the classic repertory and a schedule packed with world-class grand sopranos and tenors; the Metropolitan Opera ranks first in the world.

The opera house also hosts the **American Ballet Theatre** (www.abt.org) each spring as well as visiting companies such as the Kirov, Royal, and Paris Opera ballets.

The **New York State Theater** (℗ 212/870-5570) is the home of the **New York City Opera** (www.nycopera.com) a superb company, that not only attempts to reach a wider audience than the Met with its more "human" scale and lower prices, but is also committed to new productions of classics, new work, and occasional avant-garde work.

Symphony-wise, you'd be hard pressed to do better than the phenomenal **New York Philharmonic** ★ (℃ **212/875-5656;** www. newyorkphilharmonic.org) performing at Avery Fisher Hall.

Other resident companies include: the **Chamber Music Society of Lincoln Center** (℃ **212/875-5788;** www.chambermusicsociety. org), which performs at Alice Tully Hall or the Daniel and Joanna S. Rose Rehearsal Studio; the **Film Society of Lincoln Center** (℃ **212/875-5600;** www.filmlinc.com), which screens a daily schedule of movies at the Walter Reade Theater and hosts annual film and video festivals as well as the Reel to Real program for kids, pairing silent screen classics with live performance; and the **Lincoln Center Theater** (℃ **212/362-7600;** www.lct.org), which consists of the Vivian Beaumont Theater, a modern venue with great sightlines that has been home to much good Broadway drama, and the Mitzi E. Newhouse Theater, a well-respected Off-Broadway house that has also boasted numerous triumphs.

Most of the companies' **major seasons** run from about September or October to April, May, or June. **Special series** like Great Performers and the new American Songbook, showcasing classic American show tunes, help round out the calendar. Indoor and outdoor events are held in warmer months: Summer kicks off with the **JVC Jazz Festival** in June; July sees **Midsummer Night's Swing,** with partner dancing, lessons, and music on the plaza; August's **Mostly Mozart** attracts talents like Alicia de Larrocha and André Watts; **Lincoln Center Festival** celebrates the best of the performing arts; **Lincoln Center Out-of-Doors** is a series of free alfresco music and dance performances; there's also the **New York Film Festival,** and more. Check the "New York City Calendar of Events" section in chapter 1, or Lincoln Center's website to see what special events will be on while you're in town.

Lincoln Center is also home to the **New York Public Library for the Performing Arts** (℃ **212/870-1630;** www.nypl.org), which is now reopened after a major renovation.

Offered daily, 1-hour **guided tours** of Lincoln Center tell the story of the great performing-arts complex, and even offer glimpses of rehearsals; call ℃ **212/875-5350.** 70 Lincoln Center Plaza (at Broadway & 64th St.). ℃ **212/546-2656** or 212/875-5456. www.lincolncenter.org. Subway: 1 to 66th St.

Madison Square Garden   U2, Springsteen, the Stones, Santana, and other monsters of rock and pop regularly fill this 20,000-seat arena, which is also home to pro sports teams such as the Knicks, the Rangers, and the Liberty. A cavernous concrete hulk, it's better

Moments A Midsummer's Night in Central Park

Shakespeare in the Park, a New York institution since 1957, is as much a part of a New York summer as fireworks on the Fourth of July. The outdoor free event at the open-air Delacorte Theater in Central Park was the brainchild of the late Joseph Papp, who founded the Public Theater. Each summer usually features a revival of a Shakespeare play featuring a large company, including at least one or more "names" from film or television. The 2008 slate featured *Hamlet* and that other Shakspearean classic rock musical (I'm kidding) *Hair*. Productions run from June to early September. Depending on the star power, tickets can be quite scarce.

The Delacorte Theater, next to Belvedere Castle near 79th Street and West Drive, is a dream—on a starry night, there's no better stage in town. Tickets are distributed at the theater free on a first-come, first-served basis (two per person) at 1pm on the day of the performance. The Delacorte might have 1,881 seats, but each is a hot commodity; whatever the show, people line up next to the theater 2 to 3 hours in advance (even earlier if a big name is involved). You can also pick up same-day tickets between 1 and 3pm at the Public Theater, at 425 Lafayette St. For more information, call the Public Theater at ✆ **212/539-8500** or the Delacorte at ✆ **212/535-4284**, or visit **www.public theater.org**.

Free concerts by the **New York Philharmonic** and the **Metropolitan Opera** are held under the stars on Central Park's Great Lawn and in parks throughout the five boroughs. For schedules, call the Philharmonic at ✆ **212/875-5656** or the Metropolitan Opera at ✆ **212/362-6000**. The Philharmonic lists its upcoming gigs at www.newyork philharmonic.org, under "Attend Concerts."

suited to sports than to concerts, or in-the-round events such as the Ice Capades, Ringling Bros. and Barnum & Bailey Circus. If you end up with seats in the back, you'd better have binoculars.

You'll find far better sightlines at the **Theater at Madison Square Garden,** an amphitheater-style auditorium with 5,600 seats. Watch for annual stagings of *The Wizard of Oz, A Christmas Carol,* and family shows such as *Sesame Street Live.* Newest at MSG is the Wamu Theater, for events such as comedy shows, the NFL and NBA Drafts and family programming.

Note that MSG's owners have announced a massive renovation project which will take place in the summers of 2009-10. For information on the changes, visit **http://msg.com/renovation**.

The box office is at Seventh Avenue and 32nd Street. You can purchase tickets there or through **Ticketmaster** (℗ **212/307-7171;** www.ticketmaster.com). On Seventh Ave. from 31st to 33rd sts. ℗ **212/465-MSG1.** www.thegarden.com. Subway: A, C, E, 1, 2, 3 to 34th St.

92nd Street Y–Tisch Center for the Arts *⁄Value* This generously endowed community center offers a phenomenal slate of top-rated cultural happenings, from classical to folk to jazz to world music to cabaret to lyric theater and readings. Great classical performers—Isaac Stern, Janos Starker, Nadja Salerno-Sonnenberg—give recitals here. In addition, the full concert calendar often includes luminaries such as Max Roach, John Williams, and Judy Collins; Jazz at the Y from Dick Hyman and guests; the long-standing Chamber Music at the Y series; the classical Music from the Jewish Spirit series; and regular cabaret programs. The lectures-and-literary-readings calendar is unparalleled, with featured speakers ranging from James Carville to Ralph Nader to Katie Couric to Erica Jong to Ken Burns to Elie Wiesel to Alan Dershowitz to A. S. Byatt to . . . the list goes on and on. There's a regular schedule of modern dance, through the Harkness Dance Project. Readings and lectures are usually priced between $20 and $40 for non-members, dance is usually $20, and concert tickets generally go for $15 to $50—half or a third of what you'd pay at comparable venues. A full calendar of entertainment targeted to an audience in their 20s and 30s—from poetry readings to film screenings to live music is offered at the Upper West Side community center **Makor.** 1395 Lexington Ave. (at 92nd St.). ℗ **212/415-5500.** www.92ndsty.org. Subway: 4, 5, 6 to 86th St.; 6 to 96th St. **Makor:** 35 W. 67th St. ℗ **212/601-1000.** www.makor.org. Subway: 1 to 66th St.

Radio City Music Hall *⚑* This stunning 6,200-seat Art Deco theater, with interior design by Donald Deskey, opened in 1932, and Radio City continues to be a choice venue, where the theater alone adds a dash of panache to any performance. Star of the Christmas season is the **Radio City Music Hall Christmas Spectacular,** starring the Rockettes. Visiting pop-chart toppers, from Neil Young to the Gipsy Kings, also perform here. Thanks to perfect acoustics and uninterrupted sightlines, there's hardly a bad seat in the house. The theater also hosts dance performances; family entertainment; a number of annual awards shows, such as the Essence Awards, the GQ Man of the Year Awards, and anything MTV is holding in town. 1260 Sixth Ave. (at 50th St.). ☎ **212/247-4777**, or 212/307-7171 for Ticketmaster. www.radiocity.com or www.ticketmaster.com. Subway: B, D, F, V to 49th–50th sts./Rockefeller Center.

3 Live Rock, Jazz, Blues & More

Arlene's Grocery This casual Lower East Side club boasts a friendly bar and a good sound system; unfortunately, music isn't always free anymore, but the quality of the artists is usually pretty high, and the cover usually tops out at $7. Arlene's Grocery primarily serves as a showcase for bands looking for a deal or promoting their own CDs. The crowd is an easygoing mix of club-hoppers, rock fans, and industry scouts looking for new blood. Monday nights the club hosts the popular "Hard Rock Karaoke," which is exactly what it sounds like. 95 Stanton St. (btwn Ludlow and Orchard sts.). ☎ **212/995-1652**. www.arlenesgrocery.net. Subway: F to Second Ave.

B.B. King Blues Club & Grill This 550-seat venue is one of the prime anchors of Times Square's "new" 42nd Street. Despite its name, B.B. King's seldom sticks to the blues; what you're likely to find instead is a bill of pop, funk, and rock names, mainly from the past. The big-ticket talent runs the gamut from George Clinton and the P. Funk All Stars and John Mayall and the Bluesbreakers to Tower of Power to Jimmy Cliff and Delbert McClinton. Tourist-targeted pricing makes for an expensive night, and word is that the food isn't as good as it was in the beginning, but there's no arguing with the quality of the talent. The Sunday gospel lunch is a slice of joy. 237 W. 42nd St. (btwn Seventh and Eighth aves.). ☎ **212/997-4144**, or 212/307-7171 for tickets. www.bbkingblues.com. Subway: A, C, E, Q, W, 1, 2, 3, 7, 9 to 42nd St.

Blue Note The Blue Note has attracted some of the biggest names in jazz to its intimate setting. Those who've played here include just about everyone of note: Dave Brubeck, Ray Charles, B.B. King, Manhattan Transfer, Dr. John, George Duke, Chick Corea, David Sanborn, Arturo Sandoval, Gato Barbieri, and the superb Ahmad Jamal. The sound system is excellent, and every seat in the house has a sightline to the stage. However, in recent years, the hard edge that once was the Blue Note has faded. Softer, smoother jazz is the domain now, so if that's your thing, enjoy. ***But be warned:*** Prices are astronomical. There are two shows per night, and dinner is served. 131 W. 3rd St. (at Sixth Ave.). ℭ 212/475-8592. www.bluenote.net. Subway: A, B, C, D, E, F, V to W. 4th St.

Bowery Ballroom   Run by the same people behind the **Mercury Lounge** (see below), the Bowery space is bigger, accommodating a crowd of 500 or so. The stage is big and raised to allow good sight-lines from every side. The sound couldn't be better, and Art Deco details give the place a sophistication that doesn't come easy to general-admission halls. The balcony has its own bar and seating alcoves. This place is a favorite with alt-rockers as well as more established acts (Neil Finn, Patti Smith, Joan Jett & the Blackhearts), who thrive in an intimate setting. Save on the service charge by buying advance tickets at Mercury's box office. 6 Delancey St. (at Bowery). ℭ 212/533-2111. www.boweryballroom.com. Subway: F to Delancey St.; J, M, Z to Bowery.

Dizzy's Club Coca-Cola ℛ   This beautiful, cozy jazz club is part of the Jazz at Lincoln Center complex in the Time Warner Center on Columbus Circle. Acoustics and sightlines are excellent and, though not nearly as dramatic as the window in the complex's Allen Room, there is a window behind the stage with views of Central Park and the city. The club attracts an interesting mix of both up-and-coming and established bands. Every Monday the club features the Upstarts, a student showcase from local schools including Juilliard and the Manhattan School of Music. My only complaint is the high $30 cover every day of the week—even for the Upstarts. Time Warner Center, 60th St. and Broadway. ℭ 212/258-9595. www.jalc.org. Subway: A, B, C, D, 1, 9 to Columbus Circle.

The Filmore New York at Irving Plaza   This high-profile mid-size music hall is the prime stop for national name rock bands that aren't quite big enough yet (or anymore) to sell out Hammerstein, Roseland, or the Beacon. Think Five for Fighting, the Eels, Jars of Clay, Badly Drawn Boy, the Reverend Horton Heat, the resurrected Television, and Cheap Trick. From time to time, big-name artists also perform—Bob Dylan, Prince, Patti Smith, and A. J. McLean of the Backstreet Boys have all played "secret" shows here. It's a very nice place to see a show, with a well-elevated stage and lots of open space even on sold-out nights. There's an upstairs balcony that offers unparalleled views, but come early for a spot. 17 Irving Place (1 block west of Third Ave. at 15th St.). ℭ 212/777-1224 or 212/777-6800. www.irvingplaza.com. Subway: L, N, Q, R, W, 4, 5, 6 to 14th St./Union Sq.

The Knitting Factory   New York's premier avant-garde music venue has four separate spaces, each showcasing performances ranging from experimental jazz and acoustic folk to spoken word and poetry readings to out-there multimedia works. Regulars who use the Knitting Factory as their lab of choice include former Lounge Lizard John Lurie; around-the-bend experimentalist John Zorn; guitar gods Vernon Reid, Eliot Sharp, and David Torn; innovative sideman (to Tom Waits and Elvis Costello, among others) Marc Ribot; and Television's Richard Lloyd. The schedule is peppered with edgy star turns from the likes of Yoko Ono, Taj Mahal, Faith No More's Mike Patton, and Lou Reed. There are often two showtimes a night in the pleasing main performance space, so it's easy to work a show around other activities. The Old Office Lounge offers an extensive list of microbrews and free live entertainment. 74 Leonard St. (btwn Broadway & Church St.). © **212/219-3132**. www.knittingfactory.com. Subway: 1 to Franklin St.

Mercury Lounge   The Merc is everything a top-notch live-music venue should be: unpretentious, civilized, and outfitted with a killer sound system. The rooms themselves are nothing special: a front bar and an intimate back-room performance space with a low stage and a few tables along the wall. The calendar is filled with a mix of accomplished local rockers and such national acts as Fat Possum, the Mekons, and Sleepy Jackson. The crowd is grown-up and easygoing. The only downside is that it's consistently packed thanks to the high quality of the entertainment and all-around pleasing nature of the experience. 217 E. Houston St. (at Essex St./Ave. A). © **212/260-4700**. www.mercuryloungenyc.com. Subway: F to Second Ave.

Smoke 🌟🌟 *Value*   A superstar in the New York jazz scene and the best place to hear it on the Upper West Side, Smoke is a welcome throwback to the informal, intimate clubs of the past—the kind of place that on most nights you can just walk in and experience solid jazz. And though it seats only 65, for no more than a $30 cover, Smoke still manages to attract such big names as the Steve Turre Quartet, Ron Carter, Eddie Henderson, and John Hicks. Sunday through Thursday there is no cover. On Sundays, the club features Latin jazz; every Tuesday it's B3 grooves and soul jazz, and Wednesdays features world jazz. There are three sets nightly, an affordable menu, and a very popular happy hour. 2751 Broadway (btwn 105th and 106th sts.). © **212/864-6662**. www.smokejazz.com. Subway: 1 to 103rd St.

S.O.B.'s   If you like your music hot, hot, hot, visit S.O.B.'s, the city's top world-music venue, specializing in Brazilian, Caribbean, and Latin sounds. The packed house dances and sings along nightly to calypso, samba, mambo, African drums, reggae, or other global grooves, united in the high-energy, feel-good vibe. Bookings include top-flight performers from around the globe; Astrud Gilberto, Mighty Sparrow, King Sunny Ade, Eddie Palmieri, Buckwheat Zydeco, Beausoleil, and Baaba Maal are only a few of the names who have graced this lively stage. The room's Tropicana Club style has island pizazz that carries through to the Caribbean-influenced cooking and extensive tropical drinks menu. This place is so popular that it's an excellent idea to book in advance, especially if you'd like table seating. Monday is dedicated to Latin sounds, Tuesday to reggae, Friday features a late-night French Caribbean dance party, while Saturday is reserved for samba. 204 Varick St. (at Houston St.). © **212/243-4940.** www.sobs.com. Subway: 1 to Houston St.

Uptown Jazz Lounge at Minton's Playhouse 🕏 *(Finds* The big neon sign on 118th Street remains intact and is a cultural landmark. The 1948-mural behind the stage of a woman sleeping off a drunk while four musicians jam by her side looks as fresh as it ever did even after a 30-year hiatus while Minton's Playhouse was shuttered. In 2006, the club, where Miles Davis, Charlie Christian, Dizzy Gillespie, Coleman Hawkins, and house pianist, Thelonius Monk once reigned, reopened. The look is sparse; a few photos cover the burnt orange walls; hard-backed chairs and formica-topped tables are scattered around the small room. But who cares? The music is straight-ahead jazz and the clientele is old school Harlem along with European and Japanese tourists. At press time, Patience Higgins and the Sugar Hill Quartet hold court every Wednesday, while Thursday headlines vocalist Gerald Hayes and the Qualified Gents. No cover Monday through Thursday. 208 W. 118th St (between St. Nicholas Ave. and Adam Clayton Powell Blvd.). © **212/864-8346.** www.uptownatmintons.com. Subway: B, C to 116th St.

The Village Vanguard 🕏🕏 What CBGB was to rock, The Village Vanguard is to jazz. One look at the photos on the walls will show you who's been through since 1935, from Coltrane, Miles, and Monk to recent appearances by Bill Charlap and Roy Hargrove. Expect a mix of established names and high-quality local talent, including the Vanguard's own jazz orchestra on Monday nights. The sound is great, but sightlines aren't, so come early for a front table. If you're looking for serious jazz, this is the place. 178 Seventh Ave. South (just below 11th St.). © **212/255-4037.** www.villagevanguard.net. Subway: 1, 2, 3, 9 to 14th St.

4 Cabaret

Cafe Carlyle ★ Cabaret doesn't get any better than this. This is where the late, great Bobby Short, held court for 35 years. The club still attracts rarefied talents such as Betty Buckley and Barbara Cook. The room is intimate and as swanky as they come. Expect a high tab—admission is $65 to $75 with a $30 per-person minimum; with dinner, two people could easily spend $300—but if you're looking for the best of the best, look no further. Value-minded cabaret fans can save by reserving standing room (which usually results in a spot at the bar) for $35. On most Mondays, Woody Allen joins the Eddy Davis New Orleans Jazz Band on clarinet to swing Dixie-style ($85 cover). At the Carlyle Hotel, 35 East 76th St. (at Madison Ave.). ✆ **212/744-1600.** Closed July–Aug. Subway: 6 to 77th St.

Feinstein's at The Regency *Finds* This intimate, elegant cabaret-style nightclub is from Grammy-winning impresario Michael Feinstein. Cover charges can soar, but you can count on a memorable night of first-quality dining and song, and no other cabaret merges old-school cool and hipster appeal so well. Recent high-wattage talent has included Keely Smith, Patti LuPone, and the man himself. Call ahead to reserve; you can also purchase tickets through Ticketmaster. At the Regency Hotel, 540 Park Ave. (at 61st St.). ✆ **212/339-4095** or 212/307-4100 for Ticketmaster. www.feinsteinsattheregency.com or www.ticketmaster.com. Subway: 4, 5, 6 to 59th St.

The Oak Room Recently refurbished to recall its glory days, the Oak Room is one of the city's most intimate, elegant, and sophisticated spots for cabaret. Headliners include such first-rate talents as Andrea Marcovicci, Steve Ross, Dave Frishberg, the marvelous Julie Wilson, and cool-cat jazz guitarist John Pizzarelli, plus occasional lesser names that are destined for greatness. At the Algonquin Hotel, 59 W. 44th St. (btwn Fifth and Sixth aves.). ✆ **212/419-9331.** Closed July–Aug. Subway: B, D, F, V to 42nd St.

5 Stand-Up Comedy

Ars Nova You won't find traditional standup at this 99-seat theater. But nothing is traditional about Ars Nova, and that's the point. It's a venue for emerging artists from playwrights to cabaret acts and the comedy you'll find here, such as Viva La Diva, is of the alternative kind. 511 W. 54th St (at 10th Ave.) ✆ **212/481-9800.** www.arsnovanyc.com. Subway: B, D, E to Seventh Avenue-53rd St.

Carolines on Broadway   Caroline Hirsch presents national headliners in her upscale Theater District showroom, which doesn't have a bad seat in the house. You're bound to recognize at least one or two of the established names and hot up-and-comers any given week, like Dave Chapelle, Janeane Garofalo, Colin Quinn, Bill Bellamy, Kathy Griffin, Jimmie Walker ("Dyn-o-mite!"), Pauly Shore, or Jay Mohr. Monday is usually New Talent Night, while HOT97 radio hosts up-and-coming black comedians on select Tuesdays. 1626 Broadway (btwn 49th & 50th sts.). ✆ 212/757-4100. www.carolines.com. Subway: N, R to 49th St.; 1 to 50th St.

Comedy Cellar *Finds*   This subterranean club is the venue of choice for stand-up fans in the know, thanks to the most consistently impressive lineups in the business. I'll always love the Comedy Cellar for introducing an uproariously funny unknown named Ray Romano to me some years back. 117 MacDougal St. (btwn Bleecker & W. 3rd sts.). ✆ 212/254-3480. www.comedycellar.com. Subway: A, B, C, D, E, F, V to W. 4th St. (use 3rd St. exit).

6 Bars & Cocktail Lounges

Remember: Smoking is prohibited in bars but allowed in outdoor spaces.

DOWNTOWN

Church Lounge   The big, super-stylish Larry Bogdanow–designed atrium-lobby bar and restaurant at the Tribeca Grand Hotel is a great place to enjoy a top-flight cocktail and rub elbows with the neighborhood's chic locals (which include just about anybody who has business with Miramax). Dress well and call ahead to see what's on tap that evening if you want to experience the height of the action—around 11pm. 2 Sixth Ave. (at White & Church sts.). ✆ 212/519-6600. Subway: 1 to Franklin St.; A, C, E to Canal St.

Ear Inn *Value*   There are many debates about which is the oldest bar in New York, and with its 1870s origins, Ear Inn is a serious contender for that crown. In super-chic SoHo, this pub is a welcome cranky relief. They pull an excellent pint of Guinness and make a surprisingly good margarita as well. On Saturday afternoon the poetry readings just might make you cry into your beer. In warm weather, tables are set up outside within exhaust distance of the nearby UPS depot. *Note:* Respect the no-cellphone policy or suffer the consequences. 326 Spring St. (btwn Greenwich & Washington sts.). ✆ 212/226-9060. Subway: C, E to Spring St.

Employees Only ✪ Don't let the palm reader in the doorway of the non-descript exterior of this bar fool you; though if she reads your palm, I can guarantee she will predict that you will very soon savor a tantalizing beverage. Employees Only goes to great lengths to recreate a 1920's speakeasy with a tin ceiling and bartenders in period costume. But who needs gimmicks when the cocktails are this good? The employees have been well trained and drinks are done painstakingly and made with the freshest ingredients and top label liquors. The daiquiri I tried was so good, Hemingway would be proud. In fact, it's called the Hemingway Daiquiri. There is a full menu available, but skip the entrees and order a few of the very good appetizers, the best being the ample Serbian charcuterie platter. 510 Hudson St. (btwn Christopher and W. 10th sts.) ✆ 212/242-3021. www.employeesonlynyc.com. Subway: 1 to Christopher St.

KGB Bar This former Ukrainian social club boasts a Soviet-themed decor, and free entertainment almost every night, thanks to its excellent, eclectic reading series, where a talented pack of up-and-coming and established writers read their prose in various genres (fiction, science fiction, poetry, and so on) to a receptive crowd starting at 7pm. Past readers have included playwright Tina Howe *(Painting Churches),* Janice Erlbaum *(Girlbomb),* and Dave King *(The Ha-Ha).* 85 E. 4th St. (btwn Second & Third aves.). ✆ 212/505-3360. www.kgbbar.com. Subway: 6 to Astor Place.

Marion's Continental Formerly a gathering place for artists and musicians hosted by former model Marion Nagy in the 50s and 60s, the bar was resurrected by her son in the 1990s where it now stands as a tribute to his mother. It still serves perfect martinis and offers a campy yet comfy alternative to the overwrought East Village scene. The retro décor, with plush colorful seats, "mood" lighting, and kitschy knick knacks on the walls adds to the allure. On Thursdays, it's "Girls Night Out" at Marion's while Sunday's, it's Fondue for everyone; now that's a blast from the past. 354 Bowery (btwn Great Jones and East 4th sts.). ✆ 212/475-7621. www.marionsnyc.com. Subway: B, D, F, V to Broadway-Lafayette.

Pegu Club ✪✪ Mixologist and owner Audrey Saunders, formerly of Bemelmans Bar in the Carlyle Hotel, makes magic with cocktails. In 2005, she opened her own downtown gathering spot where she can showcase her immense talents. The cocktails here change seasonally and will astound you with their creativity. It helps that the staff uses fresh squeezed juices, homemade ginger beer and the largest assortment of bitters you will find anywhere. You know you

Tips **Whiling Away the Happy Hours**

Many of the city's best bars suddenly become more affordable from 4 to 8pm or thereabouts, when it's definitely a
happy hour if you can snag one of those signature cocktails
($14 martinis, anyone?) at half-price or two-for-one; or
maybe there's some free bar food, or another value-saving
offer. Happy hour is a great time to experience those pricey
places you've heard so much about. For information on
happy hour at many of the city's watering holes, check
www.sheckys.com or **Murph's NYC Bar Guide** at **www.
murphguide.com**, updated daily.

are in serious cocktail heaven when your drinks are served with liq-
uid condiments; your Pisco Punch needs a bit more sugar, you can
squeeze a dropperful in. Or your Gin-Gin Mule just doesn't pack the
citrus tang you would like, add a dash of lime. Unless it's salty
peanuts or pretzels, I usually disdain bar food, but for the Pegu
Club's amazing Diver scallop mini burgers and addictive smoked
trout deviled eggs, I will happily make an exception. 77 W. Houston St.
2nd Floor (at W. Broadway), *(C)* **212/473-PEGU**; www.peguclub.com. Subway: A, B,
C, D, E, F, V to W. 4th St.

Rose Bar *(R)*   I usually abhor bars that are "scenes;" where you need
to be on a list to gain entry. But what Ian Schrager and artist Julian
Schabel have created in the Gramercy Park Hotel makes going
through the various humiliations it might take to get in *almost* worth
it. The space is spectacular with rose-colored velvet chairs, original
Warhols and Schnabels on the walls, a fireplace, a red and white tile
floor, and a billiards table you will be too intimidated to approach.
Sit on one of those plush chairs, sip your $20 cocktail, enjoy the
flawless sound system commandeered by top name DJs and for a few
moments you might forget that you don't belong in this swanky,
celebrity-laden environment. Reservations (hard to get) are manda-
tory after 10pm and security is tight. 2 Lexington Ave (btwn 20th and 21st
sts.). *(C)* **212/920-3300**. Subway: 6 to 23rd St.

Temple Bar   One of the first comers to New York's lounge scene,
Temple Bar is still a gorgeous Deco hangout, with a long L-shaped
bar leading to a seating area with velvet drapes, backlighting, and
Sinatra crooning in the background. Cocktails don't get any better
than the classic martini (with just a kiss of vermouth) or the smooth-
as-peignoir-silk Manhattan (Johnnie Walker Black, sweet vermouth,

bitters). Bring a date—and feel free to invite me along. Look for the petroglyph-like lizards on the otherwise-unmarked facade. 332 Lafayette St. (just north of Houston St., on the west side of the street). © 212/925 4242. Subway: 6 to Bleecker St.

MIDTOWN

Aspen   My favorite part of a ski vacation was always sipping a soothing cocktail in the warmth of the lodge while those silly skiers took tumbles in the cold snow. Now I don't have to head to the mountains to get that warming feeling, I can snow plow downtown to Aspen where the drinks are hot, but the atmosphere—mounted Lucite deer heads, a snow white dining room, Aspen birch and original barn wood and a bar around a blazing fire—even hotter. While nursing your toddy, you can munch on a variety of western-inspired small plates. And who knows, maybe a dose of Aspen, along with a cold drink, in the dog days of August will give you cool thoughts. 30 W. 22nd St. (btwn Fifth and Sixth Aves.). © 212/645-5040. www.aspen-nyc.com. Subway: F, V to 23rd St.

The Ginger Man   The big bait at this upscale beer bar is the 66 gleaming tap handles lining the wood-and-brass bar, dispensing everything from Sierra Nevada and Hoegaarden to cask-conditioned ales. The cavernous space has a clubby feel. The Cohiba fumes were ripe here before the smoking ban but the new nonsmoking laws have not stopped the crowds from coming to this popular Murray Hill hangout. 11 E. 36th St. (btwn Fifth & Madison aves.). © 212/532-3740. Subway: 6 to 33rd St.

King Cole Bar   The birthplace of the Bloody Mary, this theatrical spot may just be New York's most historic hotel bar. The Maxfield Parrish mural alone is worth the price of a classic cocktail (ask the bartender to tell you about the "hidden" meaning of the painting). The one drawback is the bar's small size; after-work hours and holiday times, the bar is jammed. At the St. Regis, 2 E. 55th St., at Fifth Ave. © 212/744-4300. Subway: E, V to Fifth Ave.

Mickey Mantle's *Kids*   Before Mickey Mantle's opened years ago, I was walking past the restaurant, peered into the window, and there was my boyhood idol, the Mick, sitting at the bar by himself. Through the window I waved—and he waved back. It made my day. And though the food's not very good and the drinks are overpriced, I still have a soft spot for Mickey Mantle's and always will. With plenty of Yankee memorabilia on the walls and sports on all the TVs, it's an ideal place to watch a game, but stick with the basics: beer and

burgers. 42 Central Park South (btwn Fifth & Sixth aves.). © **212/688-7777.**
www.theswearingens.com/mick/mmrest.htm. Subway: F to 57th St.

Monkey Bar   This legendary bar was recently renovated and looks
better than ever. The swanky space is dolled up like a Hollywood
supper club from the 1930s, the drinks are faultless, and the legendary monkey murals alone are worth a look. Skip the dining room
and head to the piano bar for the ultimate Monkey Bar experience.
At the Hotel Elysée, 60 E. 54th St. (btwn Madison & Park aves.). © **212/838-2600.**
Subway: 6 to 51st St.

Russian Samovar ⊛   Yes it's a restaurant with Russian food, but
the main attraction of this Theater District legend is the vodka.
There are over 20 flavors of house-infused vodkas including dill, garlic, ginger, tarragon and, host and impresario Roman Kaplan's
favorite, cranberry-lemon. Despite what it might do to you and how
it will affect the plans you have for the next 24 hours, it's difficult to
resist sampling them while listening to standards played by the house
pianist. You might want to soften the bite of the vodka with a few
appetizers like the Royal Fish Platter, a selection of smoked fish and
a little caviar. Don't make this a pre-theater stop—you won't make it
to the show. 256 W. 52nd St. (btwn Eighth Ave. and Broadway). © **212/757-
0168.** www.russiansamovar.com. Subway: 1 to 50th St.

Under the Volcano (Finds   If you've been shopping at Macy's or
braving the lines at the Empire State Building and want (need?) a
drink, one of the few choices in the area, but a good one, is this Mexi-
can-themed tequila bar. The decor is Mexican folk with Frida Kahlo
undertones, but the main attractions are the 16 varieties of tequila
and smooth, potent margaritas. The bar features an excellent selection of aged rums. 12 E. 36th St. (btwn Fifth & Madison aves.). © **212/213-
0093.** Subway: B, D, F, N, R to 34th St.

UPTOWN

Bemelmans Bar   This is my choice as New York's best hotel bar.
It has everything you want from a hotel bar: white-coated service;
lush seating with dark romantic corners to sink into; a nice mix of
locals and guests; and incredible cocktails, like the Old Cuban, a
mojito topped with champagne. The bar is named after children's
book illustrator Ludwig Bemelmans, who created the *Madeline*
books after he painted the whimsical mural here. At the Carlyle Hotel, 35
E. 76th St. (at Madison Ave.). © **212/744-1600.** Subway: 6 to 77th St.

Creole   Tucked away in the heart of El Barrio (also known as east
Harlem) is a relatively new and welcome addition to the uptown

The New York Dive Experience

Not all of New York nightlife means clubs with cover charges, expensive cocktails, beautiful people, and velvet ropes. There are places that you should be rewarded for braving; old, dark places where the drinks are cheap and the characters colorful. These are dive bars and they are just as New York as their trendy counterparts. Here are some of my favorites; stop in for a New York experience.

Jimmy's Corner, 140 W. 44th St., between Broadway and Sixth Avenue (© **212/221-9510**). Owned by a former boxing trainer, Jimmy's is a tough-guy's joint that has been around for more than 30 years and survived the Disneyfication of Times Square. Pictures of boxers adorn the walls, and the jukebox plays lots of R&B and '70s disco. In the pre–smoking ban days, the smoke would get so thick in Jimmy's you needed night goggles to see through the haze. Beer is cheap and drinks aren't fancy. Skip the theme bars and restaurants in the area and go for an after-theater pop at Jimmy's instead.

Rudy's Bar & Grill, 627 Ninth Ave., between 44th and 45th streets (© **212/974-9169**). This Hell's Kitchen establishment is no secret; its happy hour is legendary and the place is usually packed with slackers sucking up cheap beer, including the house brand, Rudy's Red, a weak brew served

music scene. Creole is an intimate bar/restaurant that features top-notch jazz, Latin, R&B, and on Sunday, gospel. Sit at the bar or enjoy the music while chowing down on very good Southern/Cajun specialties—the gumbo might be the best in the city. Entertainment begins at 8:30, but you might want to venture in a little early for Creole's fun happy hour from 5 to 7pm. 2167 Third Ave. (at 118th St.). © 212/876-8838. www.creolenyc.com. Subway: 6 to 116th St.

The Den 𝄞 *Finds*   For not only the most creative cocktails north of 96th Street, but also the most imaginative drink names in all of Manhattan, come uptown to the fun, funky Den. Here you can sip concoctions like the "Pimp Slap," "Sex in the Inner City," "Bahama Baby Mama Drama," and the "Harlem Ice Tea," while watching a blaxploitation flick off the bar/restaurant's brick wall. Don't ask me in a huge plastic cup for $3. My advice is to get here before happy hour, grab a seat on one of the few broken banquettes, and keep your eyes open for the guy who gives out free hot dogs. You'll need one to balance out a bucket of Rudy's Red. In the summer, Rudy's opens its cement garden for drinks "alfresco."

Subway Inn, 143 E. 60th St., at Lexington Avenue (© 212/223-8929). My all-time favorite dive, the Subway has been around for over 60 years, and I believe some of the regulars have been on their stools the whole time. The red neon sign beckons from outside while inside, no matter what time of day, it's dark. The bartender is ancient and until recently served Schaeffer on tap. The demise of Schaeffer was troubling, but not much else has changed. The booths are still wobbly and the models of Godzilla and E.T. along with other dusty junk continue to decorate the shelves behind the bar. The last time I visited, I was barred from entering the men's room by police who were patting down one of the regulars during a drug bust. You might find workers from the upscale stores in the neighborhood and writers searching for "material" slumming at the Subway, but this joint remains the pinnacle of divedom.

what's in the drinks, just know that they are colorful, sweet, and very potent. On Saturday, the brick wall is the screen for kung fu movies, while on Wednesday, it's live old- and new-school R&B. To fortify yourself from those drinks, sample The Den's kitchen creations like the "Not ya mama's chicken and waffles," "Bruce LeeRoy's popcorn shrimp," "Mississippi Burnin' wings," or a "soul roll," The Den's take on sushi stuffed with, not raw fish, but BBQ pulled pork. 2150 Fifth Ave. (btwn 131st & 132nd sts.). © 212/234-3045. www.thedenharlem.com. Subway: 3 to 135th St.

Dublin House   For years, like a welcoming beacon, the Dublin House's neon harp has blinked invitingly. This old pub is a no-frills Irish saloon and the perfect spot for a drink after visiting the Museum of Natural History or Central Park. There's a long, narrow

Cocktails Alfresco (Who's Al Fresco?)

Food and drink always *do* taste better alfresco. Here are some of my favorite places for cocktails out of doors.

The outdoor space at rowdy **Jeremy's Ale House,** 228 Front St. (© **212/964-3537;** www.jeremysalehouse.com), near the South Street Seaport, is no fairy tale, but it does have one of the best views of the Brooklyn Bridge. Maybe that's because the bar is practically under the bridge (on the Manhattan side). Jeremy's is so close to the river you may think you smell the sea, but what you are really smelling is the calamari and clams in the deep fryers and gallons of Coors beer, which are served in 32-ounce Styrofoam cups.

Some of the best outdoor drinking can be found at a few select hotels. The best of the best, way downtown at the southern tip of Manhattan, is the **Rise Bar** ℛ at the Ritz-Carlton New York, Battery Park, 2 West St., just north of Battery Place (© **212/344-0800**). On the 14th floor of the hotel, the bar boasts incomparable views of Lady Liberty and New York Harbor from the massive waterfront terrace.

barroom up front and a bigger room in the back that's good for groups. Original wood veneer detail remains, adding to the pub's charm. The Guinness is cheap and drawn perfectly by the able and sometimes crusty bartenders. Best enjoyed in the late afternoon or early evening when the regulars populate the bar. Stay away on weekend nights and St. Patrick's Day when the place is overrun with amateurs: frat boys and sorority girls on pub crawls. 225 W. 79th St. (btwn Broadway & Amsterdam Ave.). © 212/874-9528. Subway: 1 to 79th St.

Great Hall Balcony Bar *Moments*   One of Manhattan's best cocktail bars is only open on Friday and Saturday—and only from 4 to 8:30pm. The Metropolitan Museum of Art transforms the lobby's mezzanine level into a cocktail-and–classical music lounge twice weekly, offering an only-in-New York experience. The music is provided by a grand piano and string quartet. You'll have to pay the $10 "requested contribution," but the galleries are open until 9pm. At the Metropolitan Museum of Art, Fifth Ave., at 82nd St. © 212/535-7710. www. metmuseum.org. Subway: 4, 5, 6 to 86th St.

For the more trendy set, where the eye candy is not just the spectacular views, take the elevator up to the top of the Hotel Gansevoort, 18 Ninth Ave., at 13th Street (© 212/206-6700) to **Plunge,** where the you can gaze out at New Jersey, inhale the chlorine fumes from the hotel's pool (which only guests can use), all the while sipping pricey cocktails. A few blocks north at the Maritime Hotel, 363 W. 16th St., at Ninth Avenue, the scene on the roof at **Cabanas** (© 212/242-4300) is like something out of Hollywood. In fact, you'll probably recognize a few Hollywood denizens sunning themselves with colorful drinks, umbrella stirrers and all, balanced on their abnormally firm abs. Uptown, in the heart of Midtown, the **Pen-Top Bar** at the classic grande-dame Peninsula Hotel, 700 Fifth Ave., at 55th Street (© 212/956-2888), offers views of the glittering neighboring spires and the bustle of Fifth Avenue below that are not only calming but romantic, if that is actually possible.

7 Dance Clubs & Party Scenes

New York nightlife starts late. With the exception of places that have scheduled performances, clubs stay almost empty until about 11pm. Don't depend on plastic—bring cash, and plan on dropping a wad at most places. Cover charges run anywhere from $7 to $30, and often get more expensive as the night wears on.

Cafe Wha?   You'll find a carefree crowd dancing in the aisles of this casual basement club just about any night of the week. From Wednesday through Sunday, the stage features the house's own Wha Band, which does an excellent job of cranking out crowd-pleasing covers of familiar rock-'n'-roll hits from the '70s, '80s, and '90s. Monday night is the popular Brazilian Dance Party, while Tuesday night is Classic Funk Night. On the weekends, expect to be surrounded by lots of Jersey kids and out-of-towners, but so what? Reservations are a good idea. The cover runs from free to $10. 115 MacDougal St. (btwn Bleecker & W. 3rd sts.). © 212/254-3706. www.cafewha. com. Subway: A, B, C, D, E, F, V to W. 4th St.

Cain   At Cain the theme is Africa—South Africa to be specific. The front door, if you gain entry, has elephant-trunk handles, there are zebra hides everywhere, and the big game is celebrity-spotting. The DJ's spin energetic house music to keep the hordes moving, but you might be better off sampling one of the club's excellent cocktails in the "premium seating lounge." God knows what it takes to get a seat there. 544 W. 27th St. (btwn Tenth & Eleventh aves.). ℂ 212/947-8000. Subway: C, E to 23rd St.

Cielo   At Cielo you'll find the best sound system of any small club in town. House is big here and they bring in some of the best DJs from around the globe. The renowned Louis Vega is the DJ on Wednesday. There's a sunken dance floor and an authentic, glittering disco ball rotating above. What more could you want? 18 Little W. 12th St. (btwn Ninth Ave. & Washington St. ℂ 212/645-5700. www.cieloclub.com. Subway: A, C, E, to 14th St.; L to Eighth Ave.

Club Shelter   House-heads flock to this old-school disco. The big draw is the "Saturday Night Shelter Party," when late-1980s house music takes over. The crowd is racially and sexually diverse and dress is not fancy; wear whatever is comfortable for doing some heavy sweating on the dance floor. 20 W. 39th St. (btwn Fifth & Sixth aves.). ℂ 212/719-4479. www.clubshelter.com. Subway: B, D, F, Q, V, 7 to 42nd St.

Mansion   Located in the old Crobar space and after a million-dollar renovation, this club, with a sister in Miami, opened in early 2008. The dance floor is small (meaning intimate) and the music booms with a Euro beat until 4 a.m. At press time the buzz was white hot but we know the dance crowd is fickle and that heat could fade fast. 530 W. 28th St (btwn 10th and 11th aves.). ℂ 212/629-9000. www.mansionnewyork.com. Subway: C, E to 23rd St.

Pacha   No, you are not on exotic Ibiza, but in Hell's Kitchen, New York. But enter Pacha and wade through the club's four levels, marvel at the palm trees, ogle discreetly the bikini-clad gogo girls dancing in the red-lit showers and you'll for a few hours be transported somewhere a little less hellish than Hell's Kitchen. 618 W. 46th St (btwn 11th Ave and the West Side Hwy.). ℂ 212/209-7500. www.pachany.com. Subway: A, C, E, 7 to 42nd St.

13 _Value_   This little lounge is a great place to dance the night away. It's stylish but unpretentious, with a roster of fun weekly parties. Sunday night's Britpop fest Shout! lives on, as popular as ever—and with no cover. The rest of the week runs the gamut from '70s and

'80s New Wave and glam nights to progressive house and trance to poetry slams and performance art. If there's a cover, it's usually $5, occasionally $7 or $10. Happy hour offers two-for-one drinks (no cover) from 4 to 8pm. 35 E. 13th St. (btwn Broadway and University Place), 2nd floor. ✆ 212/979-6677. www.bar13.com. Subway: 4, 5, 6, L, N, R, Q, W to 14th St./Union Sq.

8 The Gay & Lesbian Scene

To get a thorough, up-to-date take on what's happening in GLBT nightlife, grab a copy of *HX* (www.hx.com), *Gay City News* (www.gaycitynews.com), the *New York Blade* (www.nyblade.com), *GONYC* (www.gomag.com) or *Next.* They're available for free in bars and clubs all around town or at the **Lesbian and Gay Community Center,** at 208 W. 13th St., between Seventh and Eighth avenues (✆ **212/620-7310;** www.gaycenter.org).

Barracuda   Chelsea is central to gay life—and gay bars. This trendy, loungey place is a continuing favorite, regularly voted "Best Bar" by *HX* readers, while *Paper* singles out the hunky bartenders. There's a sexy bar for cruising out front and a comfy lounge in back. Look for the regular drag shows. 275 W. 22nd St. (btwn Seventh and Eighth aves.). ✆ **212/645-8613.** Subway: C, E, 1 to 23rd St.

Boiler Room   This down-to-earth East Village bar is everybody's favorite gay dive. Despite the mixed guy-girl crowd, it's a serious cruising scene for well-sculpted beautiful boys and a perfectly fine hangout for those who'd rather play pool. 86 E. 4th St. (btwn First and Second aves.). ✆ **212/254-7536.** Subway: F to Second Ave.

The Cubby Hole   They call it a fusion bar, but chicks know it as a longtime lesbian hangout/watering hole. It's small, but rather than detract from its appeal, it's size only adds to it. Look for drink specials every night, from Bloody Marys to Pomegranate Martinis. 281 W. 12th St (at W. 4th St) ✆ **212/243-9041.** www.cubbyholebar.com. Subway: A, C, E, L to 14th St.

Splash/SBNY   Beautiful bartenders, video screens, New York's best drag queens—Splash has it all. Theme nights are a big deal. The best is Musical Mondays, dedicated to Broadway video clips and music. Musical Mondays' singalongs are a blast. 50 W. 17th St. (btwn Fifth and Sixth aves.). ✆ **212/691-0073.** www.splashbar.com. Subway: F, V to 14th St.; 4, 5, 6, L, N, Q, R, W to 14th St./Union Sq.

Cross over to Cattyshack in Brooklyn

In Park Slope (aka "Dyke Slope") NYC's favorite lesbian bar is **Cattyshack** ☆ (249 Fourth Ave., between Carroll and President sts.; © 718/230-5740; www.cattyshackbklyn. com; Subway: R to Union St.; F to Fourth Ave./9th St.).

The two-level club offers several kinds of ambience, ranging from casual pool playing, beer sipping, and TV watching downstairs to upstairs dance parties where DJs play all genres of music, frequently featuring go-go girls.

Theme nights are popular, with regularly scheduled trivia contests, country nights, Guitar Hero competitions, and (of course) *The L Word* viewing parties and events.

On Sundays there's all-you-can-eat pizza and beer during football season (and after). In good weather, everyone heads for the back patio, where a weekly barbecue/beer bust (with vegetarian selections!) draws crowds all summer.

Stonewall Bar   Where it all began. A mixed gay and lesbian crowd—old and young, beautiful, and great personalities—makes this an easy place to begin. At least pop in to relive a defining moment in queer history. 53 Christopher St. (east of Seventh Ave.). © 212/463-0950. Subway: 1 to Christopher St.

Appendix: Fast Facts: New York City

American Express Travel-service offices are at many Manhattan locations, including 295 Park Avenue South at 23rd Street (℄ **212/691-9797**); at the New York Marriott Marquis, 1535 Broadway, in the eighth-floor lobby (℄ **212/575-6580**); on the mezzanine level at Macy's Herald Square, 34th Street and Broadway (℄ **212/695-8075**); and 374 Park Ave., at 53rd Street (℄ **212/421-8240**). Call ℄ **800/AXP-TRIP**, or check **www.americanexpress.com** for other locations or information.

Area Codes There are four area codes in the city: two in Manhattan, **212** and **646;** and two in the outer boroughs, the original **718** and the new **347.** Also common is the **917** area code, which is assigned to cellphones, pagers, and the like. All calls between these area codes are local calls, but you'll have to dial 1 + the area code + the seven digits for all calls, even ones made within your area code.

Business Hours In general, **retail stores** are open Monday through Saturday from 10am to 6 or 7pm, Thursday from 10am to 8:30 or 9pm, and Sunday from noon to 5pm (see chapter 8). **Banks** tend to be open Monday through Friday from 9am to 5pm, with many open Saturday mornings, and some even open on Sundays.

Doctors For medical emergencies requiring immediate attention, head to the nearest emergency room (see "Hospitals," below). For less urgent health problems, New York has several walk-in medical centers, such as **DOCS at New York Healthcare,** 55 E. 34th St., between Park and Madison avenues (℄ **212/252-6001**), for non-emergency illnesses, and 202 W. 23rd, at Seventh Avenue ℄ **212/352-2600**. The clinic, affiliated with Beth Israel Medical Center, is open Monday through Friday from 8am to 7pm, Saturday from 9am to 1pm, and Sunday from 9am to 1pm. The **NYU Downtown Hospital** offers physician referrals at ℄ **212/312-5800**.

Drinking Laws The minimum legal age to purchase and consume alcoholic beverages in New York is 21. Liquor and wine are sold only in licensed stores, which are open 6 days a week, with some choosing to close on Sunday, others on an early or midweek day. (You can usually find an open liquor store on Sundays). Liquor stores are closed on holidays and election days while the polls are open. Beer can be purchased in grocery stores and delis 24 hours a day, except Sunday before noon. Last call in bars is at 4am, though many close earlier.

Electricity   Like Canada, the United States uses 110 to 120 volts AC (60 cycles), compared to 220 to 240 volts AC (50 cycles) in most of Europe, Australia, and New Zealand. Downward converters that change 220 to 240 volts to 110 to 120 volts are difficult to find in the United States, so bring one with you if you are coming from overseas.

Embassies & Consulates   All embassies are in Washington, D.C. Some consulates are in New York and most nations have a mission to the United Nations. If your country isn't listed, call for directory information in Washington, D.C. (© **202/555-1212**) or log on to **www.embassy.org/embassies**.

The embassy of **Australia** is at 1601 Massachusetts Ave. NW, Washington, DC 20036 (© **202/797-3000;** www.austemb.org). There is a consulate in New York City.

The embassy of **Canada** is at 501 Pennsylvania Ave. NW, Washington, DC 20001 (© **202/682-1740;** www.canadianembassy.org). There is a consulate in New York City.

The embassy of **Ireland** is at 2234 Massachusetts Ave. NW, Washington, DC 20008 (© **202/462-3939;** www.irelandemb.org). Consulates are in Boston, Chicago, New York, and San Francisco. See website for complete listing.

The embassy of the **United Kingdom** is at 3100 Massachusetts Ave. NW, Washington, DC 20008 (© **202/588-6500;** www.britain usa.com). There is a consulate in New York City.

Emergencies   Dial © **911** for fire, police, and ambulance. The **Poison Control Center** can be reached at © **800/222-1222** toll-free from any phone.

Hospitals   The following hospitals have 24-hour emergency rooms. Don't forget your insurance card.

Downtown: New York University Downtown Hospital, 170 William St., between Beekman and Spruce streets (© 212/312-5063 or 212/312-5000).

Midtown: Bellevue Hospital Center, 462 First Ave., at 27th Street (© 212/562-4141; **New York University Medical Center,** 550 First Ave., at 33rd Street (© 212/263-7300).

Upper West Side: St. Luke's Hospital Center, 1111 Amsterdam Avenue at 114th Street (© 212/523-4000).

Upper East Side: New York Presbyterian Hospital, 525 E. 68th St., at York Avenue (© 212/472-5454); **Lenox Hill Hospital,** 100 E. 77th St., between Park and Lexington avenues (© 212/434-2000).

Hot Lines   Department of Consumer Affairs © 212/487-4444; and **taxi complaints** at © 212/NYC-TAXI. If you suspect your car was towed, call the **Department of Transportation TOWAWAY Help Line** at © 311. You can also call 311 for non-emergency city matters or questions pertaining to New York City.

Insurance   Medical Insurance   Although it's not required of travelers, health insurance is highly recommended. Most health insurance policies cover you if you get sick away from home—but check your coverage before you leave.

International visitors to the U.S. should note that unlike many European countries, the United States does not usually offer free or low-cost medical care to its citizens or visitors. Doctors and hospitals are expensive, and in most cases will require advance payment or proof of coverage before they render their services. Good policies will cover the costs of an accident, repatriation, or death. Packages such as **Europ Assistance's "Worldwide Healthcare Plan"** are sold by European automobile clubs and travel agencies at attractive rates. **Worldwide Assistance Services, Inc.** (© 800/777-8710; www.worldwideassistance.com) is the agent for Europ Assistance in the United States.

Canadians should check with their provincial health plan offices or call **Health Canada** (© 866/225-0709; www.hc-sc.gc.ca) to find out the extent of their coverage and what documentation and receipts they must present if they are treated in the United States.

Travelers from the U.K. should carry their **European Health Insurance Card** (EHIC), which replaced the E111 form as proof of entitlement to free/reduced cost medical treatment abroad (© 0845/606-2030; www.ehic.org.uk). Note that the EHIC only covers "necessary medical treatment," and for repatriation costs, lost money, baggage, or cancellation, travel insurance from a reputable company should always be sought (**www.travelinsuranceweb.com**).

Travel Insurance   The cost of travel insurance varies widely, depending on the destination, the cost and length of your trip, your age and health, and the type of trip you're taking, but expect to pay between 5% and 8% of the vacation itself. You can get estimates from various providers through **InsureMyTrip.com**. more than a dozen companies.

U.K. citizens and their families who make more than one trip abroad per year may find an annual travel insurance policy works out cheaper. Check **www.moneysupermarket.com**, which compares prices from providers for single- and multitrip policies.

Trip Cancellation Insurance Trip-cancellation insurance will help retrieve your money if you have to back out of a trip or depart early, or if your travel supplier goes bankrupt. Trip cancellation traditionally covers such events as sickness, natural disasters, and Department of State advisories. The latest news in trip-cancellation insurance is the availability of **expanded hurricane coverage** and the **"any-reason"** cancellation coverage—which costs more but covers cancellations made for any reason. You won't get back 100% of your prepaid trip cost, but you will get a substantial portion. **TravelSafe** (© 888/885-7233; www.travelsafe.com) offers both types of coverage. Expedia also offers any-reason cancellation coverage for its air-hotel packages. For details, contact one of the following recommended insurers: **Access America** (© 866/807-3982; www.accessamerica.com); **Travel Guard International** (© 800/826-4919; www.travelguard.com); **Travel Insured International** (© 800/243-3174; www.travelinsured.com); and **Travelex Insurance Services** (© 888/457-4602; www.travelex-insurance.com).

Libraries The **New York Public Library** is on Fifth Avenue at 42nd Street (© 212/930-0800). This Beaux Arts beauty houses more than 38 million volumes, and the beautiful reading rooms have been restored to their former glory. More efficient and modern, if less charming, is the mid-Manhattan branch at 455 Fifth Ave., at 40th Street, across the street from the main library (© 212/340-0833). There are other branches in almost every neighborhood; most provide public computer terminals and are equipped with Wi-Fi. You can find a list online at **www.nypl.org**.

Lost & Found Be sure to tell all of your credit card companies the minute you discover your wallet has been lost or stolen and file a report at the nearest police precinct. Your credit card company or insurer may require a police report number or record of the loss. Most credit card companies have an emergency toll-free number to call if your card is lost or stolen; they may be able to wire you a cash advance immediately or deliver an emergency credit card in a day or two. Visa's U.S. emergency number is © **800/847-2911** or 410/581-9994. American Express cardholders and traveler's check holders should call © **800/221-7282.** MasterCard holders should call

ⓒ **800/307-7309** or 636/722-7111. For other credit cards, call the toll-free number directory at ⓒ **800/555-1212.**

If you need emergency cash when banks and American Express offices are closed on weekends or holidays, you can have money wired to you via **Western Union** (ⓒ **800/325-6000;** www.western union.com).

Mail   At press time, domestic postage rates were 27¢ for a postcard and 42¢ for a letter. For international mail, a first-class letter of up to 1 ounce costs from 72¢ (69¢ to Canada and Mexico), depending on size and destination; a first-class postcard costs the same as a letter. For more information go to **www.usps.com** and click on "Calculate Postage."

Always include zip codes when mailing items in the U.S. If you don't know your zip code, visit www.usps.com/zip4.

Medical Conditions   If you have a medical condition that requires **syringe-administered medications,** carry a valid prescription from your physician; syringes in carry-on baggage will be inspected. Insulin should have the proper pharmaceutical documentation. If you have a disease that requires treatment with **narcotics,** you should carry documented proof with you—smuggling narcotics aboard a plane carries severe penalties in the U.S.

For **HIV-positive visitors,** requirements for entering the United States are somewhat vague and change frequently. For up-to-the-minute information, contact **AIDSinfo** (ⓒ **800/448-0440** or 301/519-6616 outside the U.S.; www.aidsinfo.nih.gov) or the **Gay Men's Health Crisis** (ⓒ **212/367-1000;** www.gmhc.org).

Newspapers & Magazines   There are three major daily newspapers: the *New York Times,* the *Daily News,* and the *New York Post.* There are also two free daily papers, *AM-New York* and *Metro*, usually distributed in the morning near subway stations and in self-serve boxes around town.

Passports   The websites listed provide downloadable passport applications as well as the current fees for processing applications. For an up-to-date, country-by-country listing of passport requirements around the world, go to the "International Travel" tab of the U.S. Department of State at **http://travel.state.gov**.

International visitors to the U.S. can obtain a visa application at the same website. *Note:* Children are required to present a passport when entering the United States at airports. More information on obtaining a passport for a minor is at **http://travel.state.gov**. Allow plenty of time before your trip to apply for a passport; processing normally takes 4 to 6 weeks (3 weeks for expedited service) but can take longer during busy periods (especially spring). And keep in mind that if you need a passport in a hurry, you'll pay a higher processing fee.

For Residents of Australia   You can pick up an application from your local post office or any branch of Passports Australia, but you must schedule an interview at the passport office to present your application materials. Call the **Australian Passport Information Service** at © **131-232,** or visit the government website at **www. passports.gov.au**.

For Residents of Canada   Passport applications are available at travel agencies throughout Canada or from the central **Passport Office,** Department of Foreign Affairs and International Trade, Ottawa, ON K1A 0G3 (© **800/567-6868;** www.ppt.gc.ca). *Note:* Canadian children who travel must have their own passport. However, if you hold a valid Canadian passport issued before December 11, 2001, that bears the name of your child, the passport remains valid for you and your child until it expires.

For Residents of Ireland   You can apply for a 10-year passport at the **Passport Office,** Setanta Centre, Molesworth Street, Dublin 2 (© **01/671-1633;** www.irlgov.ie/iveagh). Those under age 18 and over 65 must apply for a 3-year passport. You can also apply at 1A South Mall, Cork (© **21/494-4700**), or at most post offices.

For Residents of New Zealand   You can pick up a passport application at any New Zealand Passports Office or download it from their website. Contact the **Passports Office** at © **0800/225-050** in New Zealand or 04/474-8100, or log on to **www.passports.govt.nz**.

For Residents of the United Kingdom   To pick up an application for a standard 10-year passport (5-yr. passport for children under 16), visit your nearest passport office, major post office, or travel agency or contact the **United Kingdom Passport Service** at © **0870/521-0410,** or search its website at **www.ukpa.gov.uk**.

Pharmacies   For 24-hour pharmacies in Manhattan, downtown, try **Walgreen's** at 145 Fourth Avenue (at 14th Street), © **212/677-0054.** Midtown on the East Side, head for **CVS** at 630 Lexington Ave. (at 53rd St.), © **917/369-8688. Duane Reade** has a 24-hour pharmacy on the Upper East Side at 1279 Third Ave. (at 74th St.; © **212/744-2668**). On the Upper West Side there's another 24-hour pharmacy at the **Duane Reade,** 2522 Broadway (at 94th St.) © **212/663-1580.**

Police   Dial ℂ **911** in an emergency; otherwise, call ℂ **646/610-5000** or 718/610-5000 (NYPD headquarters) for the number of the nearest precinct. For non-emergency matters, call ℂ **311.**

Taxes   **Sales tax** is 8.375% on meals, most goods, and some services, but it is not charged on clothing and footwear items under $110. **Hotel tax** is 13.25% plus $2 per room per night (including sales tax). **Parking garage tax** is 18.375%.

The United States has no value-added tax (VAT) or other indirect tax at the national level. Every state, county, and city may levy its own local tax on all purchases, including hotel and restaurant checks and airline tickets. These taxes will not appear on price tags.

Time   For the correct local time, dial ℂ **212/976-1616.** New York City is on Eastern Time (GMT -5 hours).

Daylight saving time is in effect from 1am on the second Sunday in March to 1am on the first Sunday in November. Daylight saving time moves the clock 1 hour ahead of standard time.

Tipping   Tips are a very important part of certain workers' income, and gratuities are the standard way of showing appreciation for services provided. (Tipping is not compulsory if the service is poor!) In hotels, tip **bellhops** at least $1 per bag ($2–$3 if you have a lot of luggage) and tip the **chamber staff** $1 to $2 per day (more if you've left a disaster area to clean up). Tip the **doorman** or **concierge** only if he or she has provided you with some specific service (for example, calling a cab for you or obtaining difficult-to-get theater tickets). In restaurants, bars, and nightclubs, tip **service staff** 15% to 20% of the check, tip **bartenders** 10% to 15%, tip **checkroom attendants** $1 per garment, and tip **valet-parking attendants** $1 per vehicle.

As for other service personnel, tip **cab drivers** 15% of the fare; tip **skycaps** at airports at least $1 per bag ($2–$3 if you have a lot of luggage); and tip **hairdressers** and **barbers** 15% to 20%.

Transit Information   For information on getting to and from the airport, see "Getting There," in chapter 1, or call **Air-Ride** at ℂ **800/247-7433.** For information on subways and buses, call the **MTA** at ℂ **718/330-1234;** go online to **www.mta.info**.

Traveler's Assistance   **Travelers Aid** (www.travelersaid.org) helps distressed travelers with all kinds of problems, including accidents, sickness, and lost or stolen luggage. There is an office on the first floor of Terminal 6 (JetBlue terminal) at JFK Airport (ℂ **718/656-4870**), and one in Newark Airport's Terminal B (ℂ **973/623-5052**).

Visas For information about U.S. Visas go to **http://travel.state. gov** and click on "Visas." Or go to one of the following websites:

Australian citizens can obtain up-to-date visa information from the **U.S. Embassy Canberra,** Moonah Place, Yarralumla, ACT 2600 (© **02/6214-5600**) or by checking the U.S. Diplomatic Mission's website at **http://usembassy-australia.state.gov/consular**.

British subjects can obtain up-to-date visa information by calling the **U.S. Embassy Visa Information Line** (© **0891/200-290**) or by visiting the "Visas to the U.S." section of the American Embassy London's website at **www.usembassy.org.uk**.

Irish citizens can obtain up-to-date visa information through the **Embassy of the USA Dublin,** 42 Elgin Rd., Dublin 4, Ireland (© **353/1-668-8777;** or by checking the "Consular Services" section of the website at **http://dublin.usembassy.gov**.

Citizens of **New Zealand** can obtain up-to-date visa information by contacting the **U.S. Embassy New Zealand,** 29 Fitzherbert Terrace, Thorndon, Wellington (© **644/472-2068**), or get the information directly from the website at **http://wellington.us embassy.gov**.

Index

See also Accommodations and Restaurant indexes below.